Discourses of the Developing World

I0880937

Against the backdrop of overwhelming discourse scholarship emanating from the Western cosmopolitan centres, this volume offers a development-centred approach to unfamiliar, marginalized or otherwise disadvantaged discourses of the Third World or the Global South. Written by leading researchers based in Asia, Africa and Latin America, respectively, this book reconstructs Eastern paradigms of communication studies on the one hand and explores the discursive problems, complexities, aspirations, and dynamics of the non-Western, subaltern, and developing societies on the other. As methodological principles, the authors i) adopt the cultural-political stance of supporting cultural diversity and harmony at both academic and everyday levels, ii) draw upon Asian, African and Latino scholarship in critical dialogue with the existing mainstream traditions, and iii) make sense of the discourses of Asia, Africa and Latin America from their own local as well as global, historical and intercultural, perspectives. This book will particularly appeal to scholars and students in the fields of discourse studies communication and cultural studies, and development studies.

Shi-xu is Changjiang Distinguished Professor, founding Director of the Centre for Discourse and Cultural Studies, Hangzhou Normal University, China. He is founding and former Director of the Centre for Contemporary Chinese Discourse Studies, Zhejiang University, China, and has held teaching posts in the Netherlands, the UK and Singapore.

Kwesi Kwaa Prah is Professor Emeritus in Sociology of the University of the Western Cape. He is founder and former Director of the Centre for Advanced Studies of African Society (CASAS) based in Cape Town, South Africa.

María Laura Pardo is Researcher at the National Council of Scientific and Technical Research (CONICET), Director of the Department of Linguistics at the Philosophical and Cultural Anthropology Research Centre (CIAFIC-CONICET), Professor of Analysis of the Languages of the Mass Media at the Faculty of Arts, University of Buenos Aires.

Cultural Discourse Studies Series

Discourses of the Developing World
Researching properties, problems and potentials of the developing world
Shi-xu, Kwesi Kwaa Prah and María Laura Pardo

Discourses of the Developing World

Researching properties, problems and potentials of the developing world

Shi-xu, Kwesi Kwaa Prah and María Laura Pardo

Routledge
Taylor & Francis Group
LONDON AND NEW YORK

First published 2016 by Routledge

2 Park Square, Milton Park, Abingdon, Oxfordshire OX14 4RN
52 Vanderbilt Avenue, New York, NY 10017

Routledge is an imprint of the Taylor & Francis Group, an informa business

First issued in paperback 2018

British Library Cataloguing in Publication Data
A catalogue record for this book is available from the British Library

Library of Congress Cataloging in Publication Data
A catalog record for this book has been requested

ISBN: 978-1-138-01748-1 (hbk)
ISBN: 978-0-367-13384-9 (pbk)

Typeset in Times New Roman
by HWA Text and Data Management, London

Contents

Acknowledgements

Shi-xu gratefully acknowledges that Chapter 2 is based on the article co-authored with Feng-Bing that is published in *Culture & Psychology* under the title: 'Contemporary Chinese communication made understandable' (2012: 3-19). The current version is much revised and expanded. Also, he wishes to thank Routledge for kind permission for reproducing here as Chapter 3, with slight modifications, his paper published in *Language and Intercultural Communication*, entitled 'International city branding as intercultural discourse' (2015, 15(1): 161–178).

Kwesi Kwaa Prah thankfully acknowledges the time spent on the computer production of the three chapters by his Secretary, Grace Naidoo of the Centre for Advanced Studies of African Society (CASAS), Cape Town.

María Laura Pardo would like to express her gratitude to CIAFIC and CONICET and the University of Buenos Aires that have funded her research. Special thanks to Valentina Noblia, Alicia Carrizo, and Martín Menéndez for their comments and support. Thanks to Monica Descalzi and Matías Soich for their translations and suggestions. She is very thankful to the editor of the book series Shi-xu for all his constant guidance and to the editorial team at Routledge. Her deepest gratitude to those who voluntarily participated in the life stories and interviews that she conducted in Buenos Aires from 2003 to 2010 and which made this research possible.

Prologue

Today America-dominated globalization has firmly become an organizing and defining feature of our contemporary times. Especially in the last few years it has increasingly taken on a brutal form, going from a phase of neo-liberalism to one of militarism. Gross foreign aggression to Iraq, Afghanistan and Libya, US 're-entry' into Asia, international crisis in Ukraine, and the Israeli army's school bombings in Palestine are just obvious signs of this power-oriented globalization process under the America-almighty reign (Escobar 2004; Irogbe 2005; McGrew and Poku 2007).

In fact much scholarship has shown globalization as the ideological and geo-political and geo-economic project of the American-West and exposed its human consequences of worsening poverty, inequality and subjugation on the part of the non-Western, developing, Third World (Cho 2005; Held and McGrew 2007; Krishnaswamy 2005; Sohn 2012; Taylor 2005).

And yet it seems that equally urgent and important questions have hitherto been neglected or explained away: is there a possibility for some collective, or global, forces to arise which may be able to counter this polarizing and de-humanizing globalizing tyranny, who can be agents of such countervailing forces, and how can they shoulder the historic task and responsibility to salvage the world from spiralling down to total rule of terror?

It has been our conviction that answers ought to be sought in a revitalized, non-Western, developing, Third World. It is precisely in this regard, regrettably, that scholarship seems wanting or otherwise discouraging (Escobar 1995). Scholars of development studies, for example, have generally confined their field of search to 'poverty reduction' and 'human development'. Some of them have preferred to scrutinize the developing world from a Westcentric perspective, whereby the latter becomes but an object of control. Some have even had an alternative suggestion: we forsake notions of development, the developing world, the Third World and the like. Differences within developing countries, they argue, can sometimes be bigger than those between Third World countries and advanced capitalist ones (Reeves 1993).

Indeed it is high time that a new cultural approach to the developing world was formed and placed at the centre stage of globalization enquiry, not just because scholarship has been disproportionately insufficient or cultural-politically inadequate, not just because there are countless complex and complicated issues to be examined and dealt with, but also, more importantly, because a re-emerging non-Western, developing Third World represents one major, perhaps the most powerful, agent of cultural resistance to take up the urgent human-cultural cause to redress the precarious global disorder of widening injustice and guard humanity against an irreversible abyss (Taylor 2005).

In 1960s and 1970s the developing Third World was a powerful cultural force that engendered an international fight for liberation and freedom from hegemony and poverty, but was cut short by the ensuing Cold War. Now, at the height of accelerating globalization, the developing world is yet again at the crossroads of human destiny: to disintegrate into the ultimate victim of globalization, or to forge anew a cultural Great Wall of resistance and contestation against the American-Western neo-colonialism (Cheng and Kurtz 1998; Cho 2005; Fergus and Rowney 2005; Haynes 2008; Simon 1997; Sohn 2012).

There are palpable signs of hope. The transcontinental BRICS, for one, has put a wedge in the US-dominated global hierarchy. For another, China, now the world's second largest economy, is on the one hand engaged in the diplomacy of human-cultural diversity and on the other hand calling for the establishment of a 'new type of major-country relationship' with the United States. Still other examples of the Third World project of autonomy and alliance are the African Union, the Association of Latin American Integration, South Asian Association for Regional Cooperation, and the Shanghai Cooperation Organization. And yet on the academic front, far little, culturally conscious and critical, research is being conducted on the developing world of Asia, Africa and Latin America as a countervailing force to redress the human disorder set on by globalization.

In this book, accordingly, we shall concern ourselves with the non-Western, developing, Third World and focus in particular on its development in the context of globalization. That is, despite the fact that development has often been taken to be the condition, process and aspiration of Asia, Africa and Latin America, it will not be treated as given here, but rather as researchable phenomenon. Thus, our aim, first of all, is to analyse and assess the role of the developing world in general and various facets of its development in particular in re-shaping globalization. Specifically, we shall try to identify, interpret, explain, and appraise the properties, problems and potentials of development practice of the Third World in the context of globalization. Apart from initiating a topical shift in development studies and in globalization studies, second, our objective is to effect provisionally a paradigmatic construction: namely, to outline a culturally conscious and critical system of researching development from the point of view of cultural discourse studies (Shi-xu 2015), 'development discourse studies'. A little explanation is in order here.

Conventional research on development has usually been conducted from such disciplinary perspectives as political science, economics, sociology, law, geography, demography, urban and rural studies, and so on. But in this book, the three authors, based in China, South Africa and Argentina, respectively, will use a notion of development (practice) as cultural-discursive phenomenon (or cultural-communicative event or a class thereof, activity) and so study development affairs of the developing world in terms of who are talking, what they say and how, through what mediums, with what purposes and effects and in what historical process and (inter)cultural power relations. This also means that we, as cultural members living and working within the communities under investigation, shall be able to take the native perspectives of the non-Western communities themselves and gain insights into their agencies, identities and dynamics, and so on.

At this juncture it may be noted that there has been a special strand of communication research devoted specifically to the developing Third World, often under the headings of development communication, Third World communication or communication for development (Lent 1978; Melkote 1991). This is however different from, though related to, our current concern. Emanating from the America-based tradition, Third World communication studies tend to focus on 'communication' per se, namely in terms of (use of) technology, media policies, content and information of mass communication, and to a lesser degree, cultural knowledge and norms (Reeves 1993). Wider historical processes and cultural (power) relation and interaction, detailed verbal and non-verbal strategies – which are integral parts of situated cultural communication – are usually left out of purview.

Cultural-discursive study of the developing world will not just advance research, teaching and practice in this re-emerging field, but also contribute to a better understanding of globalization. Globalization cannot be adequately understood without knowledge of the non-Western, developing, Third World which interacts and contests with it.

In this book, the notions of the non-Western, developing world, Third World, discourses and development discourse studies are essential. In one sense, they are nascent or re-emerging; in another, they are precisely the new constructs we are dedicated to creating through this book. So at the outset let us briefly describe them.

The non-Western, developing Third World

The Third World, or interchangeably, the developing world, was formed in 1960s and 1970s among Asian, African and Latin American countries and regions; politically, it functioned as a non-aligned movement in the Cold War between the North Atlantic Alliance and the Soviet Eastern bloc. But because the Third World, or the developing world, was characterized by a low level of economy, it usually meant 'poor' and 'under-developed', as opposed to the highly industrialized world.

After the disintegration of the Soviet Union, the collapse of the Berlin Wall and consequently the end of the Cold War, the developing world found itself subjected to the American-West through globalization. In this global process from neo-liberalism to militarism, the plight of the developing world has not got better but worse and the entire world order threatens to go down a spiral of militarist hegemony.

And yet, at this critical crossroad of human history, the three authors maintain, the once 'poor' and 'under-developed' Third World represents the only hope of forming anew a cultural-political Great Wall to contest with and resist against the American-Western military authoritarianism. It is out of this conviction that we insist that both globalization scholars and development scholars turn their attention to this emerging, new world.

Thus, in this book, we shall normally use the phrase *the developing world* to refer to the emerging, formative cultural-political entity composed of Asian, African, Latin American and any other non-Western communities, which is subject to, yet resistant against, the American-Western globalization in general and its world hegemony in particular. Sometimes the phrase the Third World is used to stress the historical experience of colonialism and post-colonialism; the epithet non-Western is also occasionally used in order to stress its cultural-political character of opposing the American-Western domination and exploitation.

From here it should become clear that the terms and concepts discussed above are not to essentialize or dichotomize anything; rather, through them, we are striving to create or re-affirm new, human and cultural-political identities and agencies for the sake of exploring, illuminating or re-discovering the non-Western world on the one hand and counter-balancing, undermining or neutralizing the effects and consequences of Americanized globalization on the other.

Development as discourse

'Development', like 'the developing world', is a contested term among the peoples of the developing world and scholars of different persuasions alike (say, modernist, critical or monastic, see Melkote and Steeves 2001: 34–6). So the term development will be used in a narrower sense in this book to refer specifically to any form of social-cultural life and practice of the developing world as defined above. This means, as the primary object of our investigation and evaluation, we shall be focusing on socially, culturally broad and significant phenomena, issues, events and activities happening in the developing world.

As alluded to earlier, phenomena of the developing world will not be examined from conventional points of view, but from the special perspective of cultural discourse: culturally differentiated and cultural power saturated forms of human communication (Shi-xu 2015). That is, they will be examined in terms of communicative or discursive events or activities (i.e. series of interrelated events) in which participants (speakers and hearers) interact with each other using verbal and non-verbal symbols through particular channels (time and space) and in particular historical and (inter)cultural relations. Thus, cultural discourse not only offers a window onto, but also constitutes, the realities of the developing world. To study the developing world, then, is to study the discourses of development, hence development discourse studies. But as to why and how we should and can study the discourses of the developing world, let us turn now.

Development discourse studies

As mentioned earlier on, the current book project is designed partly to open up new ground and construct a new paradigm in the scholarship on development in general and the developing world in particular. For one thing, mainstream communication studies and (critical) discourse analysis that emanate from the Euro-American metropolis have largely been Westcentric (Shi-xu 2014), both as an academic discourse as a whole and as philosophical, theoretical, methodological and topical frameworks. Such ethnocentric myopia and academic hegemony that result in reproduction of biased, stereotypic and colonialist knowledge and marginalization of non-Western scholarship are detrimental not only for the well-being of the developing world but also for human intellectual growth itself, as many a critic has pointed out (Asante 2009; Chen 2006; Miike 2004; Shi-xu 2009, 2014, 2015). For another, development communication studies has usually been concerned with the conventional topics of the (mass) media and such research is often conducted within general, mainstream communication scholarship (e.g. Lent 1978; Melkote 1991). For still another, development studies has too often neglected the discursive or communicative dimension of development practice (but see Grillo and Stirrat 1997; Mickelson 1998; Rao and Sanyal 2010; Warah 2011).

So, in order to draw attention to the vitally important force of human-cultural growth and resistance to world hegemony, we propose in this book to initiate 'development discourse studies' within the broader framework of cultural discourse studies. Under this heading, we suggest the following general principles of research:

- To study development from the points of view of the peoples of the developing world, i.e. by listening to the voices and accounts of the peoples under study and learning from them in research.
- To overcome scholarly Westcentrism and practice, where possible, locally grounded and globally minded and culturally conscious and critical frameworks of and approaches to development by, among other things, using thorough cultural knowledge and experience
- To collaborate in building a common research programme of development discourse studies that may be instrumental not only to the societal pursuits of the peoples of the developing countries, but also the human-cultural cause of redressing the hegemonic and dehumanizing processes of globalization.

Nowadays there is increasing recognition in discourse and communication studies of the importance of taking a cultural, or multicultural, stance. It should be noted in this regard that there is a growing culturally critical and constructive literature that undermines the West-and-White-centric, colonialist discourse on the one hand and on the other hand discusses principles and ways for multiculturalist research and re-discovers the particularities, diversities and unique aspects of the discourses of the peoples of Asia, Africa, Latin America as well as other diasporic cultures (e.g. Asante 1998; Carey 1992; Chen 2004; Collier 2000; Briscoe, Arriaza and Henze 2009; Dissanayake 1988; Gavriely-Nuri 2010; Kincaid 1987; Miike 2009; Pennycook 1998). The present project draws on this body of work.

It should be noted, too, that there is a growing number of young scholars and students from developing countries, who travel between and are versed in both Eastern and Western cultures and scholarship and who are therefore equipped with the essential qualities and skills to construct culturally critical and innovative, or in-between-cultural (Shi-xu 2005), concepts, perspectives and techniques. It will be realized also that to date there are increased and enhanced facilities and mechanisms for intercultural exchange, dialogue, critique and collaboration, for example, international travel, the Internet, publications, translations, conferences, workshops, and international teaching and research programmes. Given the new conditions and potential for cross-cultural learning and fertilization, we should expect that there will be many more scholars and students of discourse and communication research who become champions of multicultural scholarship on development.

Of course, given the current general, international and cultural imbalance and disorder in the social sciences and humanities, it will still be a long and arduous struggle resisting the cultural-intellectual hegemony in social science in general and (re)colonization in discourse scholarship in particular. More specifically, the construction and practice of the envisaged development discourse studies here will have to be embarked on as a long-term objective which requires concerted efforts of many groups of scholars and students from all over the world. But we may expect that, because of the faster changing pace of international scholarly exchange and increased multicultural awareness in social science in general and language/communication/discourse studies in particular, let alone the continuing ascendancy of the developing world, the formation and growth of development discourse studies will only be an inevitable trend.

Native researchers, cultural perspectives and major countries

The discourses of the developing world, despite their commonalities, are as diversified as they are complex. So, to collect typical and sufficient data and then represent them convincingly and productively pose serious challenges to the present enterprise. One may expect the discourses of many developing countries to be studied; one may also anticipate a unified approach to those discourses which is based on a diversity of lineages.

However, the present book is but an initial and largely illustrative attempt at constructing a paradigmatic and empirical approach to development discourse and so does not aspire to be an all-encompassing study. Yet we have made a number of minimal methodological considerations that may underpin the present endeavour. First of all, the three authors live and research respectively in Asia, Africa and Latin America, and more particularly, in the major countries of these continents. Further, the authors have had wide research experience in the relevant discourses. Second, development discourse studies as a system of research is to be represented from three broad, emerging or established, Asian, African and Latin American perspectives. This way, not only commonality may be more effectively found, but also relative international diversity and complexity may be reflected. Third, one or two in-depth case studies are rendered of one or a few major countries in Asia, Africa and Latin America apiece as a way to represent not only a broad, continent-oriented, empirical category of culture or cultural community, say, Asia, but also development discourse as a whole. It is our belief that cases of major developing countries can serve as important indicators.

Organization of the book

The project of development discourse studies carried out here is divided into three parts: Asian, African and Latin American approaches, respectively, which are composed of three chapters apiece. Thus, Part I presents an Asian paradigm of development discourse studies with three kinds of approaches – paradigmatic, theoretical and empirical – which in turn are undergirded by three genres of methodology – inductive, illustrative and case-study based. Specifically, Chapter 1 argues that it is not only necessary but also possible to construct an Asian form of development discourse studies. After pointing out the cultural and intellectual limitations and consequences of Westcentric (critical) discourse analysis, it enumerates Asian cultural traditions, scholarly resources and contemporary realities and thereupon outlines an Asian-development-oriented system of research (composed of philosophical, theoretical, methodological and topical propositions) for studying present-day Asian affairs. In this account, Asia is no longer conceived of as a geo-political or social=psychological entity or a passive object of globalization as has been routinely treated in development studies of 'poverty reduction' or 'improvement of human rights', but as a cultural-power oriented community with its own properties, perspectives and potentials in line with the rest of the developing world; further, the research system is equipped with Asian wisdoms and the researcher is required to help with Asian development goals.

Against the particular backdrop of Asian communication being hitherto neglected, misunderstood or distorted, Chapter 2 illustratively re-describes and re-explicates contemporary Chinese society by taking a cultural-psychological perspective on its social practice. Drawing on insights from indigenous Chinese cultural psychology as well as Chinese communication studies, the chapter expatiates with empirical examples on how Chinese worldviews (e.g. 天人合一 (holism)), ways of thinking (e.g. 辩证 (dialectic)), concept of communication (e.g. 言不尽意 (meaning-beyond-language)), moral values (e.g. 和为贵 (harmony) and 中庸 (moderate)), collective memories (e.g. subjugation to colonialism and imperialism), attitudes towards other cultural groups (e.g. opposition to hegemony and empathy with Third World countries), love of one's country (e.g. 爱国主义 (patriotism)) and national aspirations (e.g. socio-economic development), and so on, organize, guide and constitute their conduct and communication as opposed to those of Western counterparts. Such culturally grounded accounts are supposed to help with understanding of developing societies on the one hand and contribute to paradigmatic construction of development discourse studies on the other.

The third chapter goes on to examining, as Asian cultural case of urban development, international city-branding practices of Hangzhou, an ancient capital and tourist city on the east coastal region of China. It starts by outlining a brief conceptual framework of international branding of developing world cities in terms of its cultural-communicative properties and corresponding methodology that is characterized by a holistic, multi-site and multi-categorical approach. Based on data obtained from a plethora of mega-events, the media and other information sources (the Internet, institutions, interviews, newspapers, expos, museums, etc.), the chapter provides a synthesis and appraisal of the city's diverse branding practices ranging from municipal management, expos, festivals, international visits, to contests for awards. It is shown that, in its international branding, the city has a municipality-leading approach, engages a diversity of sectors, and resorts to a variety of forms of branding tactics and tools. At the same time, however, the city has had difficulties of establishing outlets of branding abroad because of inability to meet local standards and that compared with other world-class cities it has not been able to offer culturally distinct and rich contents.

Part II showcases an African form of development discourse research. Chapter 4 makes the point that current indications by policy and practice suggest that African countries are beginning to realize that the language question in Africa in general and more particularly the use of African languages in education and social intercourse are crucial in any attempt to developmentally transform African societies. The chapter looks at the impact of colonialism on language-use in Africa and describes how colonial policies placed Western languages at the centre of African education and general social practice. It proceeds to examine the evidence of cultural and linguistic subservience to Western languages and discourse produced by the legacy of colonial language impositions. In discussion of the way forward towards African development, it points in the direction of the intellectualization of African languages and the simultaneous harmonization of African-language orthographies which will enable a better, and more rational economic basis for the production of literature to serve large constituencies. An argument which is made from the start of the chapter is that the use of African languages for education and development is directly linked to the emancipation principle and the democratic empowerment of mass African society.

Chapter 5 records an African academic experience on African-language harmonization and standardization for development by the Centre for Advanced Studies of African Society (CASAS) based in South Africa. The peculiarities of language and literacy in the acquisition of knowledge in the African context differ in many respects from large parts of Asia and Latin America. Partly for this reason the use of languages in education in Africa is trapped in a neo-colonial time-warp which is not easily rolled back. The situation has created particular problems which need to be resolved if African languages can be directed towards the purposes of educational, scientific and technological development. The chapter shows how CASAS has for the past decade and a half been working in the area of the harmonization and standardization of African linguistic orthographies to enable their languages and empower their users to develop them for purposes of education, intellectualization and development more generally.

The sixth chapter looks at problems linked with linguistic policies and power relations within countries as well as between countries in Africa. It provides a narrative account of how language policies have evolved over the past 100 years in Africa and how these language policies have reflected the changes in power relations in African societies. It presents a number of pointed insights with examples from countries ranging from Tanzania, Madagascar, Kenya, Namibia, Ethiopia, Ghana, Nigeria, to Sierra Leone. It explains how power relations and group interests affect policy and practice with regard to language-use in African countries and draws implications for policy change.

Part III of the book introduces a Latin American discursive approach to development. Chapter 7 presents a framework of Latin American discourse studies featuring centrally modernity, postmodernity and academic life. Modern and postmodern cultures of Latin America affect its everyday life and scholarly practice alike. We must therefore reconsider the roots of research, as well as the role of globalization and neo-liberalism in the continent as a whole. The cultural-critical discourse study of extreme poverty carried out by a network of Latin American academics is discussed here with a particular focus on the cultural challenges it poses to team members. It is argued that the place of cultural studies in the neo-liberal cultural model must be continually re-examined and avenues for resistance to homogenization explored. Cultural resistance cannot be reduced to a set of educational practices that reproduce theories, methods and themes of the core countries of the West. We must seek new horizons and look for alternative ways of contesting colonial Westernization, primarily through reviewing our own actions as teachers, researchers and particularly specialists in cultural studies.

Chapter 8 discusses the thirtieth anniversary of the Malvinas/Falklands War as marked by Argentine television. The corpus consists of four television programmes, broadcast by over-the-air television channels to commemorate its anniversary in 2012. Proceeding from the notion that cultural studies should account for the particular ways in which each country or region builds the events related to its memories (in this case, of the Falklands War), we identify five kinds of discourse: (1) the triumphalist nationalist story; (2) sympathy or lack of it; (3) a narrative that focuses on the correlation between the dictatorship's crimes against humanity and the qar; (4) the 'new vision' which sees the War as against neither the British people nor the islanders; and (5) the 'false way' view. Further, there appears a coexistence of modern and postmodern commemorative discourses, which allow different actors in the media to create different options according to their ideological interests.

Chapter 9 analyses the cultural differences between modern and postmodern capitalist logics in relation to the way in which work is represented in the discourse of homeless inhabitants of Buenos Aires. Modern society is slowly but surely turning postmodern, thereby changing from a producer society into a consumer one, from work ethic-oriented society into one ruled by consumer aesthetics. The theoretical framework of the study is provided by cultural discourse studies and qualitative methods are applied. The Information Hierarchy notion is also used as conceived by the Prague School and reformulated by Pardo (2011). The corpus is made up of life-story interviews with over 60 homeless people over 17 years of age living in the city of Buenos Aires. Research results show that homeless people have a culturally oriented conception of modern work. Consequently, policies of both the government and NGOs disregarding this cultural differentiation between modern and postmodern work would fail and be challenged by people who do not feel the alternatives proposed by them (e.g. selling newspapers on the street) as real jobs.

In sum, the three parts of the volume combine to show the contours and terrains of development discourse studies. While the topics and approaches are related though different, they are all linked by a common theme and concern, namely, a discourse research programme of the developing world striving to identify, explicate, illuminate, and critique Asian, African and Latin American – and more generally the developing world's – practices and experiences with a view to fostering its development on the one hand and neutralizing the consequences of mounting globalization on the other.

References

Asante, M. K. (2006). The rhetoric of globalisation: The Europeanisation of human ideas. *Journal of Multicultural Discourses*, 1(2): 152–158.

Briscoe, F., Arriaza, G. and Henze, R. C. (2009). *The Power of Talk: How Words Change Our Lives*. Thousand Oaks, CA: Corwin Press.

Carey, J.W. (1992). *Communication as Culture: Essays on Media and Society*. New York: Routledge.

Chen G-M. (2004). The two faces of Chinese communication. *Human Communication*, 7: 25–36.

Chen, G-M. (2006) Asian communication studies: What and where to now. *Review of Communication* 6: 295–311.

Cheng, S. J. A. and Kurtz, L. R. (1998). Third world voices redefining peace. *Peace Review: A Transnational Quarterly*, 10(1): 5–11.

Cho, H. Y. (2005). 'Second death', or revival of the 'third world' in the context of neo-liberal globalization. *Inter-Asia Cultural Studies*, 6 (4): 497–509.

Collier, P. and Dollar, D. (2002). *Globalization, Growth, and Poverty: Building an Inclusive World Economy*. Washington, DC: World Bank.

Dissanayake, W. (ed) (1988). *Communication Theory: The Asian Perspective*. Singapore: Asian Mass Communication Research and Information Center.

Escobar, A. (1995). *Encountering Development: The Making and Unmaking of the Third World*. Princeton, NJ: Princeton University Press.

Escobar, A. (2004). Beyond the third World: imperial globality, global coloniality and anti-globalisation social movements. *Third World Quarterly*, 25(1): 207–230.

Fergus, H. T. and Rowney, J. I. A. (2005). Sustainable development: lost meaning and opportunity? *Journal of Business Ethics*, 60, 17–27.

Gavriely-Nuri, D. (2012). Cultural approach to CDA. *Critical Discourses Studies*, 9(1): 77–85.

Grillo, R. D. and Stirrat, R. L. (1997). *Discourses of development: anthropological perspectives*. New York: Berg.

Haynes, J. (2008). *Development Studies* (Polity short introductions). Cambridge: Polity.

Held, D. and McGrew, A. (2007). *Globalization/Anti-Globalization*. Cambridge: Polity.

Irogbe, K. (2005). Globalization and the development of underdevelopment of the Third World. *Journal of Third World Studies*, XXII(1): 41–68.

Kincaid, D. L. (ed) (1987). *Communication Theory: Eastern and Western Perspectives*. San Diego, CA: Harcourt Brace Jovanovich.

Krishnaswamy, R. (2005). Globalization and its postcolonial (dis)contents. *Journal of Postcolonial Writing*, 41(1): 69–82.

Lent, J. A. (1978). *Mass Communications in the Third World: Some Ethical Considerations*. Washington, DC: Distributed by ERIC Clearinghouse.

McGrew, A. and Poku, N. K. (2007). *Globalization, Development and Human Security*. Cambridge: Polity.

Melkote, S. R. (1991). *Communication for Development in the Third World: Theory and Practice*. London: Sage Publications.

Melkote, S. R. and Steeves, H. L. (2001). *Communication for Development in the Third World*. London: Sage.

Mickelson, K. (1998). Rhetoric and rage: Third World voices in international legal discourse. *Wisconsin International Law Journal*, 16(2): 353–419.

Miike, Y. (2006) Non-Western theory in Western research? An Asiacentric agenda for Asia communication studies. *The Review of Communication* 6(1–2): 4–31.

Miike, Y. (2009). New frontiers in Asian communication theory: an introduction. *Journal of Multicultural Discourses*, 4(1): 1–5.

Pardo, L. (2010). Latin-American discourse studies: state of the art and new perspectives. *Journal of Multicultural Discourses*, 5 (3): 183–192.

Pennycook, A. (1998). *English and the Discourses of Colonialism*. London: Routledge.

Rao, V. and Sanyal, P. (2010). Dignity through discourse: poverty and the culture of deliberation in Indian village democracies. *The Annals of the American Academy of Political and Social Science*, 629(1): 146–172.

Reeves, G. (1993). *Communications and the 'Third World'*. London: Routledge.

Shi-xu (2009). Reconstructing eastern paradigms of discourse studies. *Journal of Multicultural Discourses*, 4(1): 29–48.

Shi-xu (2014). *Chinese discourse studies*. Basingstoke: Palgrave Macmillan.

Shi-xu (2015). Cultural discourse studies. In K. Tracy, C. Ilie and T. Sandel (eds) *International Encyclopedia of Language and Social Interaction*. Oxford: Wiley-Blackwell.

Simon, D. (1997). Development reconsidered: New directions in development thinking. *Geografiska Annaler*, 79B(4): 183–201.

Sohn, I. (2012). After renaissance: China's multilateral offensive in the developing world. *European Journal of International Relations*, 18(1): 77–101.

Taylor, I. (2005). Globalisation studies and the developing world: making international political economy truly global. *Third World Quarterly*, 26(7): 1025–1042.

Warah, R. (2011). Afro-Pessimism in the discourse on urban east Africa. *Development*, 54(3): 325–329.

Part I
Asian discourse studies

1 Asian discourse for development

This first chapter has two interrelated or complimentary objectives. In one perspective, it attempts to consolidate the nascent paradigm of cultural discourse studies (CDS) by showing that it is not only necessary but also possible to construct a culturally conscious and critical paradigm of discourse studies within the international arena on discourse and communication studies. In another, it strives to contribute to development discourse studies (DDS) as a particular, arguably most typical, constituent strand of CDS by carving out Asian discourse studies (ADS), a development-oriented approach on a par with African and Latin American discourse studies (which will be found in Parts II and III of the book). To these ends, the chapter will begin with a cultural critique of the limitations and consequences of Western/centric discourse analysis, then enumerate the foundations for a paradigmatic articulation in terms of the cultural conditions of Asian communities on the one hand and the Asian intellectual resources on the other. After that, it formulates a provisional system of philosophical, theoretical, methodological and topical components for the study of Asian discourses. In conclusion, suggestions are offered for a common research agenda of Asian development discourse studies.

Introduction

The Asian community, which accounts for nearly 60 per cent of the human population and extends for over 30 per cent of the world's land, is by far the most complex, diverse and dynamic one in the world. There is no greater urgency to re-examine, re-evaluate and reorient Asia since WWII than right now, when globalization of capitalism and imperialism has accelerated with America's military 're-entry' into Asia as a most recent example and when the talk of an 'Asian century' during the past two decades has quickly given way to America's 'rebalancing' of Asia (David 2012; Nissanke and Thorbecke 2010). Indeed, reassessment of Asia's development, peace and unity has become an utmost important and urgent task for students and scholars of Asian studies and of development studies more generally (Oga 2004; Wang 2007; Wang 2010; Yoichi 1993).

To make sense of Asia – its past and present, whether in terms of its actions, agency, or aspirations, and to positively impact upon its potential future, there is no better way perhaps than to study its communication or discourse, namely the social events or activities in which people engage in meaning-making through verbal and other mediums in historical and cultural contexts. ('Discourse' is preferred here to 'communication' because the latter is often narrowly conceptualized in linear, non-verbal and a-cultural terms; but both will be used interchangeably for variable contextual emphasis.) For, a discursive perspective, as will be explicated shortly, offers a most comprehensive, careful and concrete vantage point through which to view human actions and their meaning-making (Shi-xu 2015).

There has been a growing, culturally critical and distinct, tradition of building an Asian approach to communication and discourse – which may be traced back at least to the mid-1980s (e.g. Chu 1986). This tradition makes critical reflections upon the Western etic, pan-cultural and universal paradigm and offers new theoretical prisms as well as methodological tools to look into Asian cultural communicative practices and complement existing communication research more generally (Chen 2003, 2006; Dissanayake 1988, 2003, 2009b; Hasnain 1988; Irwin 1996; Ishii 2001, 2006, 2009; Jia 1997; Jin 2009; Miike 2002, 2006, 2007; Shi-xu 2009a, 2014; Tehranian 1988; 陈光兴 2006; 施旭 2010; 周光庆 2002).

As yet there are still serious limitations and challenges to this evolving scholarship which call for urgent solutions, however. It has been suggested that there are tendencies of binarism, overgeneralization and eurocentrism (Chen 2010; Dissanayake 1988a, 2003, 2009; Kim 2009, 2010; Wang and Shen 2000). Further, as will be argued shortly, the theoretical and methodological constructive work has largely focused on the traditional and philosophical aspects of Asian communication and culture and not adequately reflected present-day issues, concerns and aspirations of the Asian peoples and societies. A comprehensive paradigmatic system of research, complete with methodology and empirical research agenda, has yet to be formulated. In addition, much of the research has been focused on displaced migrant Asians in the Western world and questions asked are more often than not to do with living in the West, for example, multilingualism and interethnic interaction in Europe or America.

Against this large problem, we shall in the present chapter take a modest initiative: to sketch out a provisional Asian framework of communication or discourse research – in terms of interrelated philosophical, theoretical, methodological and investigative components, call it Asian discourse studies, in critical dialogue with the existing cultural counterparts. Previously, we have suggested the motives, foundations and directions of such an endeavour (Shi-xu 2006, 2009a, 2009b). To that end, we shall first identify the practical reasons and foundational resources for the paradigmatic construction. Next, we shall consider the realities of Asian communication in its global context. Then, as the central objective of this chapter, we shall canvas the paradigm itself. In conclusion, some suggestions will be made regarding the directions for future research efforts.

If the mainstream (critical) discourse analysis is Westcentric in the sense of 'being' culturally specific yet 'doing' universalistic and hegemonic, how would the proposed Asian paradigm overcome possible Asia-centrism? If the proposed Asian paradigm of discourse studies is to be constructed as an alternative or a new speaker in the international-intellectual arena, would it be completely unique and unconnected to the Western counterpart? If a generalism or univeralism and a particularism are equally binary in conception, why is ADS not bi-polar?

Obviously, these are interrelated questions and so my answer below to one can have implications for another. First of all, it is out of the recognition of the Western intellectual domination that the need for an alternative has arisen. Therefore, the present proposal to construct and consolidate an Asian-culturally-grounded paradigm is, not to repeat the same mistake, but to help diversify and so enrich and enliven our field. To that end, ADS will not exclude other cultural approaches or impose itself on other cultural realities; on the contrary, it will strive as a distinct identity and voice to enable cultural-intellectual dialogue and debate. In this sense, the proposed paradigmatic shift is not merely a theoretical and methodological turn, but also a cultural-political movement (Shi-xu 2005, 2009a, 2009b). Thus, it should also be clear that my notions of Asia and for that matter of an Asian paradigm are *cultural-politically* defined. This leads to my next answer.

Second, while an Asian paradigm is designed to enable an Asian intellectual identity, voice and perspective, it will assimilate insights and techniques from other disciplines and traditions. For, in the age of globalization, Asia is, complex and diversified as it is, already interwoven with the rest of the developing world and the wider international community. Thus, the construction of an Asian paradigm is a culturally dialectic process: in order to enrich and empower itself, ADS draws upon the useful elements and concepts of the existing Western counterparts and upon those from other non-Western counterparts, whether African or Latin American. This also implies that the Asian paradigm in question is not (to be) a closed system, but rather a globally minded one.

Third, as should become clear by now, ADS does not assume a reified, fixed and homogenous 'Asia', 'East/West', 'developing world'; to speak of an Asian paradigm or for that matter the African/Latin American/Western paradigms is meant neither to dichotomize nor essentialize these entities. Just as there are cultural-critical intellectuals within the Western tradition, there can also be culturally domineering elements in the Asian/Third World discourse. Many Western businesses can and do operate in the place we call Asia and many Asian communities can and do have their diasporas in America and Europe. There are internal differences and complexities, between rich and poor, men and women, urban and rural, connected or displaced, and so on. So the construction and practice of an Asian paradigm are designed also as a *cultural-political,* domination-resistant move counter-balancing or overcoming the rampant universalizing but Westcentric tendencies in discourse and communication scholarship.

With such an Asian paradigm of discourse studies, it is hoped, we shall have a culturally productive apparatus with which to interpret, evaluate and engage with current Asian practices of discourse and communication. Besides, a cultural-intellectual Asian identity is created in the sphere of international communication and discourse research. Further, what is being proffered here may serve as a reference point for colleagues and students of other cultures to (re)construct other parallel paradigms of discourse studies, whether African, Latin American, Feminist or Black. Furthermore, what is being explored here may provide not only a framework for the founding of 'lower-level' intra-Asian research systems but also a basis for the establishment of 'higher-level' Third World or Eastern or Global-Southern paradigms of discourse studies (Shi-xu 2009b). In addition, the present attempt is intended to contribute to the Asianization of Asian Studies by offering a development-oriented, at once locally grounded and globally minded, approach to Asian discourse and communication.

Western bias on human discourse and its globalization

At the outset of the paradigmatic construction, let me summarize the reasons identified earlier (Shi-xu 2005, 2006, 2009a, 2009b; see also Asante 2006; Miike 2002, 2006, 2007). First, the mainstream Western discourse and communication studies is steeped in binarism which is against the grain of the Asian way of thinking (Miike 2006, 2007). For example, in Western discourse analysis, language is treated as separable from context, the researcher from the researched, good from bad, true from false, right from wrong, standard from deviant, and so on. The West is assumed to be democratic whereas the East, Asia or China is totalitarian. Similarly, researchers often adjudicate discourses in terms of whether statements or representations therein are true or false in relation to reality. Despite its theoretical recognition of the relation of context to text, practitioners of discourse studies tend to indulge in analysing observable, 'objective' linguistic forms – singular (segments of fragments of) texts – drawing on aspects of context as unproblematic or given tools for justifying interpretation.

In close connection with that Western mental habit, second, concepts, values, theories, models, methods, and so on, as developed in the Euro/American-Western context, are neither universal nor neutral as they are often indirectly or explicitly presented. Therefore, they may not be applicable to Asian, or any other, cultural contexts. For instance, the speaker is privileged in Western research over the hearer; for, the former is seen as the originator, producer and determiner of meaning; further, s/he is a self-centred and manipulative and his/her primary goal to persuade others or get them under control. Consequently, communication is studied, taught and evaluated in terms of effectiveness in achieving that goal. But for Asians, such a model of discourse is only partial and the norm of discourse inappropriate for Asian contexts, where care for others and long-term interpersonal relationship are valued over immediate individual interests. Another example is that Western theory of meaning and hence analytic methods emphasize observable forms; but for Asians, the role of language in meaning-making is limited and action, as well as imagination, are much more important. Blind application of Western discourse studies would not just fail to register cultural dimensions but also possibly distort or demean cultural life. Therefore, discourse analysis without taking account of Asian histories and cultures, as well as of its contextual global order, will not advance cross-cultural or human understanding, but only serve to reproduce more misunderstandings and perpetuate existing stereotypes and inequalities.

Third, the preference of Western discourse studies for privileging certain phenomena or questions – often Western, isolated, minute (say 'identity', politeness, metaphor or nominalization) – over others is something that developing Asian societies at this stage of their history can ill-afford. For industrially advanced welfare states, it is well understandable that professors and research students can have all the time, interest and resources to ask and answer scientific questions. Asia has its own realities, issues, problems, interests, concerns, and so on: poverty, environmental disasters, lack of education and low literacy, lack of health care, corruption, poor information services, and so on. And they have their own aspirations: peace, development and cooperation. All of these call for urgent, concerted and comprehensive research efforts on the part of the students and staff of higher education and research institutions – 'real' problems that call for 'real' solutions.

Finally but most importantly, the current mainstream forms of (Critical) Discourse Analysis emanating from Western industrialized metropolitan centres have become a globalized discourse thanks to powerful Western corporate publishing, marketing and distribution on the one hand and border crossings, the internet and international educational programmes on the other. In its global campaign, this discourse has not rendered the non-Western world – Asia, Africa, Latin America and diasporas – understandable, worthy of support and generative of new meaning, but instead it has more often than interrogated, adjudicated, or criticized it as substandard, deviant, or simply wrong; think of the stereotypes of 'Yellow Peril' or 'Dragon Lady' (Curran and Park 2000; Reeves 1993; Shi-xu 2007; Shi-xu *et al.* 2005). It may be noted, too, that in the process the non-Western World scholarship rarely has its own identity or voice (Cooks and Simpson 2007; Lauf 2005; Shi-xu 2009b). Scholars and students based in the global South and diasporas, many of whom are trained in the West, find themselves in a cultural-intellectual dilemma. While realizing the limitations and inappropriateness of Western scholarship for understanding non-Western discursive practice, they do not yet have a coherent research system available that can be readily applied, on the one hand, and, on the other, in order to publish internationally, they have to emulate Western scholarship by conforming to Western concepts, values and interests, completing the circle of the Western-global discourse thereby.

There are many causes of this sorry cultural-intellectual state. To be sure, the prevalent Westcentric attitude vis-à-vis the rest on the one hand and ignorance of non-Western intellectual heritages on the other are the important subjective factors behind this. But the Westcentric discourse cannot become rampant and devastating without Western dominance and control over the international scholarly communication system (Shi-xu 2005, 2009b, 2014). It has become imperative then that a cultural alternative must be found to counterbalance this totalizing academic discourse and to addressing Asian discourse from its own perspective.

Asian intellectual heritages

The construction of an Asian paradigm of discourse studies does not have to start from scratch, fortunately. There are special and foundational Asian cultural and intellectual resources for use. Asian cultures have unique philosophical insights, for instance, that cannot only underpin the paradigm-constructive work but also compliment the Western approaches (one may think of the *Analects* of Confucius of China, the *Natya shastra*, one of the most important works on dramaturgy in India, and the works of Dogen and Zeami of Japan). Furthermore, there is a strong tradition of Asian communication studies which emerged from the late 1980s (Chu 1986); it contains an impressive array of concepts and principles of Asian communication. Besides, there is continued work in linguistics, pragmatics, rhetoric, comparative literature, intercultural communication, and so on, which explores characteristics of Asian contexts. When these strands of knowledge are synthesized, they should constitute exquisite bases for creation of an Asian framework of discourse research.

Let me begin with possible contributions from Asian philosophy. The Asian cultural traditions of Confucianism, Buddhism, Daoism, Hinduism, and so on, share an ontological view of the universe as unified One, which is composed of manifold, variously interconnected parts. In Chinese philosophy, for example, this worldview is expressed in such terms as 和 (unity in diversity) and 天人合一 (nature and man in one) (Chen 2003, 2006; Chu 1986; Zhang 2002). In Indian culture, the relatedness of everything is basic (Dissanayake 1988b; Oliver 1976: 137). In relation to that, there is a typical Asian dialectic approach to knowledge. That is, epistemologically, Asians tend to see things as a unity of two or more interdependent, interpenetrating and interchanging parts, in contrast to the Western binary, bi-polar and essentialistic way of thinking. In Indian philosophy, people are taught to see things in terms of their relations with one another (Dissanayake 1983, 1987). This mental habit is epitomized in the Chinese *yin-yang* dialectics. So given a problem, Asian peoples are likely to see the inter-infiltration of things, possibility of dynamic change between them and above all the wholeness of all relations. For example, the economic crisis started in late 2008 may well be interpreted as a window of opportunities for economic reform or self-re-invention. In close connection with the holistic worldview, furthermore, Asian peoples are morally expected to achieve and maintain harmony and balance in social interaction (Xiao and Chen 2009). In a Buddhist perspective, humans are required to exercise responsibilities, self-reflection and restraint (Ishii 2009).

The tradition of Asian communication studies is another rich resource to be tapped into for the construction of Asian discourse studies. It gathered momentum when Dissanayake's *Communication Theory: the Asian Perspective* was published in 1988 and Kincaid's *Communication Theory: Eastern and Western perspectives* in 1987. Since then, a body of research work on Asian concepts and principles of communication has been steadily growing (Chen 2003, 2006; Dissanayake 2003, 2009; Gunaratne 2008; Ishii 2001; Miike 2002, 2006, 2007). Conceptually and theoretically, this tradition has explored 和谐 (harmony, Chen 2001, 2004), 中

庸 (moderation), 面子 (face, Jia 1997), 缘 (predestined connection, Chang and Holt 1991), 客气 (politeness, Feng 2004; Gu 1990) in China, *dhvani* (suggestion, Dissanayake 2009a; Chari 1977) in India, *uye-ri* in Korea (proper interpersonal relationships, Yum 1987), enryo-sasshi and *amae* (message-expanding and message-accepting needs) in Japan (Ishii 1984; cf. Hara 2003), *kreng jai* in Thailand (being extremely considerate, Chaidaroon 2003) and so on and so forth and proffered a rich and diversified picture of the principles, ideals and images of Asian forms of communication.

Of course, cultural concepts, principles, values, rules, strategies for action and communication are relevant only if and when they are realized in symbolic and communicative practice and this is where studies in Asian discourses can offer important vantage points. There is a growing body of linguistically and literarily oriented studies on Asian concepts and theories of communication and methods of research. One important lineage regards the core Asian notion of language in relation to meaning. In Chinese scholarship, meaning is and has always been understood as limitless but language as limited in its meaning-making capacity, such that there is but a marginal relationship between language and meaning and the latter is imaginative, open-ended and dynamic; these cultural concepts are typically expressed in such terms and sayings as道, 意境，神韵，弦外之音，言不尽意，言有意而意无穷 (Cao 2008). The wariness of the limitation of language in regard to meaning is similarly reflected in Indian, Japanese and Korean scholarship (Dissanayake 1988b; Ishii 1984; Yum 1987). The Indian notion of *dhvani* is a case in point: it implies that language is to be understood as pertaining to suggestive meaning or transfer of poetic meaning, involving active participation of the recipient; in order to achieve non-form-bound, suggestive meaning of language, the reader and so the researcher are required to resort to verbal resourcefulness, maturity of understanding and depth of imagination (Dissanayake 1988a; 2009). Given the intractable problem of how to relate language to meaning, there is a body of scholarship on Asian rules and techniques for understanding language, too: e.g. resorting to classics, imagery, intuition, sudden enlightenment through (inter)subjectivity (e.g. 顿悟，*satori*), meditation (e.g. 静思), watching actions, examining personality, endless circle of understanding life through words (逆文通志) and understanding words through life (得志通文), and so on (Cao 2008; 钱钟书 2007; 周光庆 2002). In addition to these, there is a number of major conferences and publications on the topic. A special issue in *Journal of Multicultural Discourses* (2009: (4)1) updates the achievements and new directions of Asian discourse studies.

An Asian cultural paradigm: Asian discourse studies

In the present study, the term 'discourse' is used to refer to a situated event or activity (i.e. an interrelated string thereof) in which social actors interact with one another through natural and/or mediated use of linguistic as well as other symbols in cultural and historical context (Shi-xu 2014). This broad concept draws on insights from discourse analysis, pragmatics, sociolinguistics, ethnography of communication and cultural studies but differs in that it emphasizes the historical and hence cultural-political nature and dimensions of discourse and dialectic relations of the manifold constituents of discourse.

Asian discourse studies is envisaged here as a system of interrelated research frameworks – philosophical, theoretical, methodological and topical – that reflects Asian cultural traditions, realities and aspirations and is devoted to the goals of Asian development. By implication, it is a sister paradigm so to speak to those of African and Latin American discourse studies. In this context then, 'Asian discourse' is also used in a particular way to refer to any form of contemporary cultural-communicative practice by Asian peoples and communities closely connected with their historical and cultural conditions of development, so most particularly with developing countries. Thus, any hegemonic, American-controlled but otherwise 'Asian' discourse counter to Asian people's development goals, would not belong to this category. It may be noted that ADS is open-ended because it is evolving and dialogic, for example, with regard to other sub-paradigms of the Eastern paradigm and the Western mainstream; it is dynamic because there is internal diversity and complexity (e.g. between Chinese, Indian and Japanese approaches). In the following, we shall sketch out an outline of this system.

Philosophical assumptions

Our philosophical component contains propositions at three levels, ontological, epistemological and axiological which will answer the basic questions of ADS: namely, what it studies, how and why. Thus, first, from the earlier mentioned Asian holistic point of view, it may be stated that ADS takes Asian discourse, its ontological object of enquiry, to be any historically and (inter)culturally situated communicative practice (event or activity, i.e. a series thereof) since the end of the Cold War which involves Asian socio-cultural life, real or potential, by any Asian people or society. Underlying this definition is a view or understanding of Asian discourse that stresses the multiplicity of its constituent parts and complex relationships and in particular the differential value and power dimensions: it is a culturally and historically unique entity (diversity, complexity, disparity, (post) coloniality, etc.) on the one hand and on the other, part of the discourses of the Eastern, developing, Third/Fourth, world, as opposed to those of the Western, developed world. Such a view distinguishes ADS from the Western mainstream discourse analysis tradition in that the former is concerned with a culturally particular object of study though with a global dimension, that it appreciates diverse and complicated relations within and without and especially that it recognizes the culturally differentiated and competing nature of human discourses.

This definition and view of Asian discourse would enable ADS researchers to look into for example who are (not) speaking in Asian culture, what problems they experience, what aspirations they have, as opposed to those of the American-Western world, how Asian people communicate (e.g. under what moral principles), in relation to their own history and to the contemporary Western counterpart, what kind of mediums (e.g. languages are channels of communication) are at their disposal, with what effect, and so on.

Second, thanks to the Asian dialectic, and hence culturally grounded, epistemology as alluded to earlier, and given the unique scope and identity of Asian discourse, ADS takes it for granted that study of Asian discourse must be conducted from an Asian cultural, intra-Asian cultural and multicultural or intercultural perspective. In this light, what ADS seeks and produces is cultural understanding.

This implies that researchers should try to acquire wide and deep Asian historical and cultural knowledge and experience and that they should learn from different Asian cultural scholarships (see also 陈光兴). This would also require that Asian discourse scholars and students must keep a modest and persistently-searching attitude towards their research community and enterprise as a whole. Such an epistemological stance distinguishes ADS from the mainstream Western discourse analysis in that it goes beyond its hierarchical division of knowledge (e.g. objective vs. subjective, universal vs. cultural) and seeks knowledge and judgement through a continuous process of search, reflection and dialogue, especially from the point of view of the Asian peoples and cultures.

Third, considering especially the untold Asian history, its current place in the broader unequal, unjust global order and more particularly the post-'Asia-century' uncertainty and instability, we suggest that ADS should strive to help advance the Asian goals of development, and along with it, unity, peace and prosperity. That means that Asian discourse researchers should take a culturally conscious and critical stance towards the Asian community and its discourse, with special reference to its development as at once condition, concern and objective. Specifically, it would mean, for example, that their topic of concern, theoretical attention and methodological tools must be grounded in and tailored to Asian realities, needs and aspirations.

Theoretical assumptions

I would like to canvass Asian discourse in the form of a number of propositions which may be taken as theoretical prisms with which to examine, evaluate and escort Asian practice. First of all, unlike Western societies, the Asian peoples share a modern history of untold sufferings at the hands of colonialism, imperialism and the Cold War. Permeating in social, cultural, political, economic, scientific, military, and many other spheres, this historical experience has resulted in a collective memory which is profoundly embedded in Asian contemporary communication. A case in point is the patriotic, or call it anti-imperialist, discourse for territorial integrity, national self-determination and aversion to neo-colonial hegemony. For research practice, this would mean that scholars and students of Asian discourse should attempt to rewrite the Asian past and present from the Asian people's own point of view, reformulate Asia's future from a historically-reflexive-and-critical perspective and carry out debate and dialogue for new principles of inter- and intra-cultural communication.

Second, in contrast to Western societies, Asian communities are faced with particular socio-economic problems as well as potentials: poverty, low-level industrialization, high-rates of illiteracy, socio-economic contradictions, environmental pressures (Lerner and Schramsm 1967; Reeves 1993) on the one hand and on the other huge markets, cheap labour and possibilities of great economic expansion. These and other socio-economic conditions are embodied in the ways that Asian discourse is organized and functions in local and global society. Empirically, this would mean that investigations should be made into what particular discursive factors impact on socio-economic performance (e.g. participation and efficacy in public and international communication, flow of information), what kinds of problem they cause to socio-economic growth, and how Asian peoples can discursively stimulate, sustain and support socio-economic development.

Third, given their shared historical experience and contemporary environment, the Asians have their own aspirations and objectives, namely, development (Melkote and Steeves 2001). This is a complex and contested goal, as should be realized, however, which is closely linked with other major issues such as security, sovereignty, environmental protection and human rights. Asian discourse researchers should then probe into Asian people's own understanding of and attitude towards the concept, their perception of the relevant barriers, needs and strategies in relation to the objective of development.

Fourth, as part of this developmental nature, Asian discourse is embedded in an uneven, viz. US-Western-dominated, international order of communication as a disadvantaged participant, where Asians have less power to speak and their cultures, like other non-Western ones, are more often than not portrayed as backward, repressive, authoritarian, corrupt and so on, in contradistinction to the modern, democratic, free West. This ethnocentric hierarchy has tremendous consequences on the ways Asian discourse is received, understood and responded to and ultimately on their development (Chomsky 1993; Cooks and Simpson 2007; Croteau and Hoynes 1994; Hawk 1992; Herman and Chomsky 1988; Iwabuchi 2010; Pratt 1992; Said 1978, 1993; Tanno and Jandt 1994; Van Dijk 1993). In this order, too, the majority of the Asian communities do not speak English (or other European languages) as the mother tongue; at the same time, their own native languages are often discriminated against at a national and international level. This linguistic racism or linguisticism is particularly worth noting, partly because international research is done largely in and through English (Lauf 2005; Pennycook 1998). Empirical studies should then be directed at exposing and undermining the unequal and unjust international system of communication, illuminating possibilities of change, and contriving new ways of consolidating and reclaiming the Asian community as equal global participant.

Besides, Asian worldviews, values, ways of thinking, languages and so on, in contrast to those of Western cultures, are an important and special part of Asian tradition constituting their contemporary discourse. Influenced by (versions of) Confucianism, Buddhism, Daoism, Hinduism, Shintoism and so on, for example, Asians have a holistic view of the universe, that is as a unified whole of interrelated parts; further, they approach things dialectically, namely by noticing therein complex relations of interconnection, interdependence, inter-opposition, interpenetration, interchange, and so on; consequently, their discourse is oriented towards the primary value and principle of societal harmony and balance, or *equilibrium* (Shi-xu 2007; Shi-xu *et al.* 2005), in contrast to the Western value of individual reason and control (Chen 2001, 2004; Dissanayake 1987; Hara 2003; Hasnain 1988; Tehranian 1988; Yum 1988). Thus for example, the Indian model of communication suggests how important listening is for understanding communication (Dissanayake 1983: 29). The Japanese dual mode thinking and Mahayana Buddhism can explain their modal expressions, particularly honorifics, beyond Westcentric theoretical lenses. The patterns of identity construction (Saunders 2007), topic introduction (Scollon and Wong-Scollon 1991), politeness (Gu 1990), smile (Yum 1988: 79–80), silences (Miike 2003: 48–49) and so on are still other unique aspects of Asian communication. Moreover, as is virtually unknown to the Western scholarly circle, there is the typically Asian discrepancy between language and meaning. When Western researchers concentrate laboriously on observable forms and processes of language use, Asian scholars have long recognized the limitations of language and opened up the horizons of meaning. This is typically referred to as 言不尽意 (not all is and can be expressed in and through language, or there is infinite meaning beyond language). Consequently, silence, taciturnity, vagueness, indirectness, use of imagery and classics, and so on become a defining feature of Asian discourses (Dissanayake 1988a; Rahim 1987; Stowell 2003; Yum 1987). As a result, furthermore, while many meanings may be recovered from silences, many others cannot be recovered from what is said. Consequently, intuition, heightened sensitivity, instantaneous enlightenment, circular and endless reading between language and life, and so on are required as strategies of interpretation. Asian discourse researchers should then try to excavate such cultural values and rules, render them understandable internationally, and make possible intercultural dialogue and critique over them.

Last but by no means least, Asian discourse, or discourses, are as diversified as they are complex. Dynamic, hybridized and multifarious, Asian discourses are internally competing, economically, socially, religiously, linguistically, and in many other spheres (Irwin 1996; Shan 2004; Tu 1994). Just think of the mainstream religions such as Buddhism, Islam, Christianity, Hinduism and Shintoism. It is imperative then for Asian discourse students and scholars to identify and tease out intra-Asian particularities, interconnections, commonalities; they should search in particular for points of possible synergy for an empowered and prosperous Asia.

Methodological assumptions

Until recently study of Asia in general and of Asian communication in particular has been confined to so-called area studies which is conducted mainly from outside Asia, that is in the United States and Western Europe. Consequently, the models, methods and moral stances are more often than not Westcentric, or anyway out of touch with Asian realities.

As indicated above, Asia is unique as it is complex, diversified and complicated in history and culture; more particularly, it is at the crossroads of globalization as the US military re-enters Asia under the guise of 'rebalancing Asia'. If development, peace and unity should remain the central goals of Asian peoples, then we must take Asian stances, Asian perspectives and Asian techniques.

陈光兴 (2006) has argued for he calls 'Asia as method', meaning that, first of all, to study an Asian community one must use other Asian communities as frame of reference and that, further, one can use Asian experience to understand human affairs (see also Dissanayake 2003). Basically, this two-fold strategy places Asian context, knowledge and experience at the core of the methodology of Asian studies. In conformity with this general principle, we suggest some more specific tools for Asian discourse studies.

First and foremost, ADS takes the explicit cultural-political stance of supporting Asia's development, peace and unity as central principles of its investigation, evaluation and instruction. While what exactly constitutes Asia's development, peace and unity will remain open for continuous dialogue, ADS takes it for granted that its position is ultimately for the reconstruction and consolidation of the Third or Developing World as the guarantor of world peace and prosperity. This methodological stance would mean that researchers should use Asian's concepts of development, peace and unity to identify, describe, critique and guide Asian practice.

Second, ADS emphasizes local cultural concerns, experience and perspectives as topics of interest, starting point and frame of reference. This means that the researcher must try to acquire as much Asian insider, native knowledge, scholarly as well as ordinary, and make use of it for data collection, problem explication and interpretation. For example, Asian colonial, anticolonial and postcolonial history must become not only the object of (re-)interrogation, but also a comparative tool. Likewise, Asian scholarly resources, whether in terms of analytic notions or interpretative strategies, should also be mobilized in order to more appropriately and effectively discover, describe and decipher Asian experience and practice.

Third, ADS will use the notion of cultural discourse (Shi-xu 2014, 2015) as a special and specific way of conceptualizing Asian phenomena or problems and accordingly research Asian discourse in terms of a set of interrelated categories of social communicative action: subjects, intent, form or relation, mediums, purpose or effects, culture and history. It may be added here that, following from our holistic conception of the object of enquiry, ADS studies a problem not through one or two singular phenomena but a diversity of interrelated or relevant events or activities, where the notions of the front stage and back stage, to borrow Goffman's (1959) terms, and of words and deeds, play an important role.

Research agenda on Asia's development

As alluded to earlier, Asia has manifold, complex and grave issues and problems that require our attention urgently. This imperative comes from the accelerated process of globalization in general and the current critical conjunctures of Asia

Pacific in particular. Accordingly, we suggest the following priority tasks and topics for ADS.

First, we must re-examine and reflect on various forms of narratives and ignorance of especially modern Asian history in order to help decolonize and rebuild Asian identity for the future. Understanding history is one essential way for and step towards adequate interpretation of the present and future. 陈光兴 (2006) has argued for de-colonization, de-cold-war and de-imperialization as badly needed prerequisites for reclaiming Asia. For discourse research, this would mean that we study whether people talk about Asian history, what they say about it and how, how people respond to it and what effects discourses of Asian history bring about, and so on.

Second, we must look into the diversity and specificity of Asian discourse in order not only to understand Asian complexity and dynamics, but also to find synergy for collective objectives and opportunities for common good. As indicated earlier, one of Asia's hallmarks is its heterogeneity and disparity, whether in politics, economy, religion, language, customs or tradition. It is imperative then for Asian discourse scholars and students to find ways of communication that can accommodate differences, empower the deprived, disregarded or otherwise disadvantaged, and undermine forms of discourse that discriminate against or dominate over difference.

Third, we should of course centrally focus on issues of Asia's development as is both the defining condition and primary aspiration of the Asian community. Thus, we may investigate into the Asian discursive practice of development, whether in the political, social, economic, educational, medical, rural, urban, academic, technological, regional, or legal spheres; we should also try to identify and characterize Asian experiences of development, whether positive or negative, so that lessons can benefit all Asian communities and beyond in the developing, Third World.

Fourth, in relation to, or rather, as an integral part of, the Asian discourse of development, we must be attentive to the (sub-) discourse of peace, conflict and disunity, with a view to achieving common security and prosperity in Asia and the world at large. Development cannot proceed or sustain without peace and security. One must not forget, at the time of writing, foreign aggression and mass killings are of daily occurrence in in Palestine, Afghanistan and Iraq; maritime disputes loom large in the South China Sea; nuclear threat is real in the Korean peninsula. Asian (discourse) scholars and students have the obligation and responsibility therefore to actively engage in critiques of discourses of imperialism, militarism, and separatism on the one hand and advocacies of discourses of dialogue, reconciliation, coexistence and harmony on the other.

In addition, Asia's links with Africa and Latin America as well as with the rest of the world should become integral part of ADS's research agenda. What are the commonalities in their philosophies, values, histories, places in the current world order (of communication), the peoples' aspirations and barriers to their independence, self-determination and development? How may such shared experiences be turned into a unified discourse of identity, voice and power to foster their development, security and prosperity?

There are just too many topics of interest regarding Asia and Asian discourse to be listed here and research questions will have to shift as Asia and the rest of the (developing) world move. But by now it should be clear that ADS is an emerging paradigm designed to confront issues of Asian development in the context of globalization.

Conclusion

From the above exposition, it will have been seen that, while the international discourse scholarship is culturally and intellectually exclusionary and restricted, Asian scholarly heritages are left on the margins or in decay. At the societal level, Asia is at the crossroads as America re-enters it militarily and the situation is critical but at the same time offers an opportunity for change. What we have tried to show is that it is also a situation full of possibilities and opportunities. One of the biggest and unique assets is that many Asian scholars and students of Asian culture and communication are versed in both Western and Asian societies and languages on the one hand and on the other both Western and Asian scholarship. In addition to them, there is a growing number of culturally reflexive and critical individuals in the mainstream who become increasingly concerned with the ways that culturally singular and exclusive scholarship operates in the multicultural world and its consequences for humanity in general and human knowledge in particular. No less important, as must be added immediately, is the new stage of the social sciences we are at now: a postmodern, postcolonial and globalizing era when truths and universal values are no longer taken for granted but understood as saturated with power and when intellectual and cultural, or multicultural, democracy is on the way to becoming the norm. Most important of all perhaps, Asia is in its most dynamic and vibrant, though still rather uncertain and precarious, phase in its history, with China, India, South Korea playing pivotal and ascending roles in the world economy. In this context, Asian scholars and students of culture and communication have the historic opportunity to re-envision, reclaim and reformulate Asia's path to development, peace and unity. For this we propose the following strategic agendas:

1 To pay urgent attention to and study Asian discourses reflecting the concerns and aspirations of Asian and diasporic societies themselves which account for more than 60 per cent of the world's population.
2 To engage in critical and constructive dialogue with the Western mainstream at the philosophical, theoretical, methodological and empirical levels, and, in particular, in major social scientific debates over postcolonialism, postmodernism, Black studies, feminist studies, and so on, for a comparative and contrastive approach will not only help generate innovations but also sharpen the Asian paradigmatic identity itself.
3 To tap into historical concepts and perspectives in order to regain and enrich contemporary paradigmatic identity, as Asian cultures are replete with wisdoms and vitality that the contemporary world so badly needs.

4 To mutually learn from the scholarships, traditional as well as contemporary, of intra-Asian cultures and communities and, no less importantly, to learn from African and Latin American scholarships.
5 To internationalize Asian discourse scholarships by speaking and writing about them in the international arena.

I do not mean to say that all students and scholars concerned should take up these tasks all at the same time. Some of them should work on one or the other projects but often achieving one goal may contribute to another or more of the others and work on all these fronts will ultimately contribute to the construction of the collective system of Asian paradigms of discourse studies.

References

Asante, M. K. (2006). The rhetoric of globalisation: The Europeanisation of human ideas. *Journal of Multicultural Discourses*, 1(2): 152–158.

Cao, S. Q. (2008).The discourse of Chinese literary theory and the dialogue between Western and Chinese literary theories. *Journal of Multicultural Discourses*, 3(1): 1–15.

Chaidaroon, S. (2003). A case of Thai communication competence. *Intercultural Communication Studies*, XII (4): 195–208.

Chang, H-C and Holt, G. R. (1991). The concept of *yuan* and Chinese interpersonal relationships. In S. Ting-Toomey and F. Korzenny (eds), *Cross-cultural Interpersonal Communication*. Newbury Park, CA: Sage, pp. 28–57.

Chari, V. K. (1977). The Indian theory of suggestion (dhvani). *Philosophy East and West*, 2(4): 391–399.

Chen G. M. (2001). Towards transcultural understanding: a harmony theory of Chinese communication. In V. H. Milhouse, M. K. Asante and P. O. Nwosu (eds), *Transculture: Interdisciplinary Perspectives on Cross-cultural Relations*. Thousand Oaks, CA: Sage, pp. 55–70.

Chen G. M. (2003). Asian approaches to human communication: a dialogue. *Intercultural Communication Studies*, XII(4): 1–16.

Chen G. M. (2004). The two faces of Chinese communication. *Human Communication*, 7: 25–36.

Chen, G. M. (2006). Asian communication studies: what and where to now. *The Review of Communication*, 6(4): 295–311.

Chen, G. M. (2010) Beyond the dichotomy of communication studies. *Asian Journal of Communication*, 19(4): 398–411.

Chomsky, N. (1993). *Year 501: The Conquest Continues*, Boston, MA: South End Press.

Chu, G. C. (1986). In search of an Asian perspective of communication theory. *Media Asia: An Asian Mass Communication Quarterly*, 13(1): 3–5.

Cooks, L. M. and J. S. Simpson (eds) (2007). *Whiteness, Pedagogy, Performance*. Lanham, MD: Lexington Books.

Croteau, D. and W. Hoynes (1994). *By Invitation Only: How the Media Limit Political Debate*. New York: Common Courage Press.

Curran, J. and M. J. Park. (eds) (2000). *De-Westernizing Media Studies*. London: Routledge.

David L. (2012) Imperial modernity: history and global inequity in rising Asia. *Third World Quarterly*, 33(4): 581–601.

Dissanayake, W. (1983) Communication in the cultural tradition of India. *Media Development*, 30(1): 27–30.

Dissanayake, W. (1987) The guiding image in Indian culture and its implications for Communication. In D. L. Kincaid (ed.), *Communication Theory: Eastern and Western perspectives*. San Diego, CA: Academic, pp.151–158.

Dissanayake, W. (ed.) (1988a) *Communication Theory: The Asian Perspective*. Singapore: Asian Mass Communication Research and Information Center.

Dissanayake, W. (1988b) Foundations of Indian verbal communication and phenomenology. In W. Dissanayake (ed.), *Communication Theory: The Asian perspective*. Singapore: Asian Mass Communication Research and Information Center, pp.39–55.

Dissanayake, W. (2003) Asian approaches to human communication: retrospect and prospect. *Intercultural Communication Studies*, XII(4): 16–37.

Dissanayake, W. (2009a) The desire to excavate Asian theories of communication: one strand of the history. *Journal of Multicultural Discourses*. 4(1): 7–27.

Dissanayake, W. (2009b) The production of Asian theories of ommunication: contexts and challenges. *Asian Journal of Communication*,19(4): 453–468.

Feng, H. R. (2004) *Keqi* and Chinese communication behaviours. In G. M. Chen (ed.), *Theories and Principles of Chinese Communication*. Taipei, Taiwan: WuNan, pp.435–450.

Goffman, E. (1959). *The Presentation of the Self in Everyday Life*. Garden City, NY: Doubleday.

Gu, Y. G. (1990) Politeness phenomena in modern Chinese. *Journal of Pragmatics*, 14: 237–257.

Gunaratne, S. A. (2008). Falsifying two Asian paradigms and de-Westernizing science. Communication, *Culture and* Critique, 1(1): 72–85.

Hara, K. (2003). Aspects of Shinto in Japanese communication. *Intercultural Communication Studies*, XII(4): 81–104.

Hasnain, I. (1988). Communication: An Islamic approach. In W. Dissanayake (ed.), *Communication Theory: The Asian Perspective*. Singapore: Asian Mass Communication Research and Information Center, pp.183–189.

Hawk, B. (1992). *Africa's Media Image*. New York: Praeger.

Herman, E., and Chomsky, N. (1988). *Manufacturing Consent*. New York: Pantheon Books.

Irwin, H. (1996). *Communication with Asia: Understanding People and Customs*. New South Wales, Australia: Allen and Unwin.

Ishii, S. (1984). Enryo-sasshi communication: A key to understanding Japanese interpersonal relations. *Cross Currents*, 11(1): 49–58.

Ishii, S. (2001). An emerging rationale for Triworld communication studies from Buddhist perspectives. *Human Communication*, 4(1): 1–10.

Ishii, S. (2006) Complementing contemporary intercultural communication Research with East Asian sociocultural perspective and practices. *China Media Research,* 2(1): 13–20.

Ishii, S. (2009). Conceptualizing Asian communication ethics: a Buddhist perspective. *Journal of Multicultural Discourses,* 4(1): 49–60.

Iwabuchi, K. (2010). Globalization, East Asia media cultures and their publics. *Asian Journal of Communication,* 20(2): 197–212.

Jia, W. (1997). Facework as a Chinese conflict-preventive mechanism – a cultural/discourse analysis. *Intercultural Communication Studies,* VII (1): 43–58.

Kim, S. (2009) Cultural bias in communication science: challenges of overcoming ethnocentric paradigms in Asia. *Asian Journal of Communication,* 19(4): 412–421.

Kim, M. S. (2010) Intercultural communication in Asia: Current state and future prospects. *Asian Journal of Communication*, 20 (2): 166–180.

Kincaid, D. L. (ed.) (1987) *Communication Theory: Eastern and Western Perspectives*. San Diego, CA: Academic Press.

Lauf, E. (2005) National diversity of major international journals in the field of communication. *Journal of Communication*, March, 139–151.

Lerner, D. and Schramm, W. (1967). *Communications and Change in Developing Countries*. Honolulu, HI: East-West Center Press.

Melkote, S. R. and Steeves, H. L. (2001) *Communication for Development in the Third World: Theory and Practice for Empowerment*. India: Sage.

Miike, Y. (2002). Theorizing culture and communication in the Asian context: an assumptive foundation. *Intercultural Communication Studies*, XI(1): 1–22.

Miike, Y. (2006) Non-western theory in western research? An Asiacentric agenda for Asian communication studies. *Review of Communication*, 6(1–2): 4–31.

Miike, Y. (2007). An Asiacentric reflection on Eurocentric bias in communication theory. *Communication Monographs*, 74(2): 272–278.

Nissanke, M. and Thorbecke, E. (eds) (2010) *The Poor under Globalization in Asia, Latin America, and Africa*, Oxford: Oxford University Press.

Oga, T. (2004). Rediscovering Asianness: the role of institutional discourses in APEC, 1989–1997. *International Relations of the Asia*-Pacific, 4: 287–317.

Oliver, R.T. (1976). Rhetoric and the social matrix: reflections from the Asian classics. *Communication*, 4(2): 134–151.

Pennycook, A. (1998). *English and the Discourses of Colonialism*. London: Routledge.

Pratt, M. L. (1992). *Imperial Eyes: Travel Writing and Transculturation*. London: Routledge.

Rahim, A. (1987). The practice of Antyodaya in agricultural extension communication in India. (pp. 173–182) *Communication Theory: Eastern And Western Perspectives*. London: Academic Press.

Reeves, G. (1993). *Communications and the 'Third World'*. London: Routledge.

Said, E. W. (1978). *Orientalism*. London: Routledge & Kegan Paul.

Said, E. W. (1993). *Culture and Imperialism*. New York: Alfred A. Knopf.

Saunders, J. B. (2007). 'I don't eat meat': Discourse on food among transnational Hindus. *Contributions to Indian Sociology*, 41(2): 203–23.

Scollon, R. & S. W. Scollon (1995). *Intercultural Communication: A Discourse Approach*. Oxford: Blackwell.

Shan, B. (2004). Xiandai Chuanmei Yu Shehui Wenhua Fazhan [Modern Media and Social Development]. *Xiandai Chuanmei* [*Modern Media*], 1: 10–16.

Shi-xu (2005). *A Cultural Approach to Discourse*. Houndmills, England/New York: Palgrave Macmillan.

Shi-xu, M. Kienpointner and J. Servaes (eds) (2005). *Read the Cultural Other: Forms of Otherness in the Discourses of Hong Kong's Decolonisation*. Berlin/New York: Mouton de Gruyter.

Shi-xu (2006). A multiculturalist approach to discourse theory. *Semiotica*, 158(1/4): 383–400.

Shi-xu (ed) (2007). *Discourse as Cultural Struggle*, Hong Kong: Hong Kong University Press.

Shi-xu (2009a). Asian discourse studies: foundations and directions. *Asian Journal of Communication*, 19 (4): 384–297.

Shi-xu (2009b). Reconstructing Eastern paradigms of discourse studies. *Journal of Multicultural Discourse*, 4(1): 29–48.

Shi-xu (2014) *Chinese Discourse Studies.* Basingstoke: Palgrave Macmillan.

Shi-xu (2015) Cultural discourse studies. In K. Tracy, K., C. Ilie and T. Sandel (eds), *International Encyclopedia of Language and Social Interaction.* Oxford: Wiley-Blackwell. pp. 284–297.

Stowell, J. (1996). The changing face of Chinese communication: a synthesis of interpersonal communication concepts. Paper presented at the Speech Communication Association Convention, San Diego, CA.

Tanno, D. V. and Jandt, F. E. (1994). Redefining the 'other' in multi-cultural research. *The Howard Journal of Communication*, 5: 36–45.

Tehranian, M. (1988). Communication theory and Islamic perspectives. In W. Dissanayake (ed.), *Communication theory: The Asian perspective*. Singapore: Asian Mass Communication Research and Information Center, pp.190–203.

Tu, W. M. (1994). Auletter cultural China: The periphery as the center. In W. M. Tu (ed.), *The Living Tree: The Changing Meaning of Being Chinese Today* (pp. 1–34). Stanford, CA: Stanford University Press.

Van Dijk, T. A. (1993). *Elite Discourse and Racism*, London: Sage.

Wang, G. and Shen, V. (2000) East, west, communication, and theory: searching for the meaning of searching for Asian communication theories. *Asian Journal of Communication*, 10(2): 14–32.

Wang, H. (2007) The politics of imagining Asia: a genealogical analysis (trans. A. H. Matthew) *Inter-Asia Cultural Studies*, 8(1): 1–33.

Wang, X. M. (2010) The concept of 'Asia' in modern China: some reflections starting with the 2007 Shanghai conference (trans. L. Petrus) *Inter-Asia Cultural Studies*, 11(2): 197–201.

Xiao, X. S. and Chen, G. M. (2009). Communication competence and moral competence: a Confucian perspective. *Journal of Multicultural Discourses*, 4(1): 61–74.

Yin, J. (2009). Negotiating the center: toward an Asiacentric feminist communication theory. *Journal of Multicultural Discourses,* 4(1): 75–88.

Yoichi, F. (1993) The Asianization of Asia. *Foreign Affairs*, 72(5): 75–85.

Yum, J. O. (1987). Korea Philosophy and Communication. In D. L. Kincaid (ed.), *Communication Theory*. New York: Academic Press, Inc., pp. 71–85.

Yum, J. O. (1988).The impact of Confucianism on interpersonal relationships and communication patterns in East Asia. *Communication Monographs*, 55: 374–488.

Zhang, D. N. (2002). *Key Concepts in Chinese Philosophy* (trans. E. Ryden). Beijing: Foreign Languages Press.

References in Chinese

陈光兴 (2006)《去帝国 ––亚洲作为方法》台北：行人出版社。

钱钟书 (2007)《管锥编》（1–4）北京：三联书店。

施旭 (2010)《文化话语研究：探索中国的理论、方法与问题》北京：北京大学出版社。

周光庆 (2002)《中国古典解释学导论》北京：中华书局。

2 Contemporary Chinese communication from a cultural psychological perspective

In international communication scholarship, Chinese discourse or communication, whether in the form of the media, political documents, literature, or everyday conversation, has often continued to be misunderstood, misrepresented and misjudged. In this chapter, we attempt to re-explicate contemporary Chinese communication from a Chinese cultural psychological perspective, drawing on insights from Chinese psychology (e.g. Wang and Zheng 2005; Yan 1998) as well as communication studies (e.g. Chen 2001; Jia *et al.* 2002; Shi-xu 2005). It is assumed here that cultural psychological properties, as may be manifested in such forms as norms for language use, rules of language use and patterns of thinking in speaking and writing, not only impact on the ways of using language, but also constitute them; cultural psychological and discursive properties are dialectically interwoven. The Chinese worldview (e.g. 天人合一 (holism)), ways of thinking or reasoning (e.g. 辩证统一 (dialectic)), moral values (e.g. 和为贵 (harmony), 中庸 (moderate), collective memory (e.g., of the subjugation to colonialism and imperialism in modern history), attitudes toward other cultural groups (e.g., opposition to hegemony, empathy with Third World countries), feelings about one's country (e.g., 爱国主义 (patriotism), and so on, are all found in one way or another in the Chinese forms of language and communication. It is from this perspective that I argue that contemporary Chinese discourses, as part of Eastern/Asian culture but in contradistinction with the Western counterparts, are characterized by the propensities to be dynamic, tacit, balance-harmonious, face-minded, dialectic, authority-conscious, patriotic, and aesthetic. I illustrate these with examples of a diversity of Chinese discourses. In conclusion I suggest that this framework can be used for not just making new sense of Chinese texts and talk, but also evaluating them critically and constructively.

Introduction

Cultural psychology is designed ultimately to help understand and to help guide cultural practice (Ratner 2008; Schweder 1990; Valsiner 2009). In this chapter we attempt to present a version of Chinese cultural psychological make-up that accounts, to some extent at least, for contemporary Chinese linguistic communication, or discourse. Specifically, we canvass a number of important components of the Chinese cultural psychological system with special reference to discursive practice in contemporary China. Further, we spell out these Chinese cultural psychological constituents in terms of particular strategies of speaking or listening and writing or reading. To elucidate this discourse-oriented Chinese cultural psychological approach, we shall supply empirical examples from diverse settings and analyse them accordingly.

Here we do not intend to present a complete picture of Chinese cultural psychological organization. The particular aspects and elements that we want to highlight in this chapter include: (1) the overarching value or norm of conducting oneself, *he* ('harmony'), (2) the most crucial part of self-concept, *mianzi* ('face'), (3) the collective-memory and self-concept related emotion, *aiguo zhuyi* ('patriotism'), (4) the authority oriented emotion, *chongshang quanwei* ('respect for authority'); (5) the linguistic belief, *yan bu jinyi* ('meaning beyond language'); and (6) the overarching pattern of reasoning, *bianzheng siwei* ('dialectic way of reasoning').[1] These stand at the heart of Chinese cultural character and practice (Chen 2001; Bond 1996; Shi-xu 2010; Wang and Zheng 2005). But unfortunately they have not appeared to be generally understood among the international academia (see for example Brady 2008).

Chinese forms of communication have been studied in many perspectives, ranging from linguistics, rhetoric, literature, philosophy to political economy (Chen 1979; Chen 2001; Heisey 2000; Jia *et al.* 2002; Shen 1996; Shen 2001; Shi-xu 2007; Shi-xu, Kienpointner and Servaes 2005; Xing 2000). But they have hardly ever been considered from a Chinese cultural psychological perspective, due at least in part to want of a Chinese cultural psychological account that links explicitly and systematically with the discourse(s) of present-day China. In other words, there is hitherto little particular and precise knowledge of the relationships between Chinese cultural cognition and emotion on the one hand and Chinese discourses on the other, though Chinese cultural psychological principles for social (inter)action have been recognized more generally (Shi-xu forthcoming; Wang and Zheng 2005). This missing cultural psychological approach is probably attributable in turn to the wider lack of recognition and understanding of the essential relationship between cultural psychological make-up and human discourses (Shi-xu 2005, 2009).

The distinctiveness of the Chinese ways of thinking and feeling is well grounded in the literature (Bond 2010). There are records of a rich Chinese psychological research tradition of more than 2,000 years, with unique concepts, categories and theory (Yan 1998). There is also extant literature registering a wide spectrum of indigenous Chinese psychological experiences, for example, *ren* ('benevolent self'), *guanxi* ('acquaintance relation'), *yuan* ('predestined favourable liaison'), *jingjie* ('moral and spiritual height') (Bond 1986, 1996, 2000; Chu 1985; Wang and Zheng 2005). Further, Chinese psychology is rooted in the unique Chinese philosophical and religious traditions – Confucianism, Daoism and Buddhism (cf. Chen 2001). However, how quintessential Chinese ways of thinking and feeling fit into a picture of Chinese cultural psychology remains to be accomplished.

Re-conceptualizing a culture's discourse from the angle of a cultural psychological system and, conversely, a culture's psychological make-up from the viewpoint of discourse has a number of advantages. Frist, it will expand the horizon of both fields of study, so enrich respective disciplinary understanding, and ultimately enable systematic disciplinary cross-fertilization and sophistication. Second, it will consolidate a dialectic (viz. holistic, relational, and dynamic) approach to cultural psychology on the one hand and to discourse on the other and so perhaps lead to a much needed rethinking of the entrenched universalist discourse and cultural psychological scholarships (Shi-xu 2009; Schweder 1990; Trandis 1999). At a culturally particular level, similarly, such approaches will not only deepen our understanding of culture specific forms of psychology and discourse, but possibly also highlight existing academic ethnocentrism and so enhance scholarly intercultural rebalancing. In addition, a culturally (see below) conscious and critical study of a particular cultural psychological and discursive system as we shall pursue in this chapter can have important implications for re-orienting or transforming a culture's psychological make-up and its discursive practice as well, for, it can reveal strengths, weaknesses and challenges in addition to characteristics.

Cultural psychology and discourse studies

Cultural psychology has been growing as a discipline since at least early 1990s, but till today there has not yet been a general consensus on the object and objectives of research (Boesch 2001; Cole 1996; Schweder 1990; Valsiner 2007, 2009), let alone theory and methodology (Ratner 2008). *Culture and Psychology*, the main journal of the discipline, is witness to this (Valsiner 2009). This may not necessarily be a hindrance to development but is certainly a sign of openness and great potentials of the discipline.

In this chapter we wish to suggest a version of cultural psychology that defines its object of enquiry as the collective consciousness of a people as part of a culture. Culture, which has been variously conceived (Cole 1996; Ratner 2008; Shi-xu 2009; Valsiner 1998, 2007, 2009), is very crucially understood here, not as some separable, a-historical and practice-independent entity, but as the historically situated, interculturally competitive, and so power saturated, way of life of a people, such as subaltern, Eastern, Southern, Asian or Chinese cultures vs Westcentric, Eurocentric or Anglo-American cultures, or the dominant majority cultures vs marginalized minority cultures (Williams 1983; Shi-xu 2009). From this point of view, a cultural psychological make-up is relational: it cannot be understood and defined in isolation from the historically evolved international and intercultural relations and therefore is intrinsically *historical and intercultural* (Shi-xu 2005); in our analysis of the Chinese feelings of patriotism below, we shall highlight its historical and intercultural dimensions. Subaltern, Eastern, Asian or Chinese people's thoughts and feelings are rooted in and organized by their philosophical beliefs, historical experience and tradition, socio-economic conditions, and current international order of domination, repression and prejudice. In this sense it is different from indigenous psychology (where peoples or their cultures and minds are taken to be 'inward-looking') in that it has a *globally* minded perspective in which thoughts and feelings are considered as interculturally connected. And it is different from cross-cultural psychology and certain other forms of cultural psychology (where peoples or their cultures and minds are presumed to be on equal footing with one another) in that *human history* (e.g. of colonialism and imperialism) and so *relations of power* (e.g. of exploitation and exclusion) are taken into account as defining dimensions.

Further, the present account conceptualizes the cultural system of thinking and feeling in terms of a network of *values, strategies and resources* of social interaction, including in particular discourse (see below), namely values for things, people, actions and relations in the world; strategies for thinking, feeling, acting; and resources for thinking, feeling and acting (i.e. concepts and beliefs). Of note here is that this is not an abstract, independent and fixed set of psychological mechanisms, but rather, as hinted at above, it is in dialectic relation with socio-cultural practice. That is, cultural psychological entities and processes are formed, reproduced, maintained, utilized, and transformed in and through socio-cultural activities including especially discourse (Billig 1991; Shi-xu 2005, 2009).

Discourse, in turn, is conceived of here as linguistic practice, as of socio-cultural practice more generally (Fairclough 1992; Gee 1999; Shi-xu 2005, 2009), by thinking and feeling cultural members and groups, in interaction with particular history and cultures. In this view, discourse is a way and site in which a cultural psychological system is formed, transmitted, re-created, utilized, and changed. Because discourse is the primary, prevalent and prevailing part of our social cultural life (Shi-xu 2005, 2007), it is the main medium in which cultural psychological systems are embodied and operate. Consequently, cultural psychology should have a crucial role to play in the understanding of human discourses where and when agents of discourse, speakers, hearers, third-party over-hearers, interpreters and researchers draw upon, make use of, (re)create, and transform cultural psychological consciousness.

The present account is designed, emphatically, not to speculate about abstract cognitions, emotions, strategies, or thought processes. Rather and in particular, it is constructed as a device and resource for making sense of especially practical cultural discourses. The particular Chinese cultural psychological perspective as we shall outline in the remainder of the chapter is therefore to be understood as a descriptive, analytic, interpretative, as well as evaluative, tool to help understand and critique more adequately, and so make more transparent and accountable, present-day Chinese discourses in the present times of globalization and, paradoxically, continuing alienation.

Chinese cultural mind and its contemporary discourse

In what follows, we shall define some basic Chinese cultural psychological categories and principles and, then, spell them out in terms, and the form, of discursive rules in contemporary Chinese communication. It may be noted here that cultural psychological properties will be wider in scope than their discursive embodiment, since they are appropriated in other forms of social action as well. We shall illustrate the actual functioning of these discursive rules with examples from various socio-cultural settings. It will be realized that people may not only follow discursive rules but also take advantage of them or even break them for some pragmatic purposes. It should be borne in mind, too, that the features under discussion, whether at the cultural psychological, or discursive, level, may actually be interconnected in one way or another, but the current exposition is designed to highlight their salient qualities.

He ('harmony'): the overarching value for social (inter)action

The most basic and central social value in the Chinese cultural mind is *he* or 'harmony' (see below). This is the overriding norm or principle for conducting oneself in social life: building harmonious relationship upon egalitarianism or balance of power relations. The notion can be traced back to the classical Chinese concept 'he' as found in *He Wei Gui* (Of primary value is harmony) in the *Analects* by Confucius (551–479 BC) more than 2,000 years ago. But it should be pointed out immediately that *he* in contemporary Chinese cultural ways of thinking is different from its traditional Confucian counterpart in that, whereas before modern China *hierarchy* was the foundation of the value – for example the authority of parents over children, men over women, or the emperor over the subjects, in contemporary China, *balanced* social relationship is the basis. Further, the contemporary Chinese concept of *he* or 'harmony' is also different from what the European or Anglo-American term, harmony, suggests: whereas the latter emphasizes agreement and conformity, the Chinese notion allows for internal *differences* or even *opposition* and therefore may be best conceived of as a value of *unity in diversity* and of *balancing of contradictions*. So, from these historical and intercultural perspectives, the contemporary Chinese notion may be best translated as 'balanced harmony' or 'equilibrium' (but see Chen 2001).

Considered and re-formulated in terms of strategies in contemporary Chinese discourse, then it may be said that the value is manifested in a number of general and specific strategies for linguistic communication, which may be used separately or in combination:

- Build up harmonious relationship; avoid conflict.
- Be polite, sincere, sympathetic, convivial, generous.
- Attend to the interests of others.
- Be modest.
- Choose the middle, avoid extremes ('zhongyong').
- Be inclusive of alternative or opposite opinions.

Let us look at how these may actually be utilized in practice (all citations below are my translation unless otherwise indicated; italics highlight relevant discursive strategies):

> [Foreign Ministry Spokesperson Ma Zhaoxu's Regular Press Conference on 20 May 2010] The sinking of the ship [Cheonan] is a *tragic* event. After the incident, the Chinese side has *expressed its condolences and sympathy* over the casualties of the ROK on many occasions, which fully *shows China's understanding and sympathy* toward the grief of the ROK Government and people. China *has noted* the investigation results released by the ROK. We maintain that all parties *should stay calm, exercise restraint and properly handle relevant issues so as to avoid the escalation* of the situation. I want to stress that China has always viewed and treated international and regional issues *on their own merits in a fair and objective manner*. We have all along *stood for and committed to regional peace and stability*. We *will continue* to push forward the Six-Party Talks and the denuclearization of the Korean Peninsula and *oppose behaviors against such efforts*.
>
> (original, http://www.fmprc.gov.cn/eng/xwfw/s2510/2511/t696115.htm)

In this text, there is expression of sympathy in times of the other's suffering ('tragic'), reference to this expression of sympathy ('expressed'), calling for peace ('should stay calm') and restraint ('to avoid the escalation'), going in the middle ('noted', 'on their own merits'), expression of one's position for peace ('stood for', 'will continue') and of one's opposition to conflict ('oppose'). It may be argued, too, that, as two warring parties as well as third relevant parties are all implicated here but no one particular relevant side is left out or given extra attention, the text may be said to all-encompassing. Nearly all strategies listed above are taken up in this one single instance.

The following excerpt appeared at the start of critical Sino-Euro trade disputes, in which the EU accused China of shoe-dumping and over 4 million Chinese jobs were involved.

> Chinese Minister of Commerce Bo Xilai said at the 20th Sino-EU Economy-Trade Joint Conference that the shoe trade takes *no more than 2%* of the total of the Sino-Euro trade. "We *wouldn't want to have our harmony damaged for this little trade profit*."
>
> (http://www.gutx.com/news /jryw/151809.htm)

In the face of threats of anti-dumping from the EU, the Chinese minister of commerce understated the possible trade loss ('no more than 2%', 'this little trade profit') on the one hand and on the other evoked the Chinese most important value ('wouldn't want to have our harmony damaged'). So both 'generosity' and 'harmony' are exercised here.

Mianzi ('face'): the most valued part of self-concept

Mianzi ('face') is the most important part of the Chinese self-concept, the public image one has of oneself (cf. Gu 1990; Jia 2003). It has a number of crucial features. First, just as the Chinese self-concept itself which contains features of the family, groups, communities and the country one belongs to and is therefore broader than the Western counterpart (Goffman 1967), the Chinese face is more socially extended. One can speak of faces of the family, the group, the community and the country of which one is a member. Second, different from the Western counterpart which emphasizes freedom and control (Brown and Levinson 1987; Leech 1983), the Chinese face is composed of two parts or levels: the personal in terms of rare social resources (e.g. image, position and worth) on the one hand and the societal in terms of attainment of high moral standards on the other. Third, and more importantly, the Chinese face requires more of recognition and respect from social others and is therefore more highly valued and more strongly protected or defended than the Western counterpart.

In terms of discursive strategies, this may be observed in the fact that Chinese speakers will do much more (than 'politeness strategies', Brown and Levinson 1987) to keep (up) one's own face and to enhance or protect others' face than Westerners – sometimes even at heavy costs. In terms of discursive strategies, Chinese speakers typically create, maintain, show or highlight a positive image of themselves in character, position, worth, and so on; given the understanding of the importance of this aspect of the self-concept, they will make efforts to enhance, protect or save others' face, too (cf. Gu 1990). What we saw above in the Chinese Minister of Commerce's remarks is a case in point: a gesture of showing one's nation's noble and generous face.

When face as dignity and respect requiring recognition and respect from social others is 'lost', then Chinese may become defensive or even confrontational. Thus, they will protect or mend their 'face', counter-accuse the other, or even oppose the other vehemently (*sipo lianpi* – tear up the 'face'). So for example, after many years of US accusations of Chinese human rights problems which China deemed hegemonic, starting from 1999, the Information Office of the State Council of China published an extensive record of human right violations by the United States annually – in strict, regular tandem response to the US country reports on human rights (carried in full in major Chinese newspapers, as well as on websites more recently). In addition, the office makes positive reports on Chinese human rights progress (Shi-xu forthcoming).

Aiguo Zhuyi ('patriotism'): emotion of love of the motherland

Chinese love for the mother country or *aiguo zhuyi* ('patriotism') has usually been perceived and interpreted a negative by Western academia, as sentiments of nationalism, nationalist fanaticism or even xenophobia. This understanding ignores the Chinese historical experience of aggression, exploitation and domination by the Western colonial and imperialist powers since the Opium War in 1840s and so also the Chinese collective memory thereof. More importantly, it should be pointed out that from this memory, as well as the over 2,000-year-long tradition of patriotism, arises the valued emotion of love of the mother country. Because of this memory and history, it should be realized, too, that the Chinese cultural emotion of love for the mother country has the particular and unique dimension of cultural humiliation, bitterness and indignation from that experience and tradition.

With respect to contemporary Chinese discourse, this sentiment is used much more frequently than in Western discourses. More particularly, it occurs typically in the contexts of

- National Day commemoration
- War commemoration
- Historical patriotic movement or event commemoration
- Perceived foreign, but especially Western, aggression/provocation/repression
- Sovereign issues
- Scientific, technological breakthrough
- Remarkable personal achievements or contributions
- Crisis or disaster.

It should be noted, too, that the Chinese emotion of the love for the motherland has continuously been attributed or assigned *other, new* meanings than its conventional one. This motherland-loving emotion can be best seen as most vociferously attested to in the well-known books, *Zhongguo Keyi Shuo Bu* (China can say no, by Song Qiang and Zhang Zangzang, 1996) and *Huhuan: Dangjin Zhongguo de Wuzhong Shengyin* (The calls: five voices of contemporary China, by Lin Zhijun and Ma Licheng, 1999). The following excerpts give clear indications:

> [Editorial of *Guangming Daily* on the commemoration of the 60th anniversary of the victory of the Anti-Japanese War and the World Anti-Fascist War] *Putting the State and the Nation's interest first and never succumbing to foreign aggression* are the corner stone of our great nation's *patriotism.* In the 30's of the 20th century, *the Japanese waged a full-scale war* against China and brought it to the brink of national calamity....
>
> (http://www.gmw.cn/content/2005-09/13/content_300065.htm)

> [Jiang Zemin's Speech at the Meeting Celebrating the 80th Anniversary of the Founding of the Communist Party of China] We should advocate the ideology of patriotism, *collectivism and socialism among all people, combat and resist money worship, hedonism, ultra-egoism and other decadent ideas, enhance the Chinese people's national self-esteem, self-confidence, and the sense of pride, and stimulate them to make unremitting efforts for the rejuvenation of the Chinese nation.*
>
> (http://english.peopledaily.com.cn/200107/01/eng20010701_73927.html)

> [Party Secretary General Jiang Zemin's speech at the 16th Party Congress] We should hold high the banners of patriotism and socialism, *strengthen the great solidarity of the people of all ethnic groups, and consolidate and develop the broadest possible patriotic united front.* We need to strengthen

> our solidarity with the democratic parties and personages without party affiliation. We should handle well the work relating to ethnic minorities, religions and overseas Chinese. We should adhere to the principle of "one country, two systems" and bring into full play every positive factor in a common endeavor *to accomplish the grand cause of national reunification and the great rejuvenation of the Chinese nation.*
>
> (http://xibu.tjfsu.edu.cn/elearning/lk/16en.htm)

Chongshang Quanwei ('awe for authority'): emotion for authority

In the past 2,000 years of Chinese history, there has been a salient and valued emotion in the Chinese cultural mind, the respect for authority. That is, Chinese hold habitually anyone with awe who is the advanced in social position, age, knowledge, experience, as the arbiter of truth or correctness, the moral standard, or otherwise the decision-maker. This kind of feeling may be seen as linked with the Chinese social tradition of respecting the authoritative and further the broader traditional Chinese social system of hierarchy. Today, respect for authority is of course not the same as in the past, but as a general rule, Chinese give respect to the government, the advanced in position, the elder(ly), the knowledgeable and the experienced.

In contemporary Chinese discourse, we may find that, when truths, correctness or important choice are at stake or in doubt, Chinese will clearly and profusely express their respect for the advance in social position, age, knowledge or experience by

- Naming the relevant social position, seniority, expertise or experience
- Referring to or citing the authoritative for making judgements/decision, or acting as standard
- Exaggerating the value of their social position, age, knowledge, experience

So in the excerpt immediately following, the authoritative are resorted to for explaining why the damages of the Wenchuan earthquake are bigger than those of Tangshan earthquake which took place early in the morning more than 30 years ago.

> Experts analyze the situation and point out that, in comparison with Tangshan earthquake, fewer people died in the Wenchuan earthquake mainly because the former occurred at night when most people were asleep, whereas the latter during the day. Besides, the former took place in the urban area, whereas the latter in the mountainous countryside where the population is not dense.
>
> (http://news.xinhuanet.com/politics/2008-05/18/content_8197178.htm)

In this example, it may be reflected that experts are appropriated here, when no expert knowledge is needed and in fact what they say is mere common sense. Let us see how respect is paid in the following example:

> Yesterday, many SARS experts and UN Health Organization China officials said when interviewed by the Morning Newspaper that at present they are not certain whether the retracted virus of the suspicious SARS cases of Guangzhou originates in rats but they do not rule out the possibility.
>
> (*Eastern Morning Paper*, 05/01/2004)

SARS was first discovered in 2003 and at the time of its occurrence there were no real experts on the virus. Thus the value of the authoritative is exaggerated by conferring 'expert' on them to increase the acceptability of what they say.

Yan Bu Jingyi ('meaning beyond language'): the belief about language use

One of the central and the most practical elements in the Chinese belief system is that of the nature of language. That is, language can never express meaning entirely; it is often even deceptive. Consequently, one must use language carefully or strategically and go beyond language in search of meaning. This can be seen as linked with a Chinese-culture-constitutive notion, *Dao*, the core concept of Daoism founded by Laozi (571–471 BC) and Zhuangzi (369–286 BC). According to them, *Dao* is both the origin of all things in the universe and the basis for them. And yet we do not have direct access to it. Therefore we must seek continuously to transcend all appearances in order to ascertain the true nature or significance of existence. The Chinese belief about the relationship between language and meaning can also be traced back to the Chinese classics *Yijing* (*I Ching*, *c.* the end of the ninth century BC) and *Wenxin Diaolong* (*Dragon-carving and the Literary Mind*, 501–502), where language is considered as limited in its power but meaning is boundless and requires endless search.

With regard to this basic understanding of the nature and function of language, contemporary Chinese discourse has a range of rules or strategies of meaning production and comprehension at its disposal (Cao *et al.* 2001; Zhou 2002):

- Speak not
- Speak sparingly or little
- Speak implicitly or indirectly or vaguely
- Speak poetically (imaginatively, beautifully, etc.)
- Speak with the help of classical stories and proverbs
- Understand by reading out the text repeatedly
- Understand through empathy
- Understand by listening to one's inner voice
- Understand by watching people's action as well as listening to their words
- Understand through continuous dialogue with others and one's own praxis

The Chinese Premier Wen Jiabao is a typical example of such a strategic speaker. In the speech events where the following quotes occur, Premier Wen is speaking neither to the questions raised, not on the topics that the immediate circumstances bring up. Even the genre, viz. poetry and imagery, is 'unusual' for the occasions.

> To improve the well-being of the people, we should make people feel happy about their life. To do so, we must ensure people's democratic rights and promote social justice and fairness. *You may ask: what do you mean by being happy? Let me quote a line from Ai Qing, a Chinese poet, "Go and ask the thawing land, go and ask the thawing river."*
>
> (http://www.mfa.gov.cn/eng/zxxx/t304313.htm)

> Wen, after his arrival on Sunday, read a haiku-style poem describing his feelings about changes in China's relations with Japan. *"The ice melts into water in the spring. The rain is gone and the green mountain is extremely green and the earth is thick with grasses," he said.*
>
> (http://www.channelnewsasia.com/stories/afp_asiapacific/view/1060058/1/.html)

Given what may appear a 'transparent' text and 'obvious' context, the meaning remains left very much for open and dynamic interpretation.

Bianzheng Siwei ('thinking dialectically'): a cognitive resource for problem-solving

It is well known that Chinese people have many typical patterns or ways of thinking.[2] The dialectic way of thinking is probably the most habitual, frequently-used and highly regarded strategy. This may be expressed by the Chinese *biǎnzheng* siwei. This way of reasoning may be seen as anchored in the classical Chinese notion, and symbol, of *yin-yang*. That is, one should see

- the universe as unity, the One
- the universe is composed of parts
- the parts are interconnected
- the parts are interdependent
- the parts are interpenetrating
- the parts are opposing to one another
- because of the internal opposition, the universe is changing

In contemporary China, there are a number of typical forms of speaking and language-understanding which have been handed down through the Chinese tradition. Of course they occur also typically in particular types of context: when disasters happen, difficult situations arise, conflict, complications, problems are to be understood and resolved, criticism is to be uttered, or one's achievements are to be acknowledged. We can list the following as typical discursive strategies:

- Avoid absolute or extreme terms and statements.
- Speak of the positive opposites of the current negative situation.
- Speak of other agents in an event or relation.
- Speak of connections between things or people.

- Speak of the overall situation.
- Speak of possible change.
- Speak of preparation for crisis.
- Understand contextually and holistically.
- Understand fairly.
- Understand by comparing one's own desires.
- Understand by recognizing one's own limitations.

In the following we may be able to observe reflections of these patterns of speaking:

> At the high-level forum on innovative economy and enterprise finance in central China, the Dean of the Research Institute of Speculative Investment Chen Gongfeng said, financing is a double-edged sword. The current financial '*crisis*' is *on the one side dangerous*; if the bubbles of the financial crisis continue to grow, then China will sustain severe injuries. But on the other side, *the 'crisis' also offers opportunities.* He believed that the current financial *crisis will bring about positive effects on China's stock market. Besides, during this financial turbulence, China can try to attract some excellent overseas Chinese from the Wall Street to start business* in China.
>
> (http://www.chinahrd.net/zhi_sk/jt_page.asp?articleid=149052)

> Chinese medicine takes it for granted that human health *depends on the dynamics of balance between man and nature, man and society and man's internal* yin-yang.
>
> (Zhang *et al.* 2006: Thoughts on a Chinese-medicine approach to para-health. *New Chinese Medicine*, 38(6): 81-82)

> *No society can exist without contradictions; human societies develop and make strides forward in and through the dynamics of contradictions.*
>
> (Xinhua Newsagency, 18 October, Decision of the Chinese Communist Party Central Committee on major issues in the construction of socialist harmonious society)

In these examples, it may be observed that, consistent with the emphasis on a dialectic approach to thinking, discursively highlighted are opportunities from crisis, positive effects of negative events, balance of oppositions, complication of the positive, interconnections between things, and possible positive changes. Through these ways of reformulating problems speakers actively seek to neutralize them and achieve new outcomes.

Conclusion

The current proposal is set against the backdrop of the hitherto general lack of explicit, systematic cross-fertilization between cultural psychology and discourse studies. In addition, there is the more particular situation which the present study is directed at, namely, the growing interest in, desire for and, in an important sense, mixed sentiments against the fast changing China.

Accordingly, we argued that the communicative practice of contemporary Chinese culture cannot be understood without a cultural perspective, in particular, of its cultural psychology. At the same time, we suggested that, conversely, a proper account of Chinese cultural thinking and feeling must not lose sight of the culture's ways of linguistic communication.

One of our starting points has been that Chinese discourses, anchored in historical traditions on the one hand and international and intercultural relations on the other, construct, transmit, draw on and change Chinese cultural ways of thinking and feeling. In this sense they embody Chinese cultural consciousness. From this point of view, understanding of the historically and interculturally embedded collective consciousness provides an important perspective on the discourses. Consequently, cultural psychology can re-orient itself to explaining and evaluating practical cultural ways of life or semiotic meditational practices (Valsiner 2007).

One other related, basic assumption has been that the Chinese cultural psychological make-up, conversely, can best be conceived of as a dialectic, constituent part of its cultural practice, especially the practice of linguistic communication. As said above, language use as part of broader socio-cultural practice is the medium in which cultural psychological experience exists, operates and becomes transformed. In this way, discourse studies becomes an important method to understanding the cultural mind.

Proceeding from those alternative stances, we outlined in this chapter a version of a system of the Chinese cultural cognitions and emotions. This set of consciousness ranges from the basic Chinese principles of 'being' and 'doing' oneself, thinking and feeling about oneself and the world, and understanding the relationship between semiotic medium and meaning. In this sense it constitutes the core of the Chinese cultural psychological make-up.

Further, we have specified this cultural consciousness in terms of discursive strategies – values, principles and concepts for speaking/listening and reading/writing in relation to specific types of contexts. Thus, we saw that the Chinese cultural system of thinking and feeling takes the form of interrelated sets of rules of speaking and understanding in specific types of settings. We stressed that these are open-ended principles of linguistic communication that are followed, appropriated, oriented to, and transformed by specific agents of cultural members and groups.

In addition, we have presented selected samples of contemporary Chinese discourse and highlighted the ways that Chinese cultural psychological principles organize spoken and written texts in various settings. In this way, the otherwise vague, obscured, puzzling practices of Chinese linguistic communication are rendered transparent and understandable.

As part of a future research agenda, we would like to suggest that efforts be made to developing a broader and more elaborate understanding of how the

Chinese, Asian, Eastern-Southern, subaltern mind is interrelated to the Euro-American or Westcentric counterpart at different levels. This will lead to a deeper understanding of not just the psychological make-up of the different cultures, but also the nature of the cultural mind itself. Moreover, practical studies should be made to examine how, in particular situations of certain socio-cultural significance, cultural psychological experience is oriented to, appropriated, transmitted, (re) created, flaunted, or changed in and through ordinary, everyday, even private, discursive practices, beyond the public and institutional discourses. At the same time, similarly, research attempts may be made to find out how practical cultural discourses construct, re-create and transform cultural psychological principles and experiences.

Notes

1 There are Chinese philosophical, sociological, and historical accounts of Chinese communication which contain unique Chinese notions such as holism, *guanxi* (acquaintance relations), *yuan* (predestined liaison), *keqi* (conviviality). We think it appropriate to keep philosophical, sociological, historical notions apart from those of cultural psychology.

2 Wang and Zheng (2005: 334–352) have characterized Chinese psychology in terms of eight preferred 'ways of thinking': (1) holism, (2) dialecticism, (3) moderation, (4) intuitiveness, (5) authority-worshipping, (6) pragmatism, (7) image-prone and (8) circular-thinking.

References

Billig, M. (1991). *Ideology and Opinions*. London: Sage.

Boesch, E. E. (2001). Symbolic action theory in cultural psychology. *Culture and Psychology*, (4): 479–483.

Bond, M. H. (ed.) (1986). *The Psychology of the Chinese People*. Hong Kong: Oxford University Press.

Bond, M. H. (ed.) (1996). *The Handbook of Chinese Psychology*. Hong Kong: Oxford University Press.

Bond, M. H. (2000). Distant anguish and proximal brotherhood: using psychology to move beyond the Chinese face. *Journal of Psychology in Chinese Societies*, 1: 143–148.

Brady, A-M. (2008) *Marketing Dictatorship: Propaganda and Thought Work in Contemporary China*. New York: Rowman & Littlefield Publishers, Inc.

Brown, P. and Levinson, S. (1987). *Politeness: Some Universals in Language Usage*. Cambridge: Cambridge University Press.

Cao, S-Q. (2001). *Zhongguo Gudai Wenlun Huayu* (Chinese Classical Literary-Theoretical Discourses). Chengdu: Bashu Shushe.

Chen, G-M. (2001). Towards transcultural understanding: a harmony theory of Chinese communication. In V. H. Milhouse, M. K. Asante and P. O. Nwosu (eds), *Transculture: Interdisciplinary Perspectives on Cross-cultural Relations*. Thousand Oaks, CA: Sage, pp. 55–70.

Chen, W-D. (1979). *Xiuci Xue Fafan* (Development of rhetoric). Shanghai: Shanghai Educational Press.

Chu, G. C. (1985). The changing concept of self in contemporary China. In A. J. Maroella, G. de Vos and F.L.K. Hsu (eds), *Culture and Self: Asian and Western Perspectives*. New York: Tavistock Publications, pp. 252–277.

Cole, M. (1996). *Cultural Psychology: A Once and Future Discipline*. Cambridge, MA: Harvard University Press.

Fairclough, N. (1992). *Discourse and Social Change*. Cambridge: Polity Press.

Gee, J. P. (1999). *An Introduction to Discourse Analysis: Theory and Method*. London: Routledge.

Goffman, E. (1967). *Interaction Ritual: Essays on Face to Face Behavior*. Garden City, NY: Doubleday.

Gu, Y-G. (1990). Politeness phenomena in modern Chinese. *Pragmatics*, 14: 237–257.

Heisey, R. (ed.) (2000). *Chinese Perspectives in Rhetoric and Communication*. Greenwood, CT: Ablex.

Jia, W. (2003). Chinese conceptualizations of face: emotions, communication, and personhood. In L. A. Samovar and R. E. Porter (eds), *Intercultural Communication: A Reader* (10th ed.). East Windsor, CT: Wadsworth, pp. 48–57.

Jia, W. S., Heisey, D. R. and Lu, X. (Eds.) (2002). *Chinese Communication Theory and Research*. Greenwood, CN: Ablex.

Leech, G. N. (1983). *Principles of Pragmatics*. London: Longman.

Lin, Z-J. and Ma, L-C. (1999). *Huhuan: Dangjin Zhongguo de Wuzhong Shengyin* (The calls: five voices of contemporary China). Guangzhou: Guangzhou Publishing House.

Ratner, C. (2008). Cultural psychology and qualitative methodology: scientific and political considerations. *Culture & Psychology*, 14(3): 259–288.

Schweder, R. A. (1990). Cultural psychology – what is it? In J. W. Stigler, R. A. Schweder and G. Herdt (eds), *Cultural Psychology: Essays on Comparative Human Development*. Cambridge: Cambridge University Press, pp. 1–43.

Shen, K-M. (1996). *Xiandai Hanyu Huayu Yuyan Xue* (Modern Chinese Text Linguistics). Beijing: The Commercial Press.

Shen, X-l. (2001). *Hanyu Yufa Xue* (Chinese grammar). Nanjing: Jiangsu Educational Press.

Shi-xu (2005). *A Cultural Approach to Discourse*. Basingstoke: Palgrave Macmillan.

Shi-xu, M. Kienpointner and Servaes, J. (eds) (2005). *Read the Cultural Other: Forms of Otherness in the Discourses of Hong Kong's Decolonisation*. Berlin/New York: Mouton de Gruyter.

Shi-xu (2007). *Discourse as Cultural Struggle*. Hong Kong: Hong Kong University Press.

Shi-xu (2009). Reconstructing eastern paradigms of discourse studies. *Journal of Multicultural Discourses*, 4(1): 29–48.

Shi-xu (2012). Understanding contemporary Chinese political communication: a historico-intercultural analysis and assessment of its discourse of human rights. *Journal of Language and Politics*, 11(1): 93–114.

Song Q. and Zhang Z-z. (1996). *Zhongguo Keyi Shuo Bu: lengzhan shidai hou de zhengzhi yu qinggan jueze* (China Can Say No: Political and emotional choices after the Cold War). Beijing: China Industry and Commerce Joint Press.

Triandis, H.C. (1980). The self and social behaviour in differing cultural contexts. *Psychological Review*, 96: 506–520.

Triandis, H. C. (1999). Cross-cultural psychology. *Asian Journal of Social Psychology*, 2(1): 127–143.

Valsiner, J. (1998). *The Guided Mind*. Cambridge, MA: Harvard University Press.

Valsiner, J. (2007). *Culture in Minds and Societies: Foundations of Cultural Psychology*. New Delhi: Sage.

Valsiner, J. (2009). Cultural psychology today: innovations and oversights. *Culture & Psychology*, 15(1): 5–39.

Wang, M.J. (2009). Cultural norms informing other-conscious selfhood in Chinese relational world. *Culture & Psychology*. 15(1): 41–72.

Wang, Fengyan and Zheng Hong (2005). *Zhongguo Wenhua Xinlixue* (Chinese cultural psychology). Guangzhou: Jinan University Press.

Williams, R. (1983). *Keywords* (2nd ed.). London: Fontana.

Xing, F-Y. (ed.) (2000). *Wenhua Yuyan Xue* (Cultural linguistics) (revised). Wuhan: Hubei Educational Press.

Yan, G-C. (1998). *Zhongguo Xinlixue Shi* (History of Chinese cultural psychology). Hangzhou: Zhejiang Educational Press.

Zhou, Q-G. (2002). *Zhongguo Gudian Jieshi Xue Daolun* (Introduction to Classical Chinese Hermaneutics). Beijing: Zhonghua Shuju.

3 International city branding as intercultural discourse

Development and globalization

Problems and aims

Urban development is one of the basic conditions and central goals of the developing world. It is propelled by globalization and accomplished through a variety of forms of cultural and communicative practice. The present study enquires into a special and important dimension of urban development of the developing world, namely city branding to the international community, or international city branding for short.

Extant research has largely concentrated on Western-world and 'World' cities (Amin *et al.* 2000; Beaverstock *et al.* 1999; Ley 1995). As partial consequence, the integral, cultural and intercultural, nature of international city branding (discourse) has not received the attention it deserves. It will be necessary and urgent then to take developing-world cities' international branding seriously.

The field of city branding research is as yet a fragmented one. Generally speaking, there is a tendency to polarize the social-cultural aspect and the economic or technical aspect of city development and brand promotion; there is especially a lack of sufficient attention to the former (Lees 2004; Williams 2010). This is reflected for example in the fact that urban studies scholars have not always been clear and explicit about the notion of discourse/communication (Lees 2004: 101, 104). The division and, consequently, confusion are caused in great measure by differences and disparities in social scientific perspectives, that is perspectives that involve not only philosophical and theoretical foundations, but also research interests (Lucarelli and Berg 2011).

In the present study, I shall take a holistic and cultural-political stance and take developing-world city branding as a form of *cultural discourse*. Here, 'discourse', interchangeable with 'communication', refers, quite briefly, to social events or activities in which people communicate through linguistic and non-linguistic means with one another in given historical and cultural context. Because human communication differs between cultures, to wit, in terms of goals, values, concepts, strategies, and so on, and more importantly, is characterized by competing cultural relations and representations, I shall use the epithet 'cultural', hence cultural discourse.

As a case study and illustration of Asian or developing-world urban development, accordingly, I shall focus on the city branding of Hangzhou, an ancient provincial capital and tourist city in the east coastal region of China, for the international community. My aim is to identify and characterize some of the properties, problems, and potentials of urban development discourse of the developing world. This means that I shall be studying the elements, strategies, difficulties, challenges and opportunities involved in the international, more precisely, intercultural, discursive (co-)construction of Hangzhou's image and identity. I shall at the same time be evaluating the city branding practices in terms of their effects and outcomes for (urban) development, as is the central and most important objective of Chinese, Asian or developing-world societies.

As data for city branding research, one might take up an individual event or activity. But this way would lead only to partial answers. For, city branding takes place in varied forms and as such can have different characteristics. So I shall choose instead to observe a variety of branding practices that occur at different social and semiotic levels. Thus, different kinds of topics ranging from efforts by the municipality, mega-events to trade-oriented activities on the one hand and varied forms of data such as interviews, actual practice and secondary documentation on the other are used here. These will allow one to access a wider spectrum of samples and to flow more channels into them, such that not only the overall international branding situation of Hangzhou, but also the particular branding activities involving leisure, the landscape, food, drink, use of new media, and so on, come into purview.

To make sense of, account for and weigh up such a diversity of materials, one might take a singular, say linguistic, or social or managerial, perspective and examine one dimension of the data on the part of the municipality, or a business (enterprise), or some civil organization. But such a fragmented approach could lead to bias and consequently ineffectual or counter-productive conclusions. So I shall instead resort to multiple and multi-faceted – historical and intercultural – ways of approaching the collected data. More specifically, I shall take a cultural discourse studies perspective in looking at the different types of branding practice in the forms of first- and second-hand data and insider- and outsider-perspectives. That means that I shall examine each of them in terms of the various (interlocking) components of a((n) inter)cultural communicative event, the inter-connections between these types of practice and, where possible, in contrast to cities in non-developing world societies.

City branding discourse is central to a host of city planning, marketing and management goals: demography, population, the environment, business, tourism, talents, resources, and domestic and international investment. It can have important implications for residents, visitors and tourists. No less importantly, it can have a role to play in social-cultural development (e.g. social inclusion and harmony and cultural diversity). When seen as internationally oriented discourse, it can have impact on not just the city itself, but also on the world at large. By looking at the Chinese city's international branding discourse, we may gain insights into the conditions at the 'workplace' of urban development in the

Asian or developing world. Lessons learnt from it, whether positive or negative, may contribute to local development more generally. For, the city's branding discourse is an integral, and central, part of its urban development. By exploring the cultural and intercultural nature of city branding discourse, especially from a developing-world, Asian, or Chinese perspective, we may expect to reach a better understanding of not only the specific cultural differences and relations involved, but also the complexities of the discourse of urban development in general and of city branding in particular. As alluded to above, research has concentrated largely on cities in the Western world or otherwise proceeded from Western perspectives.

Discourses of urban development and branding

City branding is a crucial and effective tool for urban development; from another perspective, because it can serve as a guide for urban development, it is also a constitutive part of it. Research on the topic, which has spanned over more than three decades, is internationally recognized and continues to grow (Lucarelli and Berg 2011; see also Kavaratzis 2004; Keller 2012; Lees 2004; Wilson 1996; Zukin *et al.* 1998). What is particularly noteworthy is that there is increasing recognition of and attention to the discursive dimension of city branding (e.g. Lees 2004; Sevcik 2011).

Let us first attempt to carve out the theoretical and methodological frameworks that will be employed in the subsequent study. On the whole and at the outset, it may be said that extant literature suggests that city branding discourse studies is a nascent, promising and important field. On this we may quote Lees (2004: 101):

> The impact of the discursive turn on urban research (both political economic and cultural political urban research) is growing as more and more researchers seek to integrate the study of language and culture into urban geographical analysis (for a variety of examples, see Amin *et al.* 2000; Beauregard 1993; Imrie and Raco 2003; Ley 1995; McCann 2004; Mitchell 1996; Rutheiser 1996; Slater 2002; Wilson 1996; Zukin *et al.* 1998).

Further, much recent literature has recognized that city branding is not separable from other aspects or dimensions of the social practice of city promotion; it is created, conveyed and understood – constituted – in and through discourse and communication. City branding and discourse are thus dialectically integrated, hence city-branding discourse (CBD). Okano and Samson (2010: 12) point to this integral and dialectic condition of cultural discourse when they suggest:

> Culture is something that individuals or groups "create", or alternatively something that such individuals or groups "receive". In other words, in order to trace the development of culture, it is necessary to consider the mutual relations between the three parties, the "creator", the "cultural property", and the "recipients", and they cannot be discussed separately from the conditions of the society that gave them birth (Abe and Nishigaki, 2002) [...] The forms

of communication between the "creator" subject and the "receiver" subject are important.

Building on work such as these, let me formulate in what follows a discursively and culturally more explicit theoretical scaffolding. To start with, city branding is understood in this study as the communicative or discursive practice of constructing, marketing and understanding the image, identity and, arguably, 'face', of a city for the sake of increasing recognition and prestige and ultimately success, as well as self-affirmation, in the context of intensified local and global urban competition or for competitiveness for short, hence, city branding discourse or CBD for short.[1]

Second, CBD is created out the process of globalization on the one hand and urbanization on the other. Along with these there arises the need to distinguishing one city from the others and further enhancing the city's prestige. Ultimately, it is done in order to survive and succeed in today's increasingly competitive national and international contexts. Here it should be mentioned that the notion of city branding comes antecedently from that of corporate (product) branding; but from the present perspective, the city is neither a product or corporation, nor a nation and so the branding must take on its own characteristics. In contrast to the product or corporation, the city is more of a multiplex, dynamic and above all living entity; in contrast to the nation, it is less political and smaller in size but has more to do with everyday livelihood.

Third, CBD has varied stakeholders, who range from the municipality, businesses, the state, residents, to visitors. They have an important role to play. Whether they speak of the city brand and how they do so are of consequence to city branding. In this respect, it may be added that people as stakeholders may not just create city brands, but also be affected by the life changes brought about by the brands they create. From another perspective, it may be noted that CBD has not just a productive side, but also, crucially important, the receptive, responsive or evaluative side, as may be manifested in the forms of impression, perception, reputation and arguably expectation – by residents or citizens, tourists or visitors, businesses, governments. This leads to still another particular aspect of CBD centrally relevant in the present study, as follows. CBD has specific audiences: domestic and local and international and global. In the present study and in this respect, we are concerned with the international audiences, who may range from tourists, visitors, to government and business organizations.

Fourth, the practice of CBD may be achieved through a diversity of interrelated semiotic forms, strategies and mediums, including notably (1) channels of communication, (2) signs, (3) genres of communication, and (4) contents of communication. Thus, in terms of content, CBD can vary depending on the perspectives, principles and conditions of a city in question: a city may be branded as geographic space, governed and inhabited settlement, or quintessential feature(s) of the place, for example (Lucarelli and Berg 2011). This implies that virtually anything of city life can be the object of urban branding; we may think of such interrelated cultural resources as: history, heritage (e.g. festivals, cuisine), customs (e.g. tea drinking), monuments, iconic buildings, landscape, celebrities, heroes, art and design (e.g. clothing). As signs, we may refer to the language, graphics, architecture, art (e.g. music and painting), personalities that are mobilized; as genres, we may think of logos, slogans, brochures, advertisements, documents (e.g. positioning statements, mission statement), speeches, photos, expos, tourism, and mega-events. In terms of strategies, it may be observed that CBD may be produced in implicit or indirect or explicit or direct ways and so understood accordingly. As channels, we may think of the radio, television, internet, newspapers, magazines, films, posters, billboards, museums, word-of-mouth, international travel, and so on.

Fifth and very importantly, CBD has a 'workplace' dimension. It is not just social or public or ordinary; much of it is done in and by organizations, municipal, entrepreneurial and civil, and so is subject to the requirements and ethics of the particular organizations. Workplace discourse has been studied in terms of its formal features (of linguistic genres), settings (e.g. medical, legal), social interaction (e.g. conversation, intercultural communication) and contents (e.g. small talk and humour), from different disciplinary perspectives (e.g. linguistics, social theory) and through a diversity of approaches (e.g. ethnography, discourse analysis) (see Gunnarsson 2009; Holmes 2011; Koester 2010). However, this research has been conducted mainly within Western societies and special professions, on preferred aspects (e.g. linguistic texts) and over preferred topics (e.g. politeness, power, conflict resolution). From the present perspective, CBD is not simply about text or talk at work or about conversational interaction in work settings. It involves much more: it is a sort of workplace discourse that has a wide public mandate, is achieved through a nexus of communicative elements and processes, and with broad societal, cultural and global impact; in the present case we would need to assess, for example, if and how the workplace discourse of city branding is contributing to local social and cultural development.

Sixth, CBD is *culturally* differentiated in terms of e.g. historical conditions (e.g. context of late-modern Third World urbanization in global setting), representations, power relations, goals, and principles of interaction. Consequently, it is culturally competing. It may be stressed, too, that, as a cultural phenomenon, CBD is dynamic through time: it may go through culturally variable stages and paths of development (Gold and Gold 2004; Hajer 1995; Jensen 2007; Mommas 2002). Western branded and well-known cities are considerably larger in number than those in the rest of the world. Their branding is facilitated by a great variety of advantages, for example centres of world economy and their relative geographical vicinity.

Last but by no means the least, Chinese city-branding discourse, in turn, is characterized by its culture-specific condition of history on the one hand and its profound concern with social economic development on the other hand. For the current research, this implies that our analysis and assessment must take *this development condition in the global context* seriously and adopt social economic development as the most important criterion of judgement (Shi-xu 2014).

The methodology of city branding research

In a binary and universalistic way of thinking about and investigating into urban communication, researchers would normally focus on a singular event or, more typically, the textual form of a singular event, and appraise it from a culturally 'neutral' stance (e.g. Flowerdew 2004). But the problem is that one urban event is often interconnected with many others and moreover with local and global culture and history; the textual form is inseparable from interpretation and response and from still other textual forms. Another is that what is adjudicated as, for example, 'manipulative' or 'undemocratic', from the 'universal' point of view, may, from a local cultural and historical perspective, be a necessary or viable aspect of something more complex.

From our methodological perspective (Shi-xu 2015), then, we must as general principles approach our object of study holistically, dialectically and cultural-politically. More specifically, this means that we must examine and evaluate city-branding discourse comprehensively, historically and (inter)culturally, drawing on not only objective evidence (i.e. first-, second-hand and background data), but also subjective experience (i.e. the researcher's own personal knowledge and cultural-political stance).

Our specific methods concern two interconnected stages of research: data collection and data interpretation. With regard to the former, namely one in which data are searched, selected and structured, the following strategies will apply. First, the research should choose as object of investigation concrete, actual practices: major events, expos, fairs, businesses, architecture, landscape, intangible heritages, and so on, which are oriented towards the international community. Second, the researcher should seek information revolving round the agents, the intent/form, the use of channels and symbols, historical process and international relations on the part of the productive side of city branding. In that connection, attention should be paid to information on relevant international impact or response. Third, the researcher should try to obtain the information through direct observation (e.g. mega-events, exhibitions, forums) and secondary sources (e.g. the internet, journalism, documentation, and interviews).

With regard to the latter, 'reading' stage, accordingly, the practices of city branding will be studied from the point of view of (inter)cultural discourse, namely as a set of interrelated categories of the intercultural communicative event/activity: (1) communicative agents, (2) intent/form/relation, (3) mediums, (4) purposes/effects, (5) historical processes, and (6) intercultural representations and relations. Here obviously, multidisciplinary concepts, methods, standards must be applied depending on the nature of phenomena under scrutiny and the purpose of the research project. Further, comparisons, intra-cultural and intercultural, may be made where possible: for example, Hangzhou's international cuisine branding may be compared with its tea branding, or Hangzhou's international city branding with that of Paris, but all with a view to better understanding Hangzhou's case.

Although 'background' would be part of data since it itself, too, must be obtained from a certain data set, I should like to begin with this background because it functions here as the guide for collecting the focal data and subsequently understanding them. It may be elucidated in terms of five aspects. First, Hangzhou, the provincial capital of Zhejiang province, is a historical and tourist city situated in one of the most developed, east coastal regions in China, the Yangtze Delta. It has a territory of 16,596 square kilometres (the inner city as of 430 square kilometres) and a population of over 5 million people. The city has had a double-digit GDP growth for the past ten or so years and has enjoyed high-level development particularly in the past few years which may be seen in the statistics of social, cultural, economic, municipal and environmental survey results.[2] Second, the city has one of the country's most valued and internationally renowned lakes and many historical sites dating back to the Qin Dynasty over 2200 years ago. Third, it started applying for UNESCO world heritage listing in 1999 and succeeded in 2011; during this period, it embarked on a ten-year-long 'Comprehensive Development Plan' for that purpose at least in part. Along with this UN bid, it has more generally been pursuing internationalization in the context of accelerated globalization. Fourth, Hangzhou has historically been given numerous designations, official and otherwise. In 1958, for instance, Hangzhou Municipal Construction Bureau positioned the city as a 'comprehensive city of heavy industry'. In 2000, Hangzhou branded itself as 'Paradise Silicon Valley' and attracted investors like Huawei, Zhifubao and Wangyi. Last but by no means the least, in August 2006, the Municipality of Hangzhou put together an expert group of artists, writers, sociologists and city planners and launched a call for the selection of a city brand for Hangzhou. Over 2,000 people from 20 some provinces of China proposed some 4,620 items. Following a complex process of standard-setting, expert evaluation and public voting, the name of the brand of 生活品质之城 (the city of quality life) was chosen. What is historically interesting and significant in this case is that, against the former centralizing tradition in national development when decisions were made at the top, this brand 'from the bottom' was formally adopted at the tenth Congress of the CCP Hangzhou Committee (February 2007) and endorsed a few days later at the eleventh Congress in the report: *The CCP Hangzhou Committee's Decision on Maintaining and Developing Harmonious Society and the City of Quality Life* (施旭 2008). 生活品质之城, or the city of quality life, is understood to mean the standard levels of quality life in five domains: economic , cultural, political, social and environmental life (杭州市政府2007; 黄宇亮, 王竹2006). These are also dissolved and re-created in the 12 combinations of this city brand and local trade brands, such as:

东方休闲之都，品质生活之城	(Eastern leisure capital, quality life city);
天堂硅谷，品质生活	(Silicon paradise, quality life);
品质生活，中国茶都	(Quality life, tea capital of China);
文化名城，品质杭州	(City of culture, Hangzhou of quality)

It is this official city brand that will become the focal point of our research and, as indicated at the outset, our emphasis will be on the international branding, namely the communicating, marketing and interpreting of Hangzhou's city brand with respect to the international community. Here it may be noted that while the brand's meaning, development and communication are well stipulated from the productive point of view in various documents, there is no explicit mention of whom the brand is for, whether for local, national and international recipients and so no specification of how the branding practices might be differentiated as a result.

In order to examine Hangzhou's international branding, I have chosen a series of relevant phenomena at different semiotic levels. Specifically, we shall focus on the city's international branding as a whole, thus at the highest meaningful level, on the one hand; on the other hand, we shall be looking at a number of particular activities and events that contribute to and are constitutive of the city's international branding, namely the World Leisure Expo, the West Lake International Expo, the Longjing tea branding and Hangzhou culinary branding. By investigating a range of these workplaces and practices of international city branding at different levels, I hope to reveal relatively fully the current conditions, possibilities and problems of the city's international branding.

With respect to this diversity of phenomena to be scrutinized, I have opted to amass a multiplicity of forms of data, ranging from interviews with key agents, through actual branding practices, to secondary documentation and journalism. By obtaining information from different kinds of sources and from variable angles, I hope to yield deep insights into the properties of Hangzhou's city brand promotion to the international community.

Analysis and assessment

The branding practices in question will be studied each as cultural discourse, thus in terms of the communicative agent, intent, form or relation, mediums and outcomes in both historical and intercultural perspectives, where appropriate and possible, as explained in the preceding section. As these practices are in fact interrelated and supposed to be mutually complimentary, comparison will be made to highlight their merits and demerits and so possibilities for better management. In that connection, it may be mentioned that particular attention will also be paid to the shared dimension of international city branding, such as the use of the internet for city branding. Because this city's branding practices must be understood as embedded in the particular historical and intercultural juncture and relations, attempts will also be made to account for them accordingly.

Municipal management

In order to obtain an overview of the management of the city's brand, such that has an insider's perspective or 'from behind the scene', an in-depth interview with the director of the Centre for Research and Evaluation on Life Quality of Hangzhou was conducted by the present author, together with three other students (7 March 2014). The director was informed at the outset of the interview that its central purpose was to understand nature, the content and strategies of the work on Hangzhou's city branding for the international community and more particularly the difficulties, challenges, experiences or potentials involved in the city's international branding. Then questions and answers proceeded from the nature of the Centre's work, through its notion of city brand and branding, to its current international communication of Hangzhou's brand. It lasted for about one hour and a quarter.

There are a number of features in the city-brand managerial discourse to be noted from the point of view of cultural discourse. First, this city is one of the few places in China, and perhaps in the world, that has a municipal-level task force, composed of several offices, that is specifically charged with the city's perennial brand management. Second, the city has an officially designated brand as indicated above; in addition, the State government has an extra, semantically different, brand for it ('one-base-and-four-centres').[3] Third, under the auspices of this task force, a number of regular, international mega-events are organized in the city, such as the World Leisure Expo and the West Lake Expo, and the International Comics and Cartoons Festival. Fourth, such events, sometimes organized in conjunction with one another, are jointly sponsored by the municipality, businesses, the media, and so on, and attended by people from all walks of life including foreigners, notably in the form of so-called 'experiencing day' (when 'quality life' may be experienced). Fifth, the city's official brand seems to be semantically rather indistinct or vague, though this may be associated with various life-quality related, more concrete designations (see the ones in the past ten years in Table 3.1). Sixth, the set of organizations in charge of the city's brand development has a collective website (http://www.wehangzhou.cn/), but it is all in Chinese. Last, the brand-making of Hangzhou has 'cultural' difficulties when compared with other well-known Western cities like New York, Paris or Berlin. That is, although the city has relatively strong financial power for brand-making, it lacks the soft power or technical know-how. As he puts it,

> I feel the difference lies not so much in the economic conditions. These years China develops very fast. In terms of infrastructure, would you say there is much difference between Shanghai and New York? Scarcely any. Perhaps the level of modernization is even higher than that of well-known cities of developed countries. In the respect of economic foundation. I think the biggest difference lies rather in the respect of culture, soft power specifically. Take for example our cultural industry. Hangzhou pays a lot of attention to this these years. We have been trying to build the capital of cartoon and animation and we integrate this into the system of Hangzhou's city brand. We made a point of enabling interconnection and interaction of trade brands and the city's general brand. At that time it was a major aspect of (brands') interaction. But if you compared Hangzhou and Britain regarding development of cultural creative industry, there is still a large distance. We are still paying more attention to such things as hardware, value of production, quantities, etc. But in the respect of cultural import and influence, or high-level artistic design,

we still lag greatly behind. (我觉得这个差异更多的不是在它的经济基础，这两年我们国家发展也很快，就像从硬件方面来说，你说上海和纽约有很大的差别吗？基本上没什么差别，可能有些现代化的程度还高于一些发达国家的著名城市，在经济支撑这方面上，我觉得最大的差异就是在文化，这个软的方面。我举个例子讲，比如我们的文化产业，杭州这几年也是非常重视的，我们一直在打造动漫之都，我们也是把它纳入到城市品牌系统里面的。我们当时提到了一个行业品牌和城市整体品牌的联动，互动，当时这也是互动很重要的一方面，但是你看我们杭州的文创业的发展和英国的文创业的发展，它的差别就非常大，我们更多的还是注重一些硬性的东西，产值啊，数量啊，但在文化内涵的渗透方面，高端艺术的设计方面还很欠缺。)

In this part of the interview, it is clear that the director is contrasting the Chinese city with those in the Western, developed world (e.g. mention of 'New York' and 'Britain' and 'well-known cities of developed countries') and stresses in particular the deficiency in what he calls the 'soft', 'cultural' side of city branding on the part of Hangzhou and China by suggesting that the latter seeks what is not desirable but lacks in what is desirable (see the last sentence of the quote).

World expos

Within the city's branding framework as indicated above, Hangzhou has held two sets of major, serial international expos: the World Leisure Expo and the West Lake Expo, which are organized in line with and as part of Hangzhou's city branding. In the history of the World Leisure Expo, the first one was held in Brisbane, Australia, in 1988. Since then the expo was held every two or three years around the world. In 2006, the World Leisure Organization (WLO) decided that the World Leisure Expo would be held every five years and that Hangzhou would be the permanent venue for it. In 2006 and 2011, respectively, Hangzhou played the host and, in 2006, was nominated 'The Oriental Capital of Leisure'. Consistent with Hangzhou's official city brand '生活品质之城 (city of quality life)' which came into being in 2007, the World Leisure Expo 2011 (17 September to 18 November), sponsored by the World Leisure Organization and Hangzhou Municipal People's Government, adopted the theme of 'leisure – enhancing the quality of life'. For the expo of 2011, there was an official website (en.wl-expo.com), an official video (http://v.hoolo.tv/video-10039.html), promotional conferences overseas and news reports.

Let us take a look at the expo of 2011 (from 17 September to 18 November) in particular. From a cultural-discursive point of view, a number of features may be noted. First, there was a sizable international participation: 80 cities, 37 million visitors and 50 enterprises from China and abroad were involved. Second, under the theme of 'Leisure: enhancing the quality of life', the expo of 2011 was composed of a variety of organized communicative events: a summit meeting, conferences, forums. Third, the expo is rendered present in various forms of texts (ads, news reports, special columns, and publications), as well as artefacts (e.g.

souvenirs) and conducted through different channels (i.e. website and online videos) and in a number of international venues (e.g. international convention centres) and scores of spaces (i.e. routes and sites of leisure activities). More broadly, it is featured in a host of activities and events (e.g. Cultural Creative Industry Expo, International Tea Conference, Tea Product Fair). Finally, the expo has had a trade turnover of *c.* RMB 22.6 billion, foreign investment of *c.* US$1.1 billion and domestic investment of RMB 13.4 billion.

The West Lake Expo is another serial mega-event that is directly linked with the city's branding. The very first one was held in 1929 and then it was already a successful international fair. But the expo was not resumed until seven decades later in 2000. It may be noted that the logo is an expression of the characteristics and aspirations of Hangzhou: water, leisure and vegetation, and so on.

For the sake of understanding better the current state of the expo, let us compare the last one, the fifteenth, with the second. The latter, which lasted for 22 days, attracted 5 million visitors from home and abroad, held a score of professional exhibitions with 2,500 exhibitors coming over 30 countries and regions. The trade volume amounts to nearly RMB 7 billion, domestic investment to RMB 13.73 billion and foreign investment to US$ 311 million.

The most recent, fifteenth expo, initiated and funded (with at least RMB 17 million) by the Hangzhou government and executed by the Office of Hangzhou West Lake Expo Organizing Committee, lasted 29 days (12 October to 9 November 2013), under the theme of 'Innovative Expo, beautiful Hangzhou'. It has an official website: http://www.xh-expo.com/ (other relevant site: http://www.xh-expo.com/481/2013/09/16208.html). Sponsored by over 15 companies, the expo is comprised of 50 events (fairs, conferences, exhibitions and other activities), including major international events such as:

- The International West Lake Tourism Festival
- Hangzhou International Art and Culture Festival
- Hangzhou International Trail Walker Conference
- International Conference on Sensor in the Internet of Things
- World Top 500 Enterprises Roundtable Conference

The expo attracts about 8 million visitors from home and abroad; 50 different countries and regions were represented. The exhibitions and fairs were mainly held in internationally oriented venues (e.g. the White Horse Lake International Convention and Exhibition Center, Hangzhou Peace International Exhibition and Conference Centre, and Zhejiang World Trade International Exhibition Centre); 23 per cent of the spaces were allocated to foreign exhibitors. CCTV, local newspapers (e.g. a special column in 《都市快报》), radio, local television station, street posters, museums, conferences and websites (e.g. *youku* and *sohu*) were used in the promotion and visits to the official website reached 5 million. What is particularly noteworthy is that cooperation between international media outlets was achieved and about 100 domestic and foreign media outlets produced 3,500 reports. Different foreign languages were used (e.g. the guideposts in

Prince Bay Park (太子湾公园) had four in addition to Chinese: English, French, Japanese and Korean). The mega-event generated a total trade volume of RMB 15.7 billion, domestic investment of RMB 15.2 billion and foreign investment of US$1 billion.[4]

Tea exhibitions

Tea is another topic around which Hangzhou has done much in its city-branding discourse for the international community; that is, Hangzhou has presented a range of interconnected activities and artefacts for its international brand promotion. In 2011, *Longjing* tea of Hangzhou became part of city's share in the UNESCO world heritage list.[5] It has since become officially internationally known. Historically, however, Longjing tea was exported even before the Opium War (1840), though China was blocked from tea selling following the war by the British in support of India's tea trade.

There are a number of features to be noted from a cultural discourse point of view in the city's current international attempts at branding its tea, thereby branding itself as the city of quality life.[6] First, explicitly international events designed to brand the tea from Hangzhou are of relatively recent occurrence. It was only in 2005 that the first West Lake International Tea Culture Expo took place and since then it has been held once every year at the time of the first annual tea harvest; similarly, it was in 2010 that the International Expo of Hangzhou's Well-known Teas, together with the First Contemporary Chinese Tea Culture Festival, was held in the city and has since been organized once every year. Second, the city's (as well as particular prefectures') government on the one hand and the nation's international tea (culture) research organizations (e.g. China International Tea Research Association) on the other are major players as hosts and organizers behind the few international tea fairs and festivals held in Hangzhou. What is also remarkable is that on one day is set aside each year when 'all countrymen drink tea' and the very first was held on 20 April 2009. Third, the tea-promotional activities are often enriched and enhanced by being organized in connection with the city's other trade brands such as leisure and cuisine, as part of other mega-events such as the World Expo (Shanghai, 2010), or in conjunction with other activities or artefacts such as tourism, dancing and landscape. Moreover, the organizers often invite various media to participate in and report on the events. In the mediational aspect, it may be noted, too, that there is an online video: http://www.cnteaexpo.com/czqy.html and official websites on tea promotion: http://www.hangzhou.gov.cn/main/zwdt/ztzj/cwhjs/index.shtml and http://www.hangzhou.com.cn/cbhtbbd/index.htm; nevertheless, neither has an English-language page. In terms of spatial communication, Hangzhou has a few noteworthy architectural venues for tea producing, making and drinking: for example, the Tea Museum of China (中国茶叶博物馆),[7] the Home of Tea drinking (茶人之家) and the International Village of Tea drinking (国际茶人村). Fourth, in terms of intents and purposes of such events, it is clear that they are held with a view to contributing to the city's reputation as the capital of tea, but more broadly to the city's overarching brand, namely the city of quality life, and more particularly for a period of time before 2011 during the city's bid for UNESCO world heritage listing. However, it should be pointed out that, although many events are crowned with international designations, there seems little explicit effort at reaching out to the international community and *Longjing* tea is still largely unknown internationally.[8] The tea-tasting exchanges seem to have involved only some Japanese and Koreans. The tea industry does not seem to have organized any tea-promotional events overseas, let alone having any tea establishments abroad, unlike the Hangzhou cuisine trade, to which we now turn.

Travelling cuisine

Still another topic and another form of international city branding is found in the ways that Hangzhou promotes its local cuisine. Supported by the municipal government, the city's food catering association has travelled regularly to foreign countries to promote the city's own cuisine. In order to get an insider's view on this, the author of this chapter, together with three of his students conducted an interview with the former secretary and two representatives from the Hangzhou Association of Restaurants (www.hzms.org). Before the interview, the association was informed that the research project would concern itself with questions of internationalization of Hangzhou's cuisine; subsequently, one of them provided a written statement (by email) answering a few general questions regarding the association's international efforts. During the interview, the questions proceeded from the nature and function of the association, its international activities, ways of distinguishing the local cuisine style, to difficulties involved in its international outreach.

A few observations may be made based on the spoken interview as well as the written one. The association represents about 20,000 large and medium-sized restaurants in Hangzhou, accounting for about 60 per cent of the total number. Since 2008, international food festivals are regularly held every year in the city under the auspices of the municipality, often within mega-events like the World Leisure Expo. If one is held abroad, it is usually at the invitation of a local restaurant association and normally one country per year is chosen. The places they mentioned as having visited are Spain, France, Austria, Singapore, and the United States (i.e. the UN). It may also be mentioned that the city participates in food festivals in other Chinese cities as well. The cuisine is presented as specifically of Hangzhou, with names associated with features of the city, but adapted to local customs if necessary (like 'Pork of *Dongpo* (poet)' or 'Vinegar fish of West Lake' made from local fish with fewer bones). It appears that the association is well aware of the purposes of the international promotion of Hangzhou cuisine as the best method: namely, to make the city better known (also as 'capital of fine food'), to attract more visitors and tourists, and to help increase the revenue of the city as well as the restaurants themselves. Finally, on the question of why the city fails to establish its own restaurants abroad, the interviewees made it clear that it is next to impossible because the procedures in the West are too complex and Chinese practitioners are used to relying on network and cannot deal with Western restrictive measures (i.e. 'too many permits required'). On the whole, it may be argued that the range of communication and exchange is rather small (one country per year) while the number of foreigners reached is unknown, that there is a lack of verbal communication whether in the form of brochures or books, and that there is obvious and serious need to establish local outlets of Hangzhou cuisine in foreign countries (also considering that foreign culinary outlets are everywhere in this city).

The internet and international languages

As part of our discourse research, attention should be directed to the ways in which the city's international brand and branding are mediated as well, for example, the languages used and channels of communication drawn upon. A general search is thus conducted on the use of 'quality-of-life' related websites hosted by Hangzhou and it has been found that a good number of institutions have English language and other foreign languages on their websites. These organizations may be classified into three categories: (1) city-government offices and organizations under its administration, (2) provincial-government-administered institutions (note that Hangzhou is the capital of Zhejiang province), and (3) State-owned enterprises. The first group has far more websites; in parenthesis, few relevant trade associations would have a website with an English-language page (e.g. Association of Performing Arts: http://www.hzyyyxh.com/; Restaurants and Hotels Guild: www.hzms.org). The information on the three groups is arranged by order of the owner, the website and the foreign languages used; from the name of the owner it will be possible to appreciate the nature of the site in question.[9]

Municipal offices and organizations under its administration

- Municipal government portal: http://www.hangzhou.gov.cn/ (English);
- Information Office: http://www.hicenter.cn (English);
- Tourism Committee: http://www.gotohz.com/ (English, Japanese, Korean and German);
- Landscape and heritage site administrative committee: http://xhsy.hzwestlake.gov.cn/index.aspx (English);
- Liangzhu Heritage Site Committee: http://www.lzsite.gov.cn/ (English, Japanese, Korean, Spanish, German);
- Bureau of Gardens and Heritages: http://www.hzwestlake.gov.cn/ (English, Japanese, Korean);
- World Leisure Expo: http://www.wl-expo.com/ (English);
- West Lake International Expo: http://www.xh-expo.com/ (English);
- Southern-Song Imperial Kiln Museum: http://www.ssikiln.com/newEbiz1/EbizPortalFG/portal/html/index.html (English);

- Comprehensive Canal Protection Committee: http://www.grandcanal.com.cn/ (English, Japanese, Korean);
- China Tea Museum: http://www.teamuseum.cn/default.aspx (English, Japanese);
- Hangzhou History Museum: http://www.hzmuseum.com/ (English);
- China Silk Museum: http://www.chinasilkmuseum.com/ (English);
- Lingying Temple: http://www.lingyinsi.org/ (English, Japanese);
- *Hangzhou Daily*: http://www.hangzhou.com.cn/ (Japanese, Korean(.

Provincial-government supported institutions based in Hangzhou

- Zhejiang Art Gallery: http://www.zjam.org.cn/ (English);
- Zhejiang Symphony Orchestra: http://www.zjso.org/index.asp (English);
- China Cartoons and Animation Festival: http://www.cicaf.com/ (English).

State-owned enterprises

- Grand Opera House Limited: http://www.hzdjy.com/index.php (English);
- Olympic and International Expo Centre: http://www.hzoiec.com/ (English).>

From the list of the websites above it may be seen that the city's administrative organizations make available to the international community quite a large number of information platforms in connection with the promotion of the city, including its brand. Moreover, in addition to the English language, many of the sites use other foreign languages, reaching out to a wider international community. If we look at the contents of the websites, then some further features may be of note. While a few sites provide Chinese-culture-specific information as characteristic of Hangzhou, such as historical attractions and local food and drink (http://www.hicenter.cn/facts_33.asp), some sites have more or less the same information and moreover the information is rather general, that is, Hangzhou is described as unique neither in China nor in the world:

> Hangzhou, capital of Zhejiang province, has been one of China's most renowned and prosperous cities for much of the last 1,000 years. Located in the Yangtze River Delta, Hangzhou is well-known for its beautiful natural scenery, the West Lake being its most renowned location. Ranked among the most competitive cities and also named the Happiest City in China for five consecutive years, Hangzhou has a reputation for outstanding quality of life that attracts people of different ages and lifestyles to visit, live, work and learn. Hangzhou citizens take great pride in their city and value it as an urban habitat designed for great living. Hangzhou, capital of Zhejiang province, has been one of China's most renowned and prosperous cities for much of the last 1,000 years.
>
> (http://www.chinadaily.com.cn/m/hangzhou/e/2009-08/12/content_8561615.htm)

The last but least issue regarding the medium of communication concerns translation, namely translation of the brand name. The Chinese '生活品质之城' has been frequently translated in English as 'city of quality life'. From the productive point of view, the question is how Hangzhou may best represent, promote and market what such a translation may render to the international community. From the point of view of brand reception, the question is how this name itself may be perceived and understood. While surveys of some sorts may be conducted, from the present point of view it may be arguable that the English phrase could sound too vague or broad to ring true or realistic and consequently could prove difficult for effectively marketing the brand. A similar example of possibly dubious meaning of translation may be: 'there is heaven above, Hangzhou and Suzhou below'. (http://www.chinadaily.com.cn/m/hangzhou/e/2007-11/07/content_8551481.htm).

International recognition

As argued at the beginning, branding has both productive and receptive sides. How Hangzhou's brand of quality life is understood and responded to by the international community, professional and ordinary, should be part of our research. In the above, I have indicated, where possible, the role of the international target community in the branding practices examined and the extent and manner of its participation. Here it may be noted that Hangzhou has won much international recognition in the past decade and a half in the form of awards and plaques (see Table 3.1).

However, it will be realized that much more comprehensive research would be needed in order to ascertain the nature and extent of the international uptake of Hangzhou's brand as city of quality of life. For instance, research attention may be directed to what if any of Hangzhou is explicitly present in the global village, how people (visitors or otherwise) understand it, and where Hangzhou's brand has affected their lives in any way.

Conclusion

In the study of Asian/Third Word urban development in general and of international city branding in particular, I have chosen to focus on the case of the Chinese coastal historical, tourist and thriving city of Hangzhou. The project was motivated partly by the understanding that city branding is a new and crucial part of urban development and partly by the current research condition that Third World cities have been disproportionately understudied. My particular purpose is then to identify, analyse, explain and assess Hangzhou's international city-branding discourse as a developing- world case in terms of its properties, problems and potentials. To that end, I have first of all sketched out a cultural-discursive account of city branding and then methodologically sought to obtain a variety of kinds of data across a range of settings and examine them from historical and intercultural perspectives. In the remainder of this chapter, let me offer a synthesis and overall assessment based on the respective analyses so far.

First, as a result of a public campaign, the city of Hangzhou adopted an official brand, to wit, the city of quality life, with specific municipal offices overseeing, implementing and monitoring the brand's communication, management and development. Although this is rare not just in the Chinese context but also in the world at large, such a pro-active measure is all the more needed for the lesser-known Third World cities such as the one in question in the fast globalizing age. Second, in addition to the municipality, businesses and civil organizations, large numbers of citizens (as well as foreigners) actively participate in the all-year-round branding events via, for example, the so-called 'experiencing day'. So through mega-events ordinary people can also become city-brand makers and communicators. Third, the city brand of Hangzhou is articulated to the international community in and through a diversity of explicitly promotional practices both at the general and all-encompassing level (e.g. the World Leisure Expo and the West Lake Expo) and across a good number of trades (e.g. the industries of tea, cuisine, fashion, high-tech, e-commerce). Worthy of note here in particular is that different levels and types of branding practice are co-ordinated and integrated; this way greater effect may be expected. Such multifacetedness and interconnection of branding practices seem particularly necessary for a relatively vague and polysemic city brand such as Hangzhou's. Fourth, Hangzhou's branding practices draw on a variety of mediums available and possible, logos, websites, videos, posters, brochures, and so on. Relevant organizations at different levels use the English language as well as other international languages on their websites. Such broad use of communicative mediums will enhance international accessibility enormously. (Of course by the same token, it could be suggested that still more foreign languages, whether European, Asian, Latin American or African, as well as still more internationally oriented specialist websites (pages), be established, say on the city's cuisine, tea-houses and fashion.) Furthermore, as the city's culinary trade shows, it is possible for relevant trade representatives and firms to physically go in order to make known and promote their trade brand and thereby their city brand. Finally, as our case demonstrates, branding practices can be coupled with not just economic gains as in the form of domestic and foreign investment, but also various international distinctions.

In conclusion, it must be mentioned that the present study reveals shortcomings, constraints and potential with regard to the internationalization of the city's brand as well. To start with, unlike the brands of London as 'financial centre', Sydney as 'the opera house', or Hong Kong as 'Asia's world city', Hangzhou's brand of 'city of quality life' may sound rather abstract. Consequently, it would be doubly challenging to mobilize wide-ranging, domain-specific branding activities (such as the 'day of all citizens drinking tea' and fine food festivals). Moreover, there seems rarely any attempt to go abroad to brand the city (except for the culinary and tourism trades). Related to this, too, there does not seem to be an explicit distinction made in the branding for the international markets. Given the numerous foreign firm outlets (say shops, restaurants and cafés) distributed throughout Hangzhou, there is both a long way to go and great potential. For this an insider view has been that the difficulty of reaching out to the international community and having a strong impact lies in Chinese cultural conditions and conventions; this means that cultural creativity is called for to make an international breakthrough. In addition, although an impressive variety of mediums of communication have been employed, one can see that still other tools and channels may be resorted to, such as RQ code, APPs, in order to maximize international branding.

Table 3.1 Awards/plaques conferred on Hangzhou

Year	*Titles and awarding organizations*
2001	Habitat Scroll of Honour Award from the United Nations Centre for Human Settlements (habitat), UNCHS (http://cn.unhabitat.org/content.asp?typeid=19&catid=490&id=3156#Hangzhou)
2002	The International Award for Live-able communities from the LivCom Management Company (http://www.livcomawards.com/previous-winners/2006-index.htm)
2002	International Garden City the International Federation of Parks and Recreation Administration (http://www.hicenter.cn/facts_11.asp)
2003–2008	Best Investment Environment Cities of China from the World Bank (2003, 2004, 2005, 2006, 2007, 2008) (http://zjnews.zjol.com.cn/05zjnews/system/2007/09/11/008786891.shtml; http://www.hicenter.cn/facts_11.asp)
2006	Oriental Leisure Capital from the World Leisure Organization (http://www.hangzhou.com.cn/20060801/ca1218356.htm)
2006	The Best Tourism City of China from the United Nations World Tourism Organization and National Tourism Administration (http://www.hicenter.cn/facts_11.asp)
2007	China's Best Tourist City from the National Tourism Administration and the United Nations World Tourism Organization (http://www.china.org.cn/archive/2007-02/10/content_1199624.htm)
2007	Medaille d'Or from the Fédération internationale du tourisme (FIT) (http://www.federationinternationaledutourisme.eu/distinctions-en-chine.htm) 2004–9
	The Best Commercial Cities in Mainland of China from Forbes (http://eng.hangzhou.gov.cn/main/zpd/English/AboutHangZhou/T326241.shtml)
2011	"Creativity Demonstration" from the Organizing Committee of International Forum on Cultural Industry (http://en.hangzhou.com.cn/News/content/2011-08/03/content_3829959.htm)
2011	World Heritage Site from the UNESCO World Heritage Centre (http://en.gotohz.com/whyhangzhou/wlh/#sthash.euuYlZ1Q.eYD7oRC5.dpbs)
2012	UNESCO Creative Cities Network City of Crafts and Folk Art from UNESCO (http://news.ifeng.com/gundong/detail_2012_05/18/14620127_0.shtml)

Acknowledgements

Support for the present research by the Humanities and Social Sciences Fund of the Ministry of Education, No.11YJA740075, is gratefully acknowledged. Gratitude is expressed also to the participants of my course, Cultural Discourse Studies, as well as my research assistant Xie Xiuting, at Zhejiang University, who helped collect much of the data used here. Suggestions by two anonymous reviewers are greatly appreciated.

Notes

1 City branding is often defined too broadly or vague; the following is not untypical: 'the purposeful symbolic embodiment of all information connected to a city in order to create associations and expectations around it' (Lucarelli and Berg 2011: 21).
2 Relevant information may be found at: http://data.stats.gov.cn/workspace/index?a=q&type=global&dbcode=csnd&m=csnd&dimension=zb&code=A0101&region=330100&time=2012,2012. See also季靖，陈静2008, 《杭州》课题组2008, 邹身城2006.
3 http://hzfzw.hz.gov.cn/jjhz/myjs/201205/t20120507_315759.html
4 See: http://www.xh-expo.com/zt/15th/xhexpobm/
5 See http://whc.unesco.org/en/news/767/: 'The World Heritage Committee has inscribed the West Lake Cultural Landscape of Hangzhou, comprising the West Lake and the hills surrounding its three sides, into UNESCO's World Heritage List.' At the first West Lake International Tea Expo held in 2005, Hangzhou was awarded the plaque '中国茶都' (China's Capital of Tea).
6 Reference information may be found at: http://hznews.hangzhou.com.cn/chengshi/content/2013-03/27/content_4667544_2.htm (with English page); http://lxs.cncn.com/70786-news-show-68859.html.
7 It has web pages in English and Japanese: http://www.teamuseum.cn/default.aspx.
8 Some other related websites in English: www.teavivre.com,TravelChinaGuide.com; en.gotohz.com (of Hangzhou).
9 It may be pointed out, though, that some websites concerning key aspects of the 'quality life' of Hangzhou are in Chinese only (e.g. Landscape and heritage site administrative committee: http://xhsy.hzwestlake.gov.cn/index.aspx; Xiling Seal Engraver's Society: http://www.xlys1904.com/; West Lake Museum: http://www.westlakemuseum.com/).

References

Amin, A., Massey, D. and Thrift, N. (2000). *Cities for the Many not the Few*. Bristol: The Policy Press.

Beaverstock, J. V., Smith, R. G. and Taylor, P. J. (1999). A roster of world cities. *Cities*, 16: 445–458.

Beauregard, R. A. (1993). *Voices of Decline: The Postwar Fate of US Cities*. Oxford: Blackwell.

Flowerdew, J. (2004). The Discursive Construction of a World-class City. *Discourse & Society*, 15(5): 579–605.

Gold, J. R. and Gold, M. M. (2004). *Cities of Culture*. Farnham: Ashgate Publishing.

Gunnarsson, B. L. (2009). Discourse in organizations and qorkplaces. In L. Wei and V. Cook (eds), *Contemporary Applied Linguistics: Linguistics for the Real World*. London: Continuum International Publishing Group, pp. 122–141.

Hajer, M. A. (1995). *The Politics of Environmental Discourse*. Oxford: Oxford University Press.

Holmes, J. (2011). Discourse in the workplace. In K. Hyland and B. Paltridge (eds), *Continuum Companion to Discourse Analysis*. London: Continuum, pp. 185–198.

Imrie, R. and Raco, M. (eds) (2003). *Urban Renaissance? New Labour, Community and Urban Policy*. Bristol: Policy Press.

Jensen, O. B. (2007). Culture stories: understanding cultural urban branding. *Planning Theory*, 6(3): 211–236.

Kavaratzis, M (2004). From city marketing to city branding: towards a theoretical framework for developing city brands *Place Branding*, 1(1): 58–73.

Keller, K.L. (2012). *Strategic Brand Management*, 4th ed. Edinburgh: Pearson Education.

Koester, A. (2010). *Workplace Discourse*. London: Continuum.

Lees, L. (2004). Urban geography discourse analysis and urban research. *Progress in Human Geography*, 28(1): 101–107.

Ley, D. (1995). Between Europe and Asia: the case of the missing sequoias. *Ecumene*, 2, 185–210.

Lucarelli, A. and Berg, P. O. (2011). City branding: a state-of-the-art review of the research domain. *Journal of Place Management and Development*, 4(1): 9–27.

McCann, E. (2004). 'Best places': inter-urban competition, quality of life, and popular media discourses. *Urban Studies*, 41(10): 1909–1929

Mitchell, K. (1996). Visions of Vancouver: ideology, democracy, and the future of urban development. *Urban Geography*, 17: 478–501.

Mommas, H. (2002). City branding: The necessity of socio-cultural goals. In T. Hauben, M. Vermeulen and V. Patteeuw (eds), *City Branding: Image Building and Building Images*. Rotterdam: NAI Uitgevers, pp. 32–48.

Okano, H., and Samson,D. (2010). Cultural urban branding and creative cities: a theoretical framework for promoting creativity in the public spaces. *Cities*, 27 10–15.

Rutheiser, C. (1996). *Imagineering Atlanta*. London: Verso.

Sevcik, T. (2011). Strategic urban narratives: beyond conventional city branding. *Development*, 54(3): 343–344.

Shi-xu (2014). *Chinese Discourse Studies*. Basingstoke: Macmillan.

Shi-xu (2015). Cultural discourse atudies. In K. Tracy, C. Ilie and T. Sandel (eds), *International Encyclopaedia of Language and Social Interaction*. Oxford: Wiley-Blackwell.

Slater, T. (2002). Looking at the 'North American city' through the lens of gentrification discourse. *Urban Geography, 23*(2): 131–153.

Williams, K. (2010). Sustainable cities: research and practice challenges. International *Journal of Urban Sustainable Development*, 1(1): 128–133.

Wilson, D. (1996). Metaphors, growth coalition discourses, and black poverty neighborhoods in a US city. *Antipode*, 28: 72–96.

Zukin, S., Baskerville, R., Greenberg, M., Guthreau, C., Halley, J., Halling, M., Lawler, K., Nerio, R., Stack, R., Vitale, A. and Wissinger, B. (1998). From Coney Island to Las Vegas in the urban imaginary: discursive practices of growth and decline. *Urban Affairs Review*, 33(5), 627–54.

References in Chinese

季靖，陈静 (2008). 传播与城市品牌塑造 - - 以杭州、上海为例。《消费导刊》 21，16–17.
杭州市政府 (2007). 杭州"生活品质之城"城市品牌表述系统（要点）。《杭州通讯（生活品质版）》，(1), 20–21。
《杭州》课题组（2008）。《杭州》。北京：当代中国出版社。
黄宇亮, 王竹(2006). 杭州城市识别系统的诠释与实践。《华中建筑》，24 (8).
施旭 (2008). 从话语研究的视角看城市发展。《文化艺术研究》，3，32–43.
邹身城 (2006). 从研究城市个性特征出发，探讨杭州的发展定位。中国城市发展网 http://chinacity.org.cn。

Part II
African discourse studies

4 A discourse on the usage of African languages for scientific and technological education and development

Introduction: the emancipation principle

This chapter draws attention to the fact that by all indications the question of the centrality of African languages in our attempt to developmentally transform African society is beginning to resonate across the African continent and beyond in various contexts. This is a most welcome development and attests to the argument that the issue is like a piece of cork, which is pushed under water. Sooner or later, or indeed, sooner rather than later, it pops up again, with resoluteness.

The reasoning is philosophically grounded on the basis of an understanding of the emancipation principle. In brief, this principle argues that there is slow, steady and oftentimes staggered progress in the human condition, progress in which humanity as a whole by degrees, but unevenly in fits and jerks, moves forward in the achievement of greater freedom and control over the existential circumstances of everyday life. As history unfolds, and the present becomes the past, and the future becomes the present, human groups, communities, societies and cultures gain increasingly greater control over the forces and factors, which order their everyday lives.

A hundred years ago Africa was firmly in the grip of colonial domination. Slowly over a period of a century, Africans have been able to work their way out of colonial thraldom into colonial freedom and postcolonialism or neo-colonialism. This latter condition has its own forms of subjugated entrapment. In spite of the societal challenges of the present and the past century, we can still say that Africans have moved forward in progress from where they were 100 years ago.

Since the earliest times, the progressive ebb and flow of the emancipation process has been variously, described in discourses by social theorists and thinkers. As universal theoretical formulations, over the past 70 years, scholars like the American anthropologist Elman Service, the Dutch historian Jan Romein, have respectively called the mechanism of this process, the Law of Evolutionary Potential, and the Theory of Retarding Lead. Wertheim described it at length as 'waves of emancipation' (Wertheim 1974). In the times when such theories were professed, many were also attracted to the Marxian theory of Uneven Development, which more or less, says the same thing in a different way.[1] Leon

Blum, the French politician of the early twentieth century suggested that, 'Every institution; every nation, past or present, that impedes the progress of civilization, of justice, must disappear' (Fraser and Natanson 1937: 100). One is persuaded by the argument that African society will make progress and will move forward, but indeed, at some cost and socially motivated agency for planned and progressive social transformation would be needed. The upshot of this position is that there are no scientific grounds for supposing that Africans will be perpetually relegated to backwardness or under-development.

The principle implies that, although the emancipation process is valid for humanity as a whole, the societal and cultural conditions in which the process plays itself out differ for groups, cultures, societies and historical contexts. For example, while the institution of universal adult franchise was introduced at the closing stages of the colonial experience, it created citizens of African states on the basis of colonially foisted identities, which partially effaced deeper primordial, historical African identities, which predate colonialism. Another example is provided by the fact that, the ending of the Apartheid dispensation politically empowered the masses of South Africa, specifically its non-White masses. At the same time, it saw the dissolution of Bantustan identities and Bantustan claims of nationhood. Another way of making this point is that it is possible for the empowerment of Africans with civil rights to advance in a culturally hollow and denationalizing context; this way the emancipation process proceeds with Africans ceasing to be Africans, in a cultural or linguistic sense. If African languages and cultures die, Africans will cease to exist culturally as Africans. Africans will become other people, those whose languages and cultures are adopted. For the emancipation principle to have fuller meaning it must dimensionally move beyond individual civil rights and must respect collective and cultural rights of groups.

Already, we live in a world in Africa in which our physical environment has been linguistically and definitionally considerably alienated. Lake Victoria, Orange River, Hammanskraal, Ivorians, Nigerians, Gold Coasters, Kruger Park, Thompson Gazelle, Burchett Zebra and the Drakensberg are all names and designations which have come to replace things which Africans knew, and had names for, long before the Western encounter. Since the advent of Western colonialism, this new nomenclature has effaced the linguistic and cultural ownership of these realities. Thus Africans have been relocated from inside to outside the nomenclature of their environment. Their environmental reality has been linguistically appropriated, redefined and redesignated in favour of Europe-inspired images and the nostalgia of Western colonialists, bent on reproducing Europe in Africa. Since the end of the colonial era, African elites have inherited this new reality, and proceeded to largely maintain, understand and run it, like the colonial masters had hoped they would, with little, half-hearted, or no attempt to reclaim African reality and history. Operating in the shadow of the erstwhile colonial languages, primarily in the domestic and informal domains, African languages today are in social policy and practice definitively excluded from the purported modernization of African societies; they are essentially part of the ceded historical belongings, rendered so through Western colonialism. In as far as these conditions exist and persist they affirm a neo-colonial order in which the African as a historical and cultural product is silenced in favour of his colonial master's voice and languages.

The language question

Arguably, the message of the centrality of African languages to African development is registering in the present-day world. This point must however be made with caution, because the progress Africans are making in this respect is indecisive and spasmodic. Some positive steps forward in policy and practice are made and then oftentimes negative approaches follow which concede some retreat. While the idea of the criticality of African languages to African development is gaining acolytes and fellow-travellers, the social practice of the elites pulls in the opposite direction, favouring the social elimination of African-language usage in all domains.

For too long, too many observers and practitioners of African development have laboured under the illusion that development in Africa is largely a technicist and almost restrictedly economic problem measured and calculated on the basis on GDP (Gross Domestic Product), GNP (Gross National Product) and per capita indices. Elaborate models of various theories of modernization have for decades overwhelmed our thinking and practice and yielded remarkably little fruitful result. While these fixations still exercise the minds of contemporary neo-classical·African economists working with the structural adjustment credo, the critical minds and rational historicists amongst us have plenty of criticisms for these theoretically dated fixations.

In the area of education, popular but hard wisdom has confirmed the view, endorsed by UNESCO, that mental fertility and successful schooling is enabled and best enhanced by education in the primary years in the home language. The evidence is so overwhelming that few today would controvert the value of this judgement. Even then, there are many who continue to want to prove this point, spending scarce resources in repeating research to prove this point.

This issue is of course of interest to those societies which do not use the mother tongue in education and which interrogate themselves about the wisdom or unwisdom of working in a colonial language. It is an issue which is of little interest to those who use the mother tongue in education, invariably the language of the masses. For these latter societies, the question is purely academic. It would for them be difficult to imagine education, at any level, in somebody else's language. Mammino makes the succinct point that

> the use of a second language as a medium of instruction is a heritage of colonization. In all those countries where such a heritage is not present, students use their mother tongue throughout the whole instruction career. From a pedagogical point of view, the use of a second language is an objective disadvantage affecting both the easiness and, one might say, the comfort with

> which knowledge is acquired by students, and the extent and depth of the acquisition.[2]

In Africa, this issue is hardly treated with the necessary degree of seriousness because we remain trapped in the usage of colonially or imperially received languages which are treated as inherently superior and which come to us with a colonially induced acceptance of Western (or in some areas Arabic) cultural and linguistic superiority. Conquest and colonialism have dulled our native instincts for cultural self-preservation. Africans have become culturally submissive and accommodating to Western cultural and linguistic pre-eminence. Television, cinema and the print-media across the continent are dominated by non-African language usage.

In postcolonial Africa, remarkably, because of the material and social benefits of socio-economic elevation and vertical social mobility enjoyed by the elites, mass society treating the elites as a reference group copies the values and aspirations which visibly bring relative prosperity and privilege to the elites; principal amongst these institutional markers is fluency in the colonial language. The closer this fluency is to metropolitan Western usages, the more valued and esteemed the speaker becomes. In Anglophone Africa all of this comes with the mimicry of 'Anglo-Saxon attitudes'.

Language in Africa, myth and reality

Closely allied to African fixations to the colonially received languages is the implicit assumption that African languages are developmentally doomed: they cannot become languages of modernity and technical advancement. This view was implanted as a cultural consequence of the colonial project and has survived colonialism, through the agency of current elites, the inheritors of leadership of the postcolonial state. For the past half-century of neo-colonialism the view has been generationally reproduced and entrenched.

Joyce Cary, who became famous years ago for his novels *Mr Johnson, Aissa Saved* and *African Witch,* published during World War II a text entitled; *The Case for African Freedom* in which he argued that:

> What is to be the language of higher education in the African colonies: Hausa, Swahili, or English? We are about to set up new schools and universities on both sides of Africa. We know that mass education cannot be more than elementary; and that it will by itself create a need for more secondary schools, to be filled by the cleverer and more ambitious boys released from primitive discouragement by its action. […] More doctors, teachers, instructors, inspectors, clerks, and foremen will be wanted for the new schools, new social services, and new industries. […] no one has yet decided the fundamental point of language; whether, for instance, the object shall be to produce in Africa, as in India, an educated class, reading, speaking, and thinking in English as readily as in their mother tongues; or Swahili speakers, Baganda

> speakers, Hausa speakers, to whom English, if they know it at all, will be a grammar-book subject, useless for real intercourse. [...] 'What is the object of our education? What do the Africans want?' If the object of education is to maintain the traditional character of native states, then native languages will help to secure it. But it must be said that the natives themselves do not see it in that light. They think of it as an attempt to put them in an inferior position. [...] It is in historical fact a wrong suspicion. But it has for the African a logic not always perceived by the European. For he looks upon Europe and its civilization as things far superior to anything in his own inheritance; and he thinks of the English language as the sign and agent of that superiority; a key to power and prestige.
>
> (Cary 1944: 124–125)

Cary, in his time, considered himself and was considered by many to be a sympathetic voice in the cause of African freedom. But he could make such remarks and observations which would be considered today by educationists to be poorly conceived and detrimental to the long-term interests of Africans. The point he makes about the fact that Africans consider education in the colonial languages to be the desirable route forward has persisted and in many ways become popular, if misguided. This ideology of the inferiority of African languages has systematically seeped into the psychology of many Africans and has in turn induced a syndrome of cultural self-rejection.

During one of a set of lectures given by Dame Margery Perham for the British Broadcasting Corporation (BBC) in 1965, referring to African languages, she pointed out that these languages, as it has been said in East Africa, cannot translate 'leader of opposition' except as 'chief of the enemies' (Perham 1966: 47). Perham was suggesting that African languages in East Africa were beyond the pale of political modernity. But that is not the only problem with her view; as Shi-xu points out, 'meaning, like values, is open-ended, changing and full of complexities and inextricably bound up with the historically and culturally embedded' (Shi-xu 2012: 210). In a discussion with the Zambian linguist Lazarus Miti (29 November 2013), he pointed out that in Central Africa, in Nguni-related languages like CiNsenga and CiNyanja, leader of the opposition in crude literal translation can be rendered as: *mtsogoleli wa cipani cosutsa boma*; in English, 'leader of the party of attackers'. This does not mean that members of the opposition understand their role to require physically attacking members of the government. Perham's Eurocentric translation distorts meaning and is limited in scope and so inadequate. Alexander Crummell who is frequently regarded as a leading Black intellectual of the nineteenth century and who studied for a degree at Queens College, Cambridge, in 1853 had this to say about African languages:

> The worth of our fathers' language will in this way stand out in distinct comparison with the Anglo-Saxon, our acquired speech. And *first*, let us speak of the African dialects. [...] this whole class of languages, it may be

> said, in the aggregate that (a) 'They are', to use the words of Dr Leighton Wilson, 'harsh abrupt, energetic, indistinct in enunciation, meagre in point of words, abound with inarticulate nasal and guttural sounds, possess but few inflections and grammatical forms, and are withal exceedingly difficult of acquisition'. This is his description of the Grebo, but it may be taken, I think as on the whole, a correct description of the whole class of dialects which are entitled 'Negro.' (b) These languages, moreover, are characterized by lowness of ideas. As the speech of rude barbarians, they are marked by brutal and vindictive sentiments, and those principles which show a predominance of the animal propensities. (c) Again, they lack those ideas of virtue, of moral truth, and those distinctions of right and wrong with which we, all our life long, have been familiar. (d) another marked feature of these languages is the absence of clear ideas of justice, law, human rights and governmental order; and (e) lastly – These supernal truths of a personal present Deity, of the moral Government of God, of man's Immortality.[3]

These utterances say more about the colonized African mind than African languages. The implicit message is that 'please escape your backward languages and cultures, become like the Westerner for your own salvation and development'. Almost all the states of postcolonial Asia have escaped this fate while Africa continues to labour under the falsehoods of colonial educational theory and practice. Crummell's cultural and linguistic misguidedness and the psychological defeatism, which accompanied this, have lived with us from the earliest years of Western education in Africa. Its persistence continues to the present day. Fanon (1967: 18) in his *Black Skins, White Masks* warned that,

> Every colonized people […] every people in whose soul an inferiority complex has been created by the death and burial of its local cultural originality finds itself face to face with the language of the civilizing nation; that is, with the culture of the mother country. The colonized is elevated above his jungle status in proportion to his adoption of the mother country's cultural standards. He becomes whiter as he renounces his blackness, his jungle.

The African elites by their own testimony and practice of cultural and linguistic deference have in many ways extended these views as a reference group category to mass society. It is arguable that today many Africans, not necessarily of the elite group, accept the idea that their languages are unsuitable for scientific and technological advancement. Referring to South Africa some years ago Kathy Luckett observed that African languages are undervalued in the minds of most people and that there is a widespread belief that they are 'unsuitable for further education, science, technology, law, business and government' (Luckett 1995; Prah 1995: 31). Such views are prevalent in sub-Saharan Africa. This notion is economically propped up by a situation in which knowledge of African languages provides little or no economic rewards or social mobility. Oftentimes, on African university campuses, one hears from African students the view that those who choose to study African languages at university level are laughed at and derided. The question they are asked is, 'Can you not study anything better than that?'

Language, culture and development

It is possible to understand culture as the sum total of all activity and product resulting from human creativity and providing the context in which we are societally formed and adjusted to cope with social life. In this sense, culture provides a basis for development, and development takes place ultimately in a cultural context. Also, most importantly language is the main pillar within a cultural system and is therefore crucial in any discussion of development.

While development invariably translates as economic advancement and improvement in the material and social conditions of people, it needs also to be pointed out that when and wherever development takes place it is reflected in all areas of social life including the arts, science and technology. In any case few will deny the fact that economic progress in itself cannot be understood to constitute societal advancement if it is not translated into the quality of life and overall culture of society.

If development is in the end a cultural phenomenon, science and technological advancement operating at the level of the material culture of society represent an important benchmark for the estimation of progress. Invariably, in Africa the adoption of science and technology is undertaken without sufficient cognisance of the need to adapt such innovative technology into the indigenous practices and cultural framework of people. Too often, new scientific and technological inputs bypass indigenous knowledge systems and are constructed as parallel and better technology which cannot be married to what the people already know and what they do in their everyday lives. New technology and science are treated as sealed packages, which must be accepted in their entirety, without adaptation to suit the cultural specifics of Africans. Such misplaced approaches are highlighted by the fact that innovative ideas, science and technology are introduced in languages foreign to mass society. For this reason, implicitly, the idea is also passed on that the languages of the masses of Africa, the languages on the bases of which democratic cultures must be constructed, are unsuitable for scientific and technological progress. There are currently, by way of government policies, no exceptions in sub-Saharan Africa to these dominant assumptions. Over the past few years, emphatically governments in Malawi, Ghana, Benin and Namibia have enunciated policies which firmly endorse and expand the role of Western colonial languages in education.

The South African case is of interest for the peculiarities it brings up in the African context. South Africa has the most advanced technological culture in the African continent and for this and other reasons attracts the attention and serves as a reference point for many African countries. But its technological success is misleading in as far as its ability to can provide educators the correct language policies to effect technological development. South Africa's technological culture is firmly and rigidly based on the cultures and languages of its White minorities.

In other words, the cultural and linguistic bases of technological society in South Africa are seriously undemocratized. It is doubtful if in the long run the pace of technological improvement and the expansion of a democratic culture, which is technologically and scientifically advancing, can be constructed on the restricted and narrow bases of a minority culture. For the above reasons, 'high culture' and 'low culture' in South Africa are reflected on racial and colour lines. The same cleavage exists between the culture of the elite and mass culture.

Some years ago in a text which eloquently argued in favour of the use of African languages for scientific and technological education, Dowling, Miti, Seepe and Mammino, contended that 'unless African languages are developed to intervene at a level of science, mathematics, technology and commerce, they will be considered irrelevant in developmental terms' (Seepe and Dowling 2000: i). What is equally true but escapes mention is that if African languages are not intellectualized they will eventually face extinction. Furthermore, we know too well today that no language is inherently incapable of development, advancement and progress through the absorption and incorporation of scientific and technological terminology. All languages are capable of developing if the necessary resources are provided for this purpose. Indeed, we know that languages can in a short period of time develop from the status of non-scientific popular *patois*, to advanced languages with the requisite arsenals of technical lexical to accomplish the most advanced technologies of the twenty-first century. Perhaps the three most notable cases in this respect over the past 100 years are Modern Hebrew, Bahasa and Afrikaans.

The success of Afrikaans on the African continent has been often lost on people because of its association with the Apartheid system and institutionalized racism. But it is possible to note that from the 1920s when it became an official language in parliament to the end of the twentieth century, it advanced from a language, bereft of modern scientific terminology, to a language of science and technology capable of unravelling and teaching the secrets of heart transplantation and helicopter-manufacture technology. In short it was intellectualized. We see over that period the elevation of a *kombuis taal* (kitchen language) to the status and capacity of one of the most modern, scientifically endowed languages. It needs of course to be said that this was done through the untrammelled usage of resources as directed by the White speakers of Afrikaans in their favour and against the interests of the overwhelming majority of other South Africans. But the point here is that it is possible to develop a language 'from zero to infinity'.

The challenge facing Africa and Africans is whether Africans want to see their languages developed as languages of science and technology understandable by the overwhelming majorities in African countries, or wish to pursue a neo-colonial cultural and linguistic track which directly leads to the extinction of African languages and the cultural transformation of Africans into Westerners/ Europeans. In all probability, the majority of Africans do not want their languages to vanish into extinction. Arguably, Africans would want to develop and use their languages in the same way that all the technologically advanced countries of the world do.

Some positive messages are being signalled in Uganda. Oketcho (2014) points out that, today, at least 27 indigenous languages are used as mediums of instruction at lower-primary level and taught as subjects in upper primary. Ten local languages are also taught and examined in several secondary schools and tertiary institutions including universities. In short, indigenous languages have partially taken root across the various educational levels in Uganda, that is from basic to university education (Oketcho, 2014, iv). It would in time be interesting to assess the progress of the Uganda process.

Obviously in those countries where there is more or less African-language monolingualism like Somalia, Lesotho, Swaziland, or where one language enjoys sufficient supremacy as a language in which the overwhelming majority are proficient like the examples of KiSwahili in Uganda, Kenya, Tanzania, the Eastern Congo or Sango in the Central African Republic or Tswana in Botswana, one would hope that progress in the usage of African languages for education and development can take place without too many societal and political inhibitions.

The way forward

However, there is need to solve a number of basic problems which stand in the way of the effective development of African languages. Of all the detractions marshalled against the use of African languages, possibly none has been, in effect, as pernicious as the suggestion that Africa is a Tower of Babel. The most common figures suggested for African languages range between 1,000 and 2,000 plus. Indeed, it is difficult to find figures from two observers which coincide. Thus, at the beginning of the twenty-first century, it is remarkable that no clear and consensual picture exists with respect to either the number of languages on the African continent or how these languages can be usefully classified. Each researcher on African languages appears to put his or her own numbers on them.

Given the ubiquity and arbitrariness of the African languages numbers game which goes on, one can conclude that this idea has knowingly or unknowingly become a convenient argumentation instrument in the hands of those who want to see Africans work permanently in the colonial languages.

Scientific terminology is incorporated through two alternative strategies or a judicious application of both. First, it is possible to coin new terms on the basis of the meanings we wish to convey. Sometimes, this appears to be the only sensible way out; especially where we think explanatory inputs in the use of terminology is crucial for such terminology to be understood. The other alternative approach is to adopt the term as it appears in the scientifically-parent language (e.g. English) and then phonologically adapt it to the respective African language. Fridge, in this case becomes *ifrigi* in Nguni. Permit becomes *permiti*. This is rationally the easier option, and its acceptance rate is generally higher than the former approach. However as already indicated judicious and selective approaches using both methods makes good sense both literally and metaphorically.

What the evidence on the ground points to is that Africans need to co-operate and work together to make headway with the development of African languages. This is because practically all African languages are cross-border speech forms; therefore working exclusively within the framework of African neo-colonial borders cannot maximize the social and economic benefits of Africa's linguistic geography. In the name of flag and the so-called nation-state, the Kamuzu Banda administration in Malawi refused to accept the reality that ciNyanja and ciCewa are the same language. In his search for a separate identity from Zambia, his regime divided speakers of this language beyond what the colonialists had done.

Sometimes these tensions and contradictions are perceptible in the same country and can be construed as attempts to own and control linguistic territorium. In Ghana, for a good 50 years after the harmonization of Akan in the early 1960s to produce a unified Akan orthography under the Nkrumah regime, writers still persist in the name of their colonial linguistic masters in using the pre-unification orthography which separated mutually intelligible dialects like Akuapim, Asante, Fanti, Akim, and Brong.

In a report submitted to the Centre for Advanced Studies of African Society (CASAS) by Felix Banda who has co-ordinated work on the languages of south-central Africa, it was revealed that in Zambia,

> the new iciLamba orthography had adopted the graphemes [sy] instead of [sh] for the voiceless palatal fricative, because they associated the [sh] sound with iciBemba. This is clearly nonsense, as the [sh] sound has nothing to do, with iciBemba. Even our own cross-border orthography recommends [sh] rather than [sy] for the voiceless palatal fricative.[4]

In Cluver's richly researched paper entitled 'Variables determining a language plan for Namibia', he falls into the trap of misreading and misinterpreting the precise nature of the languages enjoying mutual intelligibility in Africa and their scope for harmonization. Starting with specific reference to Namibia, Cluver writes that:

Nine indigenous languages have been identified for educational purposes and they will have all been developed so that all school training can take place in these languages for the first three years of the child's education. Kwanyama, Ndonga and Lozi can be taken as a school subject until the final school examination (Standard 10) and Kwangali can be taken as a school subject until Standard 8. Nama and Herero can only be taken as subjects in the primary school (apparently because a lack of interest on the side of the pupils to continue studying their own languages). Gciriku and Mbukushu have also not been developed beyond the level of primary school education because of the small number of school children in secondary schools. Tswana has been developed outside Namibia where it is offered as a university subject. If the new language policy for schools is accepted, this situation would require that at least five indigenous languages will have to be developed so that educational material can be produced in them.[5]

Cluver puts a wrong tally on the numbers of sufficiently distinct languages in Namibia. Furthermore he misidentifies dialects for clusters and clusters for dialects. Lozi and Tswana are actually mutually intelligibly speech forms of Sotho-Tswana. Herero, Kwanyama, and Ndonga are also mutually intelligible. He writes that:

> Each of the main Namibian languages seems to form dialect clusters. A large project 'Dialect survey of the major African languages in Namibia' (under Prof. Haacke) is analysing this phenomenon. It is clearly impossible to standardize each of the dialects and therefore only the most important dialect can be developed as a regional language to be used in local government and in schools. This will unfortunately lead to the suppression and possible eradication of the smaller dialects. This policy could lead to two forms of reaction.[6]

The route to standardization Cluver suggests is obviously fraught with potential conflict. The more judicious approach is not to adopt a single dialect and regard it as standard but rather to create what can be described as 'orthographic commons', that is a spelling and writing system which can be read within a cluster of mutually intelligible speech forms, but for which each dialectal form maintains its unique pronunciation and phonological qualities. Cluver's argument continues from his point that this policy could lead to two forms of reaction. That is:

1 Resistance against artificial unification of dialect clusters as occurred against Doke's proposals for the unification of the Shona group in Central Africa or the attempts to construct a 'union' language, Akan, covering both Twi and Fante in the Gold Coast.
2 Resistance against the promotion of indigenous languages by the parents who want their children trained in English. The development of the indigenous languages is often seen as an attempt to suppress the speakers by keeping them away from the official language.[7]

The resistance to the unification of Shona following Doke's proposals must not be exaggerated. With the benefit of hindsight, one can say that it has been quite well accepted. The problem there again is that one out of eight/nine dialects was selected for standardization. Harmonization must precede standardization if conflict and tensions are to be avoided. As pointed out above, the harmonization of Akan was not systematically resisted. It was rather old habits which for a long time prevented users from working with the new unified Akan orthography. It may be of interest to point out here that CASAS was the first institution to publish a book (*Nyansapow*) using the unified Akan orthography (Gyekye-Aboagye 2000).

Resistance to the promotion of indigenous languages is advised by the social premium, economic rewards and power which the use of the colonial languages provides above African languages. It is these issues which need to be addressed. It is arguably faulty to suggest that,

> Citizens who have become literate in their own language tend to become hungry for more information and learning English is one of the most efficient ways to obtaining more information. We can see the indigenous languages as stimulants to attract people towards the official language.[8]

Rather, if anything, literacy in African languages whets one's appetite for more literature and materials in the African language. The suggestion that English could be one of the most efficient ways of obtaining more information would be only true if the information is not provided in the indigenous language or the mother tongue for the mother tongue reader.

Conclusion

The challenge we are faced with regards to the development of African languages as languages of science and technology is at the same time the challenge of African emancipation and progress. It will be impossible to advance African society and cultures until Africans implement linguistic policies which put the use of the languages of the African masses centre-stage. The greatest hindrance faced in this is caused by the entrenched interests of the neo-colonial elites who, like Shakespeare's Caliban of the colonial Prospero, are addicted to the languages and voices of the former colonial master. The promotion of African languages requires systematic intellectualization with scientific and technological lexical inputs.

Notes

1 A summary presentation of these and related ideas is provided by Marcel van den Linden. In the journal; *Historical Materialism*,15 (2007), pp.145–165, Published by Brill for the International Institute for Social History, Amsterdam.
2 See Liliana Mammino, 'Studying the details of the transition from the mother tongue to the second language (Seepe and Dowling 2000: 94).
3 See Alexander Crummell, *The English Language in Liberia*, London, pp. 10–21. Quoted here from Langley (1979: 357).
4 Report made to K. K. Prah by Felix Banda, Cape Town, 17 April 2002.
5 See August Cluver, *Variables Determining a Language Plan for Namibia* (Du Plessis 1989: 71–72).
6 Ibid.
7 Ibid.
8 Ibid.

References

Cary, J. (1944). *The Case for African Freedom*. London: Secker and Warburg.

Du Plessis, T. (ed.) (1989). Language policy: addressing the national question. (special issue) *Logos*, 9(2), 1909–1929.

Fanon, F. (1967). *Black Skin, White Masks*. New York: Grove Press.

Fraser, G. and Natanson, T. (1937). *Leon Blum: Man and Statesman*. London: Victor Gollancz.

Gyekye-Aboagye, J. (2000). *Nyansapow*. Cape Town: CASAS Book Series No. 9.

Langley, J. A. (1979). *Ideologies of Liberation in Black Africa, 1856–1970. Documents on Modern African Political Thought from Colonial Times to the Present*. London: Rex Collings.

Luckett, K. (1995). *National Additive Bilingualism: Towards a Language Plan for South African Education*. Cape Town: Mimeo.

Oketcho, P. (2014). *Language Policy and Education in Uganda*. Kampala: Ishimwe Enterprises.

Perham, M. (1966). *African Outline*. London: Oxford University Press.

Prah, K. K. (1995). *African Languages for the Mass Education of Africans*. Cape Town: CASAS Book Series No. 7.

Seepe, S. and Dowling, D. (eds) (2000). *The Language of Science*. Florida Hills, FL: Vivlia.

Shi-xu. (2012). Expand methodologies of discourse research. *Journal of Multicultural Discourses*, 7(3): 209–211

Wertheim, W. F. (1974). *Evolution and Revolution: The Rising Waves of Emancipation*. Harmondsworth: Penguin.

5 The role of language and literacy in the acquisition of knowledge

The African context

Introduction

Language is the most prominent feature of social interaction. It is the internalized code we all use to express ourselves and communicate with others. It is manifested as a set of symbols, conventions and rules that are used for conveying information. It is the written and spoken method of systematically combining words to create meaning used and understood by a particular group of people. It has been observed about its formal grammatical structure that,

> a person who knows a language has acquired a system of rules and principles – a “generative grammar”, in technical terms – that associates sound and meaning in some specific fashion [...] Furthermore, there has been a renewal of interest in “universal grammar”, interpreted now as the theory that tries to specify the general properties of these languages that can be learned in the normal ways by humans.
>
> (Chomsky 1973: 167)

We can also say that language is a system of gestures, grammar, signs, sounds, symbols, or words, which is used to represent and communicate concepts, ideas, meanings and thoughts. Another way of defining language is to regard it as a ‘semantic code‘, a system of connotation of words and their meanings. Some restrict the notion of language to vocalic expression, excluding non-vocal expression such as pantomimic expressions, demonstrative physical responses and gestures from the meaning of language. The point in this respect is that, while such acts and expressions may often be structured and sequentially processed in much the same way as vocalic responses are, and may indeed serve as a system of communicative symbols which supplement and enhance verbal expressions, they are generally not included in the definition of language because they cannot be vocalized. Drum renditions as produced by Yoruba or Ashanti ‘talking drums’ can be described as a kind of Morse Code; constructed not on the bases of individual letters but rather on cryptic syllabic tones of the spoken language. Such drum language falls outside the ambit of language as used in the narrow sense understood here. In sum we can say that language is

> a structured system of arbitrary vocal sounds and sequences of sounds which is used, or can be used, in interpersonal communication by an aggregation of human beings, and which rather exhaustively catalogues the things, events, and processes in the human environment.
>
> (Carroll 1953: 10–11)

The cataloguing function of language is a feature, which is often under-argued or under-represented. Language in this respect is a register, a compendium of all (both material and non-material) that is known or recognized in our environment. It is a record of the history of a given speech-community, bearing all the imprints and history of its users. No single area of culture is as revealing of the history of its users as language (Prah 2000: 33–34). Herein also lies the credibility of Wittgenstein's aphorism that words, rather like tools, can be defined by the use they serve, thus 'to imagine a language means to imagine a form of life' (Wittgenstein 1967). Language, or more pointedly the lexicon of a given language can tell us whether the society is pre-industrial or industrial, hunter-gatherer or sedentary-agricultural, tropical or temperate. All of these realities are captured in language. Living in snow-bound communities in which snow and ice are realities affecting life on a continuous basis, the Inuit and Yup'ik have numerous expressions for snow and ice in different conditions. Fifteen lexemes referring to snow and snow-related notions are listed in Steven A. Jacobson's (1984) Yup'ik Eskimo dictionary (Jacobson 1984). Similarly, the pastoralist Maasai have 18 words for different conditions of grass, because grass is central to their mode of livelihood. Context in space and time is important. One implication of this which Shi-xu has pointed to is that:

> [M]eaning emerges and exists only partially in linguistic forms; discourse is but an open site of infinite and continuous meaning generation and interpretation in which the researcher must rely also on subjective experience, intuition, imagination, etc. and conduct dialogue continuously with life.
>
> (Shi-xu 2012)

This is also why translations are always ultimately approximations.

For English, which possibly has the largest lexicon in the world, the vocabulary has grown from the 50,000 to 60,000 words in Old English, about 150,000 for Elizabethan English, to somewhere around a 1,000,000 now. The King James Bible of 1611 used only 6,000 words. The average English-speaking person could use about 2,000 different words per week. Technological and scientific language is continuously absorbed into the lexicon. A further half-million technical and scientific terms are uncatalogued. Today, more than 750 million people use the English language. An average educated person knows about 20,000 words and uses about 2,000 words in a week.[1] An English speaker may need about 800 words to satisfy daily needs. The rather limited number of words needed for daily usage is because the language has developed different lexicals. These are used by specialists who employ their own jargon or in-group languages. Years ago,

Driberg estimated that pre-civilizational man may have required about 2,000 words to express him or herself because all branches of knowledge were common to the whole community. In other words, they shared a common language which addressed every aspect of their culture.[2] Despite its widespread use, there are only about 500 million people who use English as their mother tongue. More than half of the world's technical and scientific periodicals as well as three-quarters of the world's mail, emails and cables are in English. About 70 per cent of the information stored in the world's computers is in English. English is transmitted to more than 100 million people every day by five of the largest broadcasting companies in the world (CBS, NBC, ABC, BBC, CBC).[3] However, it is useful to remember that this global dominance of English is not on account of any inherent superiority of English, but simply a result of the success of British imperialism. By the end of the nineteenth century as the saying goes 'the sun never set on the British empire.' The rise of the United States, a predominantly English-speaking country as the imperial power-house of the world has further strengthened the pre-eminence of English. Indeed, it is the Churchillian old English-speaking nations, which linguistically and technologically underwrite the pre-eminence of English in the contemporary world.

In Africa as in many other parts of the world the colonial powers never failed to leave their linguistic imprint in the various areas and over the peoples they subjugated. The history of Western languages in Africa also geographically demarcates the colonial fortunes of the imperial powers in Africa. All the peoples within respective colonial boundaries were made to adopt the language of the colonial masters. Apart from the early imperial history of the Arab caliphate in North Africa with the introduction and expansion of Arabic in the region and subsequently rather limited Turkish supremacy by the Ottomans in mainly Egypt and the Sudan, it is the Western colonial languages which have effectively made their mark. During the first half of the twentieth century they dominated the continent as languages of power and control. In this early part of the twenty-first century there are no indications as yet that Africans can roll back Western imperial linguicism.

Orality and literacy

Another notable feature of language is its manifestation as oral or literate forms. The connection or divide between these two manifestations has generated endless debate, which has been called 'the great divide'. Interest in the sociology of orality and literacy became intensive during the decade of African independence (1960s). Over the years, a huge body of work has developed probing different dimensions of the question. The original contributors to this debate included, Jack Goody (1963), Ian Watt (1963), Marshall McLuhan (1962), Walter Ong (1958), Eric Havelock (1963) and Claude Lévi-Strauss (1962). Some have regarded orality and literacy as social systems, to be separate and distinct, signifying the contrasts of civilization and barbarism. Others see the two realities not as totally binary phenomena which are structurally exclusive, but rather as dialectical realities and interpenetrative extensions of the same thing (continuity theories) with oral systems preceding or flowing into literate ones. The transition from one to the other, proto-literacy, implies in practice that elements of the older system linger as literacy grows. The transition from predominantly oral cultures to literate ones runs parallel to the shift from pre-modernity to modernity. In today's world, there are hardly any exclusively oral social or cultural systems except in very small and remote corners of the globe. All societies are more or less in transition from orality to literacy. In this transition process, or proto-literacy as it can be called, some achieve the transition much faster than others. All have to deal, as part of the instrumentation of this transition, to different degrees with issues of literacy, and the production and reproduction of knowledge.

There are those who suggest that the transition from orality to literacy is hardly the fate of all societies. Gellner for example argues that 'very roughly speaking, pre-industrial societies are of two kinds: tribal/illiterate, and urban/literate, non-industrial civilizations. From the present viewpoint, the former constitute no practical problem; their institutions simply do not survive in the modern world, other than in a symbolic or sentimental form. But those of the literate civilizations do' (Gellner 1964: 180).

This classification yields a lot of insight; much of Africa today would fall in the former category. But Gellner overstates his case. Rather, under present circumstances, with the availability of the technologies of language, tribal illiterate cultures can survive. The real question is 'do we have the will power to make this happen?' With the overwhelming majority of languages and cultures in the world endangered and threatened by extinction, clearly motivated and proactive action is needed if there is to be a serious turn-around. What is required is the expansion of literacy to reach tribal and illiterate societies, literacy that empowers marginalized people and lifts communities with their own languages into modernity.

Partial or total home-language or mother-tongue illiteracy which is compensated by a received or imposed colonial or imperial language effectively defines a colonial or neo-colonial cultural relationship. It is a relationship of linguistic dependence and surrender by one community to another; a master–servant linkage which extends far beyond the superficial communicative functions of simple language into the area of culture as a whole. Language is the main pillar of culture and serves as an agency for entry into the historico-cultural world of the speakers of a given language. We see that in general reactions to Western imperialism in a cultural sense vary. A good part of this variation arises out of the relationship between the languages of the colonized and the colonizers' language or languages. While the colonizers' language assimilates recruits from the colonized community; the aboriginal languages of the colonized stagnate and diminish in significance as a transactional medium. What we currently see in postcolonial Africa is that the languages of mass society; the native languages of the African peoples, are in recession, retreat and stagnation. They are in danger of extinction by the languages of the erstwhile colonizers. The absence in much of Africa of strong historical literacy traditions which held the cultural patrimony of much of Asia together, in spite of colonialism, is telling. The cultural confidence and societal resilience of much of Asia, in places like China, India, the Arab world, Japan, with long-standing traditions of literacy remained largely undented through colonialism to postcolonialism. It was in Oceania, the Americas and Africa with largely non-literate historical backgrounds that both colonialism and neo-colonialism have culturally been most deleterious. Unless strengthening and reinforcing democratic indigenous language policies are systematically effected, oral cultures today and tomorrow have little chance for survival; they can hardly hold their own in discourse with autonomously literate cultures of the world (Goody 1989: 86, Olson and Torrance 2001: 138–139). The culturally resilient societies of the Third World have been historically literate; they are societies which have enjoyed indigenous religious literacy. This is why they are not culturally neo-colonial in the same sort of debilitated way one finds in Africa, the Americas and Oceania.

Language as an oral form has a particularly significant role in African society. Because most African languages are largely preliterate, language as a 'living' oral form is practically the sole carrier of African culture. Indeed, the absence of a substantial legacy of writing places orality in African languages in an unrivalled role. Some scholars tend to glorify orality. However, as argued, orality as a predominant social condition cannot carry a modern, politically sophisticated, societally discerning, and intellectually empowered citizenry both at the individual or collective levels of social life. Where the informed knowledge base of the citizenry is limited and challenged by illiteracy, civil society is unable to fully develop as a modern institution. Illiteracy therefore structurally excludes prospective learners in the educational, political, economic and social process. For those who have entered into adulthood and who for a variety of reasons have been excluded from the ranks of the literate, reality is shrouded, knowledge is limited to immediately available memory, and memory as an individual faculty, as we all know leaks, especially with adulthood and age.[4] The point that has just been made does not detract from the great value of 'orature' in Africa as a classical and time-tested art form. Indeed, orature which includes oral literature in its various forms, such as proverbs, narratives, riddles, songs, performance, and the interactional dynamics between the performer (or performers) and audience represent an institutionalized art form common to African societies, from time immemorial, across the continent (Granqvist 1993: 109, Vansina 1976). Wherever we may stand on the issue of the merits of orality and literacy, undeniably literacy transforms the capacity of societies to accumulate knowledge, organize knowledge, create more efficient bureaucracies, advance the development of literacy-based technology and facilitate the emancipation of citizenry.

In an Africa which is challenged by facilitatory processes for the institutionalization of democracy, literacy is a factor which cannot be ignored. For democracy to flourish there is need for a constant state of social and political interrogation and debate between those in and out of authority. Representation must be accountable and must institutionally provide for eventual recall. For citizens to meet the challenge of questioning and seeking information on matters affecting them, literacy is crucial. It increases the information flow. It puts people on indelible record. Print and access to print is therefore vital for the cultivation of a citizenry, which is alive to these possibilities. In an earlier address the point was made that, conditions crucial to the cultivation of a democratic culture in which the idea of freedom of the press has a fuller meaning are that there has to be a high level of literacy in the African languages of the masses; a level high enough to make newspapers, intellectually, realistic propositions. It is also possible to say that, newspapers in languages, which come easily to them, will enhance the literacy levels of the people. For as long as media work is pre-eminently in European languages, they will be unable to reach a substantial section of mass society. This latter condition will steadily undermine the development of a more fully-fledged democratic culture. Furthermore, it will continue to inhibit the potential of the citizenry to participate in state-wide decision-making (Prah 2001: 22–23).

Over the past century and a half, humankind has developed technologies, which enhance the capacity of language to serve better and on a more complex scale the functions it has always served. We have moved from the quill as a writing technology, through the pen and nib, the pencil, the fountain-pen, the ball-point, the typewriter and on to the computer. At each stage of this journey into the technologies of literacy, our ability to make good the English lexicographer Samuel Johnson's famous epigram that 'knowledge is of two kinds. We know a subject ourselves, or we know where to get information upon it' is strengthened. The computer has vastly transformed the scope of deposition of the knowledge base of humanity. It is however literacy which enables us to use this instrument. Those that are excluded from literacy are locked out of the world of computers and modern science. Regarding music, again we see the advantages which literacy brings. Symphonic organizational forms and structural precision in the execution of musical genres in Western music are enabled by the literacy of Western musical culture. For the poorly sighted and blind, braille-based literacy with modern technology opens the doors to knowledge. The often understated point however is that for literacy to be societally empowering and universally uplifting, it has to be developed in the languages of the masses; the languages spoken and understood by the overwhelming majority of citizenry. In Africa, without doubt these are the African languages.

Since the beginnings of the industrial era no society has been able to developmentally advance on the basis of a language or languages used by a small minority of the populace. This fact has lessons for Africa. Nowhere in postcolonial Africa are the colonially inherited languages spoken by more than about 10 per cent of the populace. For even this minority creativity and facility in these languages are seriously inhibited. These languages are in effect languages used by narrow elites, which are culturally caught up in the orbit of the cultures of their erstwhile colonial masters. The heritage these elites support and perpetuate is what has been handed down through the colonial encounter. This reality is of course also true for the areas of Africa, which since the beginning of the Arab conquest of Africa have become culturally Arabized.

Indigenous knowledge and development

In the African experience arguably since the beginning of the colonial era, there exist two parallel histories of knowledge and knowledge production. The first of these is what is generally described in the literature as indigenous knowledge – knowledge that is built into African cultural thought and practice and in steadily modified forms, passed down to successive generations. It is possible to say that this sort of knowledge is generally dying out as a reproduced genre as it is superseded by received knowledge. The other history of knowledge is that which has been received through the Western encounter and which is also reproduced to narrower sections of the African population and which goes into the creation of the modern elite in African societies. These two histories are fundamentally divided by the different languages in, which they are represented. Indigenous knowledge comes with African languages while the received knowledge is based in the colonial languages. We describe these histories as parallel histories because hitherto there has been no sociological or educational mechanism, which enables them to meet or converge. Generally the social process in Africa has tended to devalue indigenous systems of knowledge. The basis of economic advancement both at the individual and collective levels, are grounded in the knowledge culture of the colonially installed knowledge systems. Little benefit has of now accrued to these social elements, which form the overwhelming majority, who are located within the cultural orbits of the knowledge systems. Most perceptive observers and students of African society suggest that if education and development in Africa is to take place in a sustained fashion which guarantees the socio-economic prosperity of mass society, it will, as of necessity, have to be built on what the masses already know, what they have inherited, what they have created and not bypass such knowledge. In other words, the received knowledge would profitably have to be indigenized as adaptations to the indigenous.

The process of marrying received and indigenous forms of knowledge poses many challenges and intrigues the imagination and creativity of interested parties. The first issue to be recognized in this respect is the fact that, in Africa, traditionally, indigenous knowledge has been orally developed and constructed. Knowledge, which is orally generationally handed down is, as earlier explained, limited. If indigenous forms of knowledge are to be strengthened and developed they need to be rendered in written forms so that the scope for consolidation and advancement is assured. Gellner has relevance in this respect when he suggests that literate or 'humanist intellectuals'

> as experts on words, and above all on written words, are the natural intermediators with the past and the future through records; similarly, with distant parts of the society; with the transcendent when the Word is held to contain the Message from it; when the recorded word contains the rules of conduct, they are the natural judges; and so forth. A literate society possesses a firmer backbone through time than does an illiterate one. It is at

> least potentially capable of consistency. The literate intellectuals become the guardians and interpreters of that which is more than transient, and sometimes its authors.
>
> (Gellner 1964: 195)

What needs to be added is that for as long as such literate abilities are the restricted preserve of a Mandarinate (classical China), a priesthood (medieval Catholicism, Coptic, Ethiopic), Hindu Brahmins, esoteric scholars or Ulamas/ Maalams (Muslim world) such societal literacy does not release the full development potential in a society, and is invariably tied to religious confession. What Gellner calls the 'loss of monopoly of literacy' of clerks, or better still the expansion of the social base of literacy is crucial for development (Gellner 1964: 197). This transition is most easily and effectively achieved when the languages of the social majorities are made the languages of literacy. Literacy in majority languages is thus also a crucial tool for what can be described as 'cultural democracy' or the fuller celebration of cultural diversity in a globalizing world.

Language, culture and knowledge

If culture is sociologically represented by language and language-community, language defines the entirety of knowledge as an expression of culture. What we know, we can speak or write about. Nothing in our individual or collective realities is beyond words. Reality in effect is represented by language and it is in language that we socially transact our interventions based on shared or divergent understandings of reality. Thus, knowledge is tied to culture. It is in culture that knowledge is provided in accessible forms. But if culture is the repository of knowledge it is through language that the opening to knowledge as a cultural attribute is accessed. Does this mean that knowledge is bound to specific cultures? That is certainly not the case. Knowledge is ultimately expressible in any language. In other words there is no language, which from Adam is entrusted with the preservation and development of knowledge as a universal human quality. Knowledge can be transferred into any cultural system and accessed through the language specific to the culture in question. The above points need to be stressed in the African context where too often it is assumed that African languages are incapable of scientific and technological development.

It has been observed that, 'the language of science may be said to have two characteristics, first, that vocabulary items and expressions have more precise and specific meanings than say, those of poetry, and are understood in the same way by those who have to study and learn in that science, such there is a language of physics' and second, that

> the language of science has a tradition which means that it can be learned because it is systematized through usage and tradition. [...] A prime requirement of scientific findings is that they shall be communicable to others. Anyone who learns any particular branch of science has to learn the

> usages and traditions of use in that science. The learner of any science has to learn the standardized meanings of the language of that particular branch.
>
> (Sibayan 1999: 397)

But this does not mean that the specific scientific language is immutably tied to any specific language. Scientific language like all language can be translated. The translation then ensures that the science becomes part of the culture, which the language of translation represents.

The route, which postcolonial Africa is persistently following, that is, the attempt to use colonial languages as languages of instruction is largely responsible for the stagnation and lack of progress in the expansion of scientific and technological knowledge in Africa. The feeding of knowledge into African culture does not take place. This process is arrested and held in check. African home-language speakers, attending schools, which operate languages of instruction in English, French, Portuguese or Arabic are inhibited and constrained by their inability to optimally understand and create ideas in the colonially bequeathed languages. The struggle for such students is in the first instance not so much to understand the knowledge, which is being offered but rather they are confronted with a tussle in understanding the language. Their problems become two-fold. First, they have to understand the language; second they have to understand the knowledge that is being offered. Most are naturally stuck with the first problem and are hardly able to proceed on to the second challenge. Birgit Brock-Utne makes telling observations in this respect based on her experience at the University of Dar es Salaam.

> Since the first day I started teaching at the University of Dar es Salaam and through all the four and a half years I worked there, the artificiality of the use of the English language in these African settings struck me daily. Sometimes when I was lecturing to big classes of a couple of hundred students, I wanted to make them more active by giving them some questions to discuss in small groups for just five minutes. I gave them questions in English but very soon heard that most the groups had started discussing the issues in KiSwahili. Naturally, so would I. I do not doubt that the students at the University of Dar es Salaam feel more comfortable speaking KiSwahili than English; they express themselves better and their understanding is far better if the teaching is in KiSwahili. This holds even truer in the secondary schools.
>
> (Brock-Utne 2000: 175)

Language of instruction (LOI) at the University of the Western Cape (UWC)

There is an important relationship between language facility and school success, perhaps because the way we impart knowledge in school is largely through language and the way we measure school success is language-based, predominately through written tests. Students who write well are also generally above average in speaking and reading. Some years ago the present author undertook a study in the

University of the Western Cape, Cape Town, which had been in the forefront in South Africa in ensuring that tertiary education reached as many of the formerly deprived under Apartheid, as possible (Prah 1998). This latter object earned for the university the sobriquet 'people's university'. While the idea of a 'people's university' was quickly accepted, and the doors of learning opened to large numbers of African-language speaking students, this was not effectively matched by infrastructural expansion or innovations in teaching methods and curricula. The basic assumptions of which languages to teach in, course structures and course content has lagged behind. Of these basic assumptions, the most vexatious has been the issue of language of instruction.

Initially, the university (created under Apartheid for 'coloureds') was supposed to cater for courses taught in both English and Afrikaans. Today in 2013, Afrikaans has been almost eliminated as a language of instruction. The dominance of English has become supreme, and African languages have hardly been under consideration as languages of instruction. But if English has assumed centrality as medium of instruction, at the same time, the English communication skills of students have hardly improved. Indeed, it is arguable that this has over the years further deteriorated. This is a phenomenon, which is noticeable in other English and French-based universities in the postcolonial African continent. The inability for students to cope with studies in English is beginning to force fresh thinking on the issue.

The ramifications of the language problem in schools remain most intimidating. In an interview granted to the author by a senior official of the secondary school system of the Western Cape on Thursday, 28 September 2010, information was provided regarding pass and failure rates in the rural schools of the Western Cape. Of the 250 best-performing schools in the Western Cape Province only one was a Xhosa-speaking school. There are 47 Xhosa-speaking schools in the province; of the 60 worst performing schools in the Province 44 were Xhosa-speaking. These statistics revealed the depth of the problems facing South African education. Apart from the wider problems of inadequate infrastructure and resources, the foundations of this problem derive from the language problems of school children. These problems are carried over into the university system.

Discussions about the above problem have over the past few years been an abiding feature of staff meetings in various departments of the university. These departments have felt a need to initiate a wider discussion within the university, with a view towards meaningful and attainable amelioration, of this condition. Over the years, these difficulties have hung as brooding shadows over the educational objectives of the University of the Western Cape.

As compared with Afrikaans-speaking students, poor English communication skills are particularly noticeable amongst African language-speaking students. However, these constraints are by no means exclusive to them. Some lecturers have also pointed out that, the quality of written Afrikaans is also deteriorating. This is happening in a society in which the governmentally engineered supremacy of Afrikaans under Apartheid has over the past 20 years been popularly reversed. It is observable that in post-apartheid South Africa, English is fast gaining ground over all the other languages. Although the government on paper has elevated the status to equality of all 11 official languages, in practice there appears to be little use of the African languages for official tasks. In a conversation held with the African National Congress (ANC) parliamentarian Duma Nkosi as far back as the 11 October 2000, he suggested that even in parliament there are members who struggle to express themselves effectively in English. Sometimes the inadequacies of their linguistic expression distort the meaning they wish to convey. In his experience during the years of inter-party rivalries and conflict on the Rand/ Gauteng on the eve of the 1994 elections, he as a principal ANC figure in the area formed the view that part of the problems triggering conflict in the area were due to misrepresentations and misinterpretations arising out of poor English-language rendering of views and positions.

Recently, Birgit Brock-Utne and Malcolm Mercer (2014) have observed that; there is universal agreement that pupils learn better when they understand what the teacher is saying. In Africa, lessons are delivered in a language most children do not master and hardly hear outside school. This situation leads to low retention and high dropout rates, lapses into illiteracy after a few years of schooling and many children not starting school at all; in other words, it is acting against equitable access to school for all children. It also makes adult education, community work and democratic parliamentary debates very difficult. (Brock-Utne and Mercer 2014). Regarding Mozambique the authors of the same paper wrote that Matsinhe reports that because of their poor command of Portuguese, some members of parliament in Mozambique have either become the laughing stock of the house or 'bench-warmers'. According to Matsinhe, 'Portuguese is therefore becoming both an instrument of exclusion and power.'

At UWC, students, on the whole, are enthusiastic about what they are taught and scholastically provided. What they reflect on paper, however, hardly matches up with what they are taught. Only a small minority of students are able to fully digest what they are taught, or critically handle the ideas presented to them during lectures. Their poor language use limits their understanding, and warps their expression. It is hardly uncommon to find third-year students struggling to formulate simple coherent sentences. Many students graduate and move on into the wider work arena with poor English communication and writing skills. The problems thus engendered in the workplace are multitudinous and often frustrating for all concerned parties.

Obviously the poor performance of students cannot be solely attributed to their weak English communication skills. The quality of staff in many departments of the university leaves much to be desired. However, it is the view of the present author that, the main problem arises from weak English-language communication skills. A good number of students are aware of the fact that, possibly, the greatest constraint in university studies for them revolves around their poor communication skills. But many regard this simply as a reality they have to live with. When, as in the case of many, they perform badly on account of poor communication skills, hardly any of them confronts the problem on the basis of this weakness. The revolution of rising expectations in the new South Africa, and the 'diploma disease' blinds many students from recognizing their linguistic inadequacies for what they are and seek solutions, for as long as they get their 'paper qualifications'.

An additional point, which needs to be made, is that social class can determine language use and language facility in various ways. Probably the most important factor in the way social class determines language use and facility is the tendency of society to attach social values to different types of language use. What was noticeable in the case of the above study was that students from relatively affluent homes and who had attended English-medium schools coped better with English LOI at university level.

The CASAS experience

What does all this mean? Going back to our earlier proposition, it means that Africans need to be educated and conduct their social lives in their own languages, in much the same way that all developmentally successful societies in the world do. We have in the past argued on the basis of enlightened evidence that African education from the primary to the tertiary level should be conducted in African languages which are close to the hearts and minds of the people. It is in these languages that the creativity of the African people is grounded and knowledge most easily accessible. Indeed, development in Africa will not take place, in our view, until Africans are in a position to use their own languages for education and social development at all levels, like all other advancing people do in the contemporary world. The use of African languages is not the only factor which will ensure African development, but African development cannot be realized for as long as African languages are not utilized as the instruments of development.

All considered, the view of the present author is that, African-language mother-tongue students should instead of being taught in English, French, Arabic or Portuguese should rather be provided the opportunity of studying in their mother tongue. This would remove the problem, root and branch. But there are a number of outstanding issues to be considered. First, if Africa as is often suggested fields a plethora of languages, a veritable 'tower of Babel', where and how do we begin to rationally use African languages? Second, are Africans ready to use their own languages for education and development? It was in response to their issues that the Centre for Advanced Studies of African Society (CASAS) initiated its work on African languages in 1997. It is often easily assumed that because of the great variety of languages in Africa even if Africans wish to use their languages for education and development this is mission impossible. For a start, Africa is the second biggest continent in the world, second only to Asia. Given its size the linguistic variation that we find on the ground compares easily to the range of languages and the range of varieties that we would find elsewhere in the world. This confusion and assumed numbers of between 1,000 and 2,000 languages becomes a convincing argument in the minds of those who then argue that there are too many languages for any to be realistically adopted. And so the argument moves forward to suggest that the colonial languages should be used. What the work of CASAS has so far revealed is that the tally of numbers of languages in Africa is seriously flawed. It is flawed mainly on account that a great many of the so-called languages are actually dialectal forms of what we call 'core languages'. It is the view of the present author that this idea of the African Tower of Babel has willy-nilly become useful ammunition in the hands of those who want to see Africans work in the colonial languages. It is remarkable that in the beginning of the twenty-first century there appears to be no consensus as to the number of languages on the African continent. If it is appreciated and understood that most of what are regarded as distant languages are actually dialectal variants of core languages the numbers conundrum becomes a problem easy to resolve.

What CASAS' research has revealed is that over 80–85 per cent of Africans, as first-, second- and third-language speakers, speak no more than 15–17 core languages, based on our clustering on the basis of mutual intelligibility. Africa, for its size is hardly a Tower of Babel. We are arguing that, if the total population of Black Africa is between 750 and 850 million (as first-, second- and third-language speakers) the Fula, Pulaar, Peul, Tuculor, Fulful, Fulbe, Fulani cluster alone would account for about 60 million. Hausa and its varieties bring up another 50 million. Oromo, Igbo, Mandeng/Bambara, Amharic, KiSwahili, Yoruba, the Gbe, would produce another 35–45 million in each instance. The Nguni variants, the Sotho-Tswana, the Akan, the Eastern and the Western Interlacustrine Bantu (Kitara) languages, Luganda/Lusoga/Lugishu and Luo, Gur, Lingala, Kikongo are between 30 and 40 million per set. Other languages, of smaller distribution, but which enjoy preponderance within existing states include, Sango, Fang, Nyanja-Cewa, Shona-Nyai, Wolof, Ovambo-Herero and Somali.

In as far as African development is concerned, the upshot of these facts are that the harmonization of African languages which show high levels of mutual intelligibility would greatly facilitate the economies of scale in the development of educational, media and cultural materials which could go a long way in strengthening the basis of society for the cultural and social development of Africa. Furthermore, it is the only way of culturally empowering the masses of African society. It is the one way we can remove the cultural cleavage between the elite and mass society. It provides the key to the methodology of eradicating the stigma of inferiority, which the colonial experience has invested in African languages.

African languages are much fewer than the figures put on them. For example, if Setswana is understood in its narrow sense, it features in Namibia, Botswana and South Africa. In a wider and more significant sense Setswana is part of the wider Sotho-Tswana cluster which includes Lozi in Barotseland. Somali for example is spoken in five countries. Evidence indeed suggests that well over 95 per cent of African languages are spoken across borders. Another example would be that if Luo is used as a restricted descriptive category it covers parts of three countries (Kenya, Uganda and Tanzania). In generic usage, in the sense in which it has been used by Crazzollara or Okot Bitek, its coverage will include in geographical scope an area as wide as parts of the Sudan, Ethiopia, Uganda, Kenya, and Tanzania. Proximate and mutually intelligible dialects of the Luo language in Eastern Africa for example are referred to under various designations as Jur (Sudan), Anyuak (Sudan and Ethiopia), Shilluk (Sudan and Ethiopia), Acholi (Sudan and Uganda), Langi (Uganda), Alur (Uganda), Chopadholla (Uganda) and Luo (Uganda, Kenya and Tanzania). Kikuyu, Embu, Meru, Akamba in Kenya are closely related dialects. The Bari-speaking people in the Sudan have been 'analytically chopped up' into Mondari, Bari, Nyangbara, Fajelu, Kakwa (Uganda, Sudan, Democratic Republic of the Congo), and Kuku (Uganda and Sudan). Kipsigi, Nandi, Pokot, Elgeyo Marakwet are not separate languages, but rather dialects of Kalengin. In Ghana, the Akan have been in the anthropological literature referred to as Ashanti, Fanti, Agona, Kwahu, Akim, Akuapim, Nzema, and even sub-units of these like Ahanta, Gomua, Edina, and so on. The Gbe/Ewe-speaking people can be found in communities all along the West African Coast from Ghana through Togo, Benin and to the Nigerian border area. In East Africa, the Teso, Nyangatom, Kumam, Karamojong, Dodos, Jie, Turkana, Toposa, Donyiro collectively cover areas in Kenya, Ethiopia, Uganda and the Sudan. The Nguni are found in Tanzania where they closely relate ethno-linguistically to the Nyamwezi, Ngoni and Konde. They are also located in Malawi. Nyanja in Zambia and Cewa in Malawi are particularly the same. In Mozambique, Shangaan/Tsonga/Ronga, is an Nguni variant. But it has phonologically and morphologically grown away from the other languages in the cluster. Nguni in Swaziland is called Swati, Kangwane in northern Natal/Zululand, Zulu in South Africa, Xhosa in South Africa, Ndebele in South Africa and Matabeleland in Zimbabwe. The Sotho-Tswana cluster is to be found as Tswana in Namibia, Tswana in Botswana, Lozi in Barotseland/Zambia, Sotho in Lesotho, and Pedi in South Africa. Again in East Africa, the Interlacustrine Bantu have a high degree of mutual intelligibility. They include the Nyoro, Toro, Haya, Ganda, Ankole, Rwanda. Rendille-Somali and Oromo and Borana are literally closely related pairs. Maasai and Samburu are equally close. Fulful, Fulfulde, Fulbe, Fulde, Fulani, Fula, Peul, Pula, Tuculor is spoken in 13 countries captured by the area within Senegambia, Darfur and the Northern Cameroon. It has about 50 million speakers. The Hausa based mainly in the Cameroon, Niger and Nigeria also number about 50 million. The Oromo speakers mainly in Ethiopia, and Kenya are a little less than the Hausa speaking peoples. In Benin and Nigeria, Yoruba is spoken by between 40–50 million people. Swahili is a shared language in Eastern and large parts of Central Africa. In short, the myth of the African Tower of the Babel has weak scientific foundations. Basic evidence refutes its tenability. The whole area of work needs to be revisited, with a view to updating and improving on the work of Joseph Greenberg and his scholastic progeny.

The confusion around African-language identification and count, defies authority. In his *The Languages of Africa* (1970 edition), Greenberg lists 730 languages in his index. The author admitted that, 'in the present state of our knowledge, any listing of languages is necessarily unsatisfactory in many respects'. Greenberg's listing is inaccurate and displays some of the problems the CASAS research project is clearing up. For example, dialects of Luo like Shilluk, Anyuak, Acholi, and Lango are listed as separate languages. Bari, Mondari, Fajelu, Kakwa are listed as separate languages when they are in fact simply dialects of the same language. Under Akan, readers are encouraged to 'see individual languages'. In the guide to his entry of languages on sectorial maps he explains that,

> languages spoken in a number of areas are only entered once on the map. Thus Fulani is only indicated in one of the main West Atlantic areas and not elsewhere. When reference is made to some other language, then the number of the language itself is not to be found on any of the maps. The reason for this may be that it is merely a variant name, that the group is too small to be indicated on a map of the present scale or that they live within the speech area of another people.

This way of representation is misleading. Fulani-speakers are to be found in at least 17 countries in the 'fragmentation belt'. It is easily one of the most widely languages in Africa, spoken by about 50 million people as either a first or second language; and it named variously as Pulaar, Fulful, Fulfulde, Peul, Tuclour, Fula and Fulani. Greenberg's manner of presentation obscures such important facts about the language and its demographics within an estimated sub-Saharan population of 800 million people. These weaknesses have been largely carried into the work of Fivaz and Scott (Fivaz and Scott 1977).

Closing remarks

CASAS has made a start on the harmonization and the standardization of African languages as a prerequisite towards the refinement and development of African languages for use in all levels of education and general social intercourse. Of the 15–17 'core languages' which have been identified by CASAS as languages spoken as first, second or third languages by about 85 per cent of the African population on the continent and spoken by at least 50 million in each instance, 12 have been successfully harmonized. These are Nguni, Sotho-Tswana, KiSwahili, Luo, Eastern Interlacustrine, Western Interlacustrine, Mandeng, Pulaar, Igbo, Ijo, Yoruba and Hausa.[5] In addition a good number of smaller clusters of closely related languages have been orthographically harmonized. These include, Tsonga, Ronga, Shangaan; the Gbe cluster (made up of Fon, Fun, Aja, Mina, Phela, Ewe); the Ateso and Karimojong cluster (including Ateso, Karamojong, Dodoth, Matheniko, Pian, Bokora, Pokot, Jie, Tepeth, Labwor, Nyapei, Nyangatom); the Shona cluster (including Kalanga, Lilima, Nambya, Karanga, Zezuru, Korekore, Manyika, Ndau, Hwesa, Utee and Barwe); Tshivenda; the South Central African languages (including ciTumbuka/ciSenga, eLomwe, ciNyanja/ciCewa, ciYao, eMakhuwa, ciNsenga/ciNgoni, ChiTonga and their related languages ciBemba, ciSena, ciBisa, ciLuvale ciTonga, iciLamba, CiIla, kiKaonde, Lunda, Namwanga); the Ma'di-Moru cluster has also been harmonized. Linguists are calling this cluster Ti'Alu. They include Ma'di, Lugbara, Olu'bo, Avukaya, Moru, Kaliko, Logo. The Bantu languages of Tanzania, Kenya, Namibia and Angola have all been separately harmonized. So have the Khoe and San languages of Namibia, South Africa and Botswana. CASAS has completed work on the harmonization of the orthography for Angola, Namibia, Botswana and South African Khoe and San languages. These include Khoe (Khoekhoegwab/Nama/Damara, Khwedam/Ani, Naro, Gui/Gana, Khomani, Kua/Tshoa, Shua/Cua/Tciretcire/Danisi) and San (Ju'hoan/Xun, Xoon, Hoan). Recent work on Sandawe and Hadja in Tanzania remains incomplete. The Dinka/Nuer languages of South Sudan, the Bari, the Kalenjin, the Kru have all been separately harmonized. The Gur languages consisting of Gurene, Kabye, Koulango, Bariba, Lokpa, Moore, nCam, Senoufo, Tem were also harmonized some years ago. The Cushitic languages of East Africa have been harmonized (Afar, Borana, Burji, Gede'o, Hadiyya, Iraqw, Kambata, Konso, Oromo, Saaho, Sidaama, Somali). The Maa cluster has been harmonized (Arusa, Ilchamus, Maasai/Kisongo, Parakuyu, Samburu). So have the Akan languages of Ghana and the Ivory Coast.[6] This work represents an important step in the right direction. It is expected that within the next four years most, if not all, of the 15–17 core languages will be successfully harmonized. CASAS has also proceeded to produce texts on the basis of the harmonized orthographies. To date (2014) eight monolingual dictionaries have been produced. These are for Ateso, Ciiyawo, Acoli, Kiikaonde, SiSwati, Silozi, Akan and Dhopadola. This could be used and fed directly into the educational systems of African countries.

Notes

1 See Johnny Ling.
2 http://hypertextbook.com/facts/2001/JohnnyLing.shtml.
3 See Driberg (1932: 44).
4 See Johnny Ling, op cit.
5 K. K. Prah. Reaching out to excluded learners: language, literacy and societal inclusivity for democracy, citizenship and development. Presentation made to the UNESCO International Adult Learners Week 2004 – Adult Learning and Literacy for Democracy and Citizenship, 6–11 September 2004. Cape Town.
6 CASAS Unified Standard Orthographies. CASAS Monograph No. 256. Cape Town.2013.

References

Brock-Utne, B. (2000). *Whose Education for All? The Recolonization of the African Mind.* New York: Falmer Press.

Brock-Utne, B. and Mercer, M. (2014). Using African languages for democracy and lifelong learning in Africa: a post-2015 challenge and the work of CASAS. *International Review of Education.* DOI 10.1007/s11159-014-9448-7.

Carroll, J. B. (1953). *The Study of Language.* Cambridge, MA: Harvard University Press.

Chomsky, N. (1973). *For Reasons of State.* New York: Pantheon Books.

Driberg, J. H. (1932). *At Home With The Savage.* London: Routledge.

Fivaz, D. and Scott, P. (1977). *African Languages: A Genetic and Decimalised Classification for Bibliographic and General Reference.* Boston,, MA: G. K. Hall.

Gellner, E. (1964). *Thought and Change.* London: Weidenfeld and Nicolson.

Goody, J. 1986 (1989 edition). *The Logic of Writing and the Organization of Society.* Cambridge: Cambridge University Press.

Goody, J. and Watt, I. (1963). The consequences of literacy. Contemporary *Studies in Society and History*, 5: 304–345. Republished in J. Goody (ed.) (1968). *Literacy in Traditional Societies*. Cambridge: Cambridge University Press.

Granqvist, R. (ed.). (1993). *Culture In Africa: An Appeal for Pluralism*. (Seminar Proceedings No. 29). Uppsala The Scandinavian Institute of African Studies.

Havelock, E. (1963). *Preface to Plato*. Cambridge, MA: Harvard University Press.

Jacobson, S. A. (1984). *Yup'ik Eskimo Dictionary*. Fairbanks, AS: Alaska Native Language Center.

Lévi-Strauss, C. (1962). *La pensée savage*. Paris: Plon.

McLuhan, M. (1962). *The Gutenberg Galaxy*. Toronto: University of Toronto.

Olson, D. R. and Torrance, N. (eds) (2001). *The Making of Literate Societies*. Oxford: Blackwell.

Ong, W. (1958). *Ramus: Method, and Decay of Dialogue*. Cambridge, MA: Harvard University Press.

Prah, K. K. (1998). *Studying in the Queen's Language*. (The Working Group on Educational Research in Africa – Conference of German Africanists, Bayreuth, 8–10 October. 1998). London: Mimeo.

Prah, K. K. (2000). (2nd ed,). *African Languages for the Mass Education of Africans*, CASAS Book Series No.7. Cape Town: CASAS.

Prah, K. K. (2001). *Language and Freedom of Expression in Africa*, Ghana Free Expression Series No. 2. Accra: Media Foundation for West Africa.

Prah, K. K. 2004. *Reaching out to Excluded Learners: Language, Literacy and Societal Inclusivity for Democracy, Citizenship and Development*. (UNESCO International Adult Learners Week 2004 – *Adult Learning and Literacy for Democracy and Citizenship*. September 6–11, 2004, Cape Town)

Shi-xu, (2012). Why do cultural discourse studies? Towards a culturally conscious and critical approach to human discourses. *Critical Arts: South-North Cultural and Media Studies*, 26(4): 484–503.

Sibayan, B. P. (1999). *The Intellectualization of Filipino and other Essays on Education and Sociolinguistics*. Manila: The Linguistics Society of the Philippines.

Vansina, J. 1976. *Oral Tradition as History*. Nairobi: Heinemann.

Wittgenstein, L. (1953) (1967, 3rd ed.). *Philosophical Investigations. Aphorism 19. Philosophische Untersuchungen* (trans. G. E. M. Anscombe). Oxford: Blackwell.

6 Language policies and power dynamics in Africa

Problems linked to linguistic policies and power relations within countries as well as between countries

Introduction

After a half-century of postcolonialism, African-language policies have not substantially changed from the policies which were inherited from the colonial era. This situation persists despite claims by successive African governments that they want, intend and are implementing change. African policy-makers are stuck in a groove of inertia. The result is that we keep asking ourselves the same questions and getting the same answers. The research we do show the answers clearly to be universal, answers which most societies in the world outside Africa know; we are however unable to take further steps towards bringing policy and practice in Africa in line with what has emerged as universal knowledge and collective wisdom in language policy for education and development.

The argument we have made regarding the stasis in African-language policies and practices is that unless and until more democratically inclined language policies are put in place, development writ large, will elude and confound Africans. (Prah 1995; Prah 1996) The argument here is that, in our times, development as a cultural process is ultimately a question of engaging mass society with the linguistic tools needed to transform the conditions and quality of their social lives. For all societies these are languages spoken by the overwhelming majority of the people; the languages in which their creativity and genius are most readily available. Nowhere in Africa are the colonial languages spoken and written with any degree of adeptness by the 10 per cent of the population who speak these languages. Knowledge therefore cannot be articulately shared or transferred to mass society in these languages. Effectively, the colonial languages in Africa are the preserve of narrowly-based social elites.

Where do African-language policies stand today, and how are they represented? After independence most African governments elevated some or all the indigenous languages to the status of 'national languages'. This was an acknowledgement, in theory, of the sociological significance of these languages. But in almost all instances hardly any further attention was paid to them. The principle was thus acknowledged but that is where the story practically ended; implementation has not been forthcoming. Kamwendo describes this condition as 'declaration without implementation'.[1] There is another category of languages which is more important, the 'official languages'. These were the colonial languages; in other words, French, English, Portuguese in most of Africa, and Spanish in Equatorial Guinea. Additionally, one should count Arabic in places like Sudan and Mauritania. These official languages are the languages of government business and education except in the Sudan and Mauritania where, once again, English and French respectively were retained as languages of tertiary education.

Cases in point

In education in postcolonial Africa, the general idea was that the colonial dispensation should be kept in place. That is, generally, indigenous languages should be used for the first few years of primary school and then a switch made to the official languages. This was in theory what was to happen. In actual fact, in one country after the other even this policy of education in the mother tongue for the first few years was gradually abandoned. It would seem that the reason for this abandonment was the fact that the pressures of elite formation favoured the official languages. These are the languages in which upward social mobility is guaranteed. They are the languages of power, privilege and influence. So in country after country, social practice has undermined official policy and conditions in favour of indigenous languages have become in most instances worse than under colonialism. The result has been that most development agencies and interested parties in African education have been advocating for a policy, which in effect, represents at best a return to the colonial dispensation, and they are having a hard battle against current practice. In countries like Tanzania and Madagascar which have important national languages spoken by overwhelming majorities in both instances, KiSwahili and Malagache, in recent years, after years of favour and elevation, these languages have become demoted in the role they play in the education system. In the case of Madagascar the French government has offered to support education in French and the British have done likewise for the production of books in English in Tanzanian schools.

Rubanza has argued that,

> specifically I suggest that Swahili should be the language of education in both primary and secondary school; that English should be a compulsory subject at all levels of schooling; and that Ethnic Community Languages should be implemented where desirable and convenient at the lower level of primary schools.
>
> (Limage 1998: 281)

He observes that while English maintains its position as language of instruction at the secondary and tertiary levels of the education system there is at the same time a growing demand for KiSwahili. He puts down as reasons for this demand; 'the extinction of the major functions associated with English, apart from being used by a minority, to the feelings of dependency that follows from the use of an "alien" language' (Limage 1998: 282). An additional point is that, KiSwahili and other ethnic community languages are widely used in everyday life. The situation with regards to language in education in Tanzania is that,

> Children in Tanzania officially begin léarning English as a subject in standard three (the third year of primary school). Fewer than 10% of these students enter secondary school education. Upon entering secondary school, they begin using English as a medium of instruction in all subjects except Swahili. Swahili and English are then taught as compulsory subjects up to and including from our, that is, the first four years of secondary school. Thereafter, English and Swahili as subjects are optional up to the university level, although English continues to be the language of instruction.
>
> (Limage 1998: 282)

Kadeghe has made a not so credible defence in favour of English, instead of KiSwahili, as language of instruction (Brock-Utne, Desai and Qorro 2003: 170–186). It is all rather confusing for a society which could easily develop KiSwahili into a language of science and technology, and in which education from primary to tertiary level could be organized to serve not only Tanzania but the whole region. Mutasa of the National KiSwahili Council of Tanzania has adduced evidence to show that the argument one often hears that KiSwahili is not yet ready to be used in the Tanzanian educational system because of its poverty in terminology is not correct. She indicates that numerous dictionaries some dealing with scientific subjects have been published (Brock-Utne, Desai and Qorro 2003: 197–202). Qorro has made a strong argument for the use of KiSwahili at the secondary and tertiary levels of education, pointing out that mother-tongue education is crucial for national development and that development discourses must engage the masses if they are to make a positive difference for national development (Brock-Utne, Desai and Qorro 2003: 187–196). Diffidence, rudderlessness and indecisiveness in language policies have been an educational hallmark of Africa.

The Kenyan example is a good case in point. The genesis of language policy in Kenya can be traced to 1895 when the British government declared a protectorate over the country. The policy was guided largely by administrative expediency and the needs of White settlers. In the period 1909–1945 under what was known as the 'Livingstone Principle', the missionaries played a crucial role in education and placed an emphasis on African-language education in the firm belief that, 'the language best known and understood by the child at the time of entry to school was the most effective medium of instruction' (Brock-Utne and Koloti 2000: 106). The argument was reinforced in the recommendations of the Phelps-Stokes Commission Report (1922) which reiterated that, 'the use of the language of the child in education was one of the chief means of preserving whatever was good in native customs, ideas and ideals. According to this principle, vernaculars were an excellent tool for preserving self-respect of the learners. The missionary view was that apart from the use of vernaculars as the mediim of instruction at least in elementary stages of schooling, it was morally sound to promote the teaching and use of KiSwahili in upper=primary classes. However, they advocated for the gradual replacement of KiSwahili by English. That was the genesis of an almost established practice where English totally reigned supreme over any other language' (Brock-Utne and Koloti 2000: 106). In 1943, the Advisory Committee on Education in the colonies had confirmed concern for the need of African languages in the education of children at the elementary school level. This committee had also stated that English was essential. The Beecher Report (1949) came back to emphasize the use of African languages in education and yet still stated that English should replace KiSwahili in prominence. In 1953 the syllabus for African Intermediate Schools observed that; 'apart from religious instruction, English should be the main subject of the curriculum, both for its general educational value and for its use when pupils leave Form II for employment' (Brock-Utne and Koloti 2000: 107). Makori points out that; 'Development after 1953 led to KiSwahili gradually fading so that by 1958, it was no longer taught extensively in primary schools' (Brock-Utne and Koloti 2000: 107). KiSwahili was made a national language after independence in Kenya; however, the Ominde Commission Report of 1964 did not help matters. It observed that 'most people wished to have English introduced in early grades' (Brock-Utne and Koloti 2000: 108). It went on further to suggest that, 'while the vernaculars were the primary languages of verbal communication within the families, they were nevertheless "ill prepared for educational purposes"' (Kenya Government Commission Report, 1964). The strongest, but overlooked recommendation of the commission was the use of KiSwahili as a vehicle for national co-ordination and unification as well as encouraging communication on an international basis' (Brock-Utne and Koloti 2000: 108). The emergence of a growing English=language based African elite in the post-independence era has strengthened further the position of English in the overall educational system in Kenya. What started as expediency in primarily the service of settler-colonial interests has been quietly, without fanfare, been inherited by a postcolonial African elite without question. With the elite operating as a reference group for the masses, KiSwahili has receded in the valuation of the broader populace.

Kurt Komarek who was for years on the staff of the GTZ (German Development Agency) in many parts of the Third World had this to say about the Madagascan experience:

> After [...] experiences in Peru, the government in Madagascar called upon us to do the same in their country. There was another leftist revolution in 1975, and they threw out French culture, language, everything. They nationalized the whole educational system by bringing in Malagasy as the only medium of instruction. So we had that for seven years. [...] after seven years of successfully nationalizing primary education, having books – proper textbooks in mathematics, reading and writing – [...] France very openly agreed to bring that down to the first two years. The scandal is that Malagasy is the only language in Madagascar. Everybody speaks one language. Of course, there are dialects, but 150 years ago the Bible was translated into Malagasy. Everybody reads this Bible. Everybody knows this higher standard

> Malagasy. Anyway, France was waiting for the opportunity to bring them down again and they succeeded. What is behind this? [...] It is not a linguistic problem. If there are twenty or fifty languages in one country, you can cope with this in a technical way. Think about Switzerland where there are four languages. What is the problem? Technically there is no problem. But there is a political problem, indeed. And I think a very heavy one. There is what I would call alienation as well.
>
> (Prah and King 1998: 39)

The Namibian example in terms of the evolution of language policies in education is closely tied to the South African colonial model. Under German colonialism the few schools which were built, were constructed with local reading and writing materials under the direction of missionaries. Until 1909 the running and financing of these schools was under missionary aegis. From that year, the German colonial administration started providing subsidies for the educational system. We may however note that the administration provided a racialized and lopsided financial backing for the educational system in favour of White, German colonial education. We are informed that in 1914–1915 the government spent 37 times the subsidy it provided for White education as what it did for Black education. By the time German colonialism was defeated in Namibia in 1915 a decentralized *de facto* situation of segregation between White, 'coloured' and Black education existed. South African administration maintained this segregated educational system and after 1948 when the Apartheid regime came into power, the segregated nature of education received official blessing. In 1951 the administration indicated that,

> in order to ensure efficient co-ordination of planning, the control of Bantu [the South African terminology for Black people in South Africa and Namibia] education should be removed from the provincial administration and be vested in a separate department under the aegis of the Central Government.

This laid the groundwork for the Bantu education which culminated in the Education of Act of 1953 (Brock-Utne and Koloti 2000: 34–35). For decades Bantu education was the showpiece of the Apartheid regime. Following the independence of Namibia in 1990, the new government adopted a multi-lingual policy which unfortunately had serious loopholes in its conceptualization. In a policy document published in June 1993 called, *The Language Policy for Schools – 1992 – 1996 and Beyond*, it was indicated that;

> The 7-year primary education cycle should enable learners to acquire reasonable competence in English, the official language, and be prepared for English medium instruction throughout the secondary cycle; Education should promote the language and cultural identity of learners through the use of Home Language medium at least in Grades 1–3, and the teaching of Home Language throughout formal education, provided the necessary resources

> are available; Ideally schools should offer at least two languages as subjects. Beyond the primary cycle (Grades 1–7) the medium of instruction for all schools shall be English, the official language.
>
> (Brock-Utne and Koloti 2000: 39–40)

As Halla Holmarsdottir observes, it is possible to assume that there is preference for a situation in which the home language or mother tongue as language of instruction is preferred for at least the first three grades of primary school and with the possibility of it being used throughout the school system. But then, as she says; 'it is odd that in this same document the official interpretation of these goals reads as follows: *Grades 1–3 will be taught either through the Home Language, a local language, or English*' (Brock-Utne and Koloti 2000: 40). Thus almost surreptitiously mother-tongue schooling is undermined in one sentence of the policy document. Clearly the implication of this statement is that English may be used as medium of instruction even from Grade 1. Immediately with the commencement of the independence era English became the official language and became medium of communication in all government business and transactions of the state (Brock-Utne and Koloti 2000: 40).

The case of Ethiopia is interesting in as far as Amharic for ages had a position of dominance in the Ethiopian state. Up until 1974 this position of dominance remained more or less unchallenged. Since then, the hegemony of Amharic has receded. The Table 6.1 provides a summary of the changes Ethiopia has seen in language policy over the years:

As can be seen from the table, the Ethiopian case is slightly encouraging in the sense that the national language or mother tongue has come to replace the dominance of Amharic at the primary school level but unfortunately English still dominates the heights of education at secondary and tertiary levels.

In the other African countries like Ghana, Nigeria and Sierra Leone the indigenous languages are in practical retreat in the face of the rising favour of the official language. Even in countries like Somalia, Rwanda, Burundi, Lesotho, Botswana and Swaziland where one African language is used and spoken by almost the whole population, no headway has been made in the use of African-language

Table 6.1 Languages of instruction in Ethiopia – a historical view

No.	*Year*	*Medium of instruction*		
		Primary	*Secondary*	*Higher education*
1	1908–1935	French	–	
2	1936–1941	Ethio-Italian War	Ethio-Italian War	Ethio-Italian War
3	1942–1952	English	English	English
4	1953–1991	Amharic	English	English
5	1992+	National language (mother tongue)	English	English

Source: Brock-Utne and Koloti (2000: 50).

mother tongue in education. Remarkably in these latter countries the tendency has been, under the leadership of the elites, to favour practically education in the colonial language. A possible exception can be made of the case in Burundi where Silue Sassongo writes that; 'reportedly, dialectal variations in KiRundi are so negligible that one not is really unjustified in distinguishing dialectal variants. Understandably, a nation like Burundi could afford to declare the single native language as the official language, eagerly, at Independence' (Silue 2000: 100; Ntahombaye 1999). Subsequently, it was then easier to take advantage of this exceptional situation to integrate KiRundi in the school curriculum, at least at the entire primary level where it is used as the medium of instruction. The Burundi higher educational system even goes as far as offering to students the possibility of learning some other African languages such as Malinke, Yoruba and KiSwahili, as subjects of the academic curriculum, besides French, English and German (Silue 2000: 100; Ntahombaye 1999).

In Botswana interestingly,

> English is still called the official language of the country, but in shops and bars and in market places all around the country Setswana is the language used. Up to very recently, English was the only language spoken in Parliament. This has just been changed, and it is now possible use Setswana as well in the debates in the Parliament. There are good reasons for this change. Many members of Parliament find it easier to express themselves in Setswana than in English. More importantly, most citizens find it easier to follow a discussion in Setswana than in English. Because of that, this shift from English into Setswana in the political sphere is beneficial for democracy. The language of conversation used in the government's office buildings and the different ministries and departments, i.e. in the corridors of power, nowadays is mostly Setswana. This represents a change from earlier decades, when the presence of a high proportion of foreign experts made it necessary to use English as the everyday language.
>
> (Granqvist 1993: 83)

The logic of the situation would be to press home the advantage and make Setswana superior to English. But that is not happening. It appears rather that, as the postcolonial elite reproduces itself and its English bias it is socially strengthening its commitment to the bias in policy and practice.

Another country which with a little effort could cross the threshold of using national languages as official languages is Niger. Here the two languages Hausa and Zarma are used by over 90 per cent of the population. As early as 1962, in the immediate wake of independence, primers were produced for non-formal education. Hausa is used extensively in non-formal education. Elementary technical literature for agriculture, specifically animal husbandry and farming has also been produced. Driving tests can be taken in Hausa and Zarma and functional literacy programmes tailor-made for women mainly on family planning are available. The two languages can be used in the National Assembly in the Courts of Law. The first bi-lingual experimental curriculum was developed in 1978; it has had pilot runs over the years but it has never been adopted (Silue 2000: 101–102). Initiative appears to have stalled.

The trepidation and inertia of language policy-makers affects countries like the Cameroon and Nigeria worst where in the words of Silue; 'the linguistic diversity argument is used in justifying the timidity in the elaboration of national language policies for national development' (Silue 2000: 104). The cases of the three East African countries Kenya, Tanzania and Uganda present another scenario altogether. In this region, KiSwahili enjoys prominence and has possibly more literature than any other African language. There are even newspapers appearing on a daily basis in KiSwahili in Tanzania and Kenya. In spite of this, little headway has been made in developing KiSwahili as a language of science and technology. To some extent KiSwahili is in competition with a language like Luganda in Uganda. Therefore, it is in Uganda that the prospects and position of KiSwahili is weakest among the three countries. It needs however to be remembered, that KiSwahili is used also limitedly in the Southern Sudan, in a good part of the Democratic Republic of the Congo, Northern Mozambique and the northern border areas of Zambia.

In the Ivory Coast, the French language in education is dominant. The situation is the same in most of the Francophone countries. In countries like Togo, Benin, Senegal and Guinea there is no serious challenge to the hegemony of French. Sassongo recalls that,

> On the fringe of a linguistic workshop in Ouagadougou in June 1999, an Anglophone participant wanted to make sure whether one of his Francophone colleagues did mean what he said when he mentioned French among the *national languages* of his home French-speaking country. The Francophone linguist fumbled into acrobatic justifications, speculating that French was a national language in some African nations insofar as the citizens use it in significant proportions, and that everyone in his country regards the French language as a uniting factor [...] The Anglophone linguist who happened to be Professor N. E. Emenanjo felt a bit impatient and authoritatively indicated that descriptive concepts such as '*national language*, *'official language'*, *'native language'*, *'mother tongue'* had very precise and unequivocal meanings. The debate was interesting because what can be interpreted as a mere terminological dispute was, in fact, a covert and yet profound ideological controversy. In French-speaking milieus, citing French as an African '*national language*' is a casual slip of the tongue that no one really cares about. By contrast, among Anglophone Africans, such a mention causes shock and embarrassment.
>
> (Silue 2000: 109)

The present author in 2005 also heard the writer Veronique Tadjo assert that 'French is an African language.'[2] Such Euro-preferential perceptions affect a wider range of matters beyond purely linguistic concerns, matters related to identity, cultural memory and expression, politics and cultural affiliation, autonomy and the celebration of diversity.

Ingse Skattum makes enlightening observations about the Malian case where although Bambara enjoys clearly a position of popularity and widespread usage it is not used as profitably as it could. She writes that,

> In Mali, all official documents, including the Constitution, state their support to all the languages of the country, while French paradoxically is being maintained as the only official language. Malian linguists are equally careful, speaking of 'favouring the development of some of the languages without neglecting the others'. None of them mention the fact that Bambara is the majority language, nor the possibility of making it a second official language.
>
> (Brock-Utne and Koloti 2000: 86–87)

The point is that no African country has been able to take that bold step. The dominant elites have not found that move to be important enough. In the Malian case Skattum adds that,

> [F]or Bambara as well as the other Malian languages, [...] they have not been taught in secondary school or at university level, not even in the teachers' colleges, where they are badly needed after the reform. Malians still have to go abroad to study their own languages and even if they come back with a Master's or Doctoral degree, there are few jobs where this competence is required.
>
> (Brock-Utne and Koloti 2000: 88)

Again, her apt commentary can be generalized to cover most if not all of Africa. This reality in fact underscores the cultural basis of neo-colonialism in Africa.

South Africa presents a situation of a different and peculiar kind, fairly distinct and unique in the African continent. Under the Apartheid settler-colonial regime in order to uphold the myth of the absence of an African majority the country was chopped up into Bantustans which were each described as a 'nation'. These so-called 'nations' were ethno-linguistic and cultural sub-units among the African-language-speaking peoples. When Apartheid was overthrown and the new dispensation came into place, the new order simply accepted the idea of 11 separate language groups and communities in the country. The languages of ethno-linguistic groups were elevated to the status of national languages. Thus, the new post settler-colonial state simply recognized on paper the equality of all the language communities invented by the Apartheid regime. What is important to remember here is that these language groups are groups, which for the most enjoy a great deal of mutual intelligibility. Most of them can be grouped in two, namely the Sotho-Tswana group consisting of the languages Sotho, Tswana, Pedi and the Nguni group consisting of Zulu, Xhosa and Ndebele. What is even more interesting is that beyond South Africa Sotho-Tswana communities exist in Namibia, Lesotho, Botswana and Zambia (as isiLozi in Barotseland). SiNdebele is spoken in Matabeleland, Zimbabwe and SiSwati in Swaziland. Therefore most of the indigenous languages of South Africa could easily be collapsed into two mutually intelligible speech clusters, which extend in the region into most of the countries of the Southern African Development Community. IsiTsonga, which is spoken in southern Mozambique, is a fairly prominent language in north-east South Africa and parts of Swaziland. What all this means is that on the basis of the economies of scale, it is rational to harmonize the orthographies and spelling systems of these languages so that literature in them are accessible to large speech communities. This situation we have described for South Africa is true for most of the continent.

In West Africa, languages like Bambara, Djula, Malinke, Kasonke, Mande, Mandingo, Mandenkan are to a large extent, mutually intelligible and they are spoken in nine countries. The mutually intelligible Gbe languages of the West African littoral include Aja in Nigeria, Aja in Benin, Gun in Benin, Mina in Benin, Fon in Benin, Mina in Togo, Ewe in Togo and Ewe in Ghana. The same is true for Fulaar, which in mutually intelligible dialectal variation exists in different countries as Peul, Pulaar, Fula, Fulful, Tuclor and Fulani. This language is extensive and is spoken in different pockets from the Sene-Gambia basin through Mauritania, Mali, Niger, Chad and parts of the Sudan, and also Nigeria, Cameroon, Guinea and Guinea Bissau; indeed in 17 countries. In East Africa varieties of Luo are spoken in Southern Sudan, Uganda, Kenya and Tanzania. Somali is spoken in Ethiopia, Somalia, Djibouti and Kenya. Yoruba is spoken in Benin and Nigeria. Akan finds expression in the Ivory Coast, Ghana and parts of Togo. Mutually intelligible Gur speech forms exist in Burkina Faso, Benin, Togo, the Ivory Coast and Ghana. Bari varieties exist as Mondari, Riverine Bari, Kuku, Kakwa, Nyangbara, and Fajelu in the Southern Sudan, the eastern Congo and Uganda. Many more examples in Africa can be found to attest to this situation of mutual intelligibility of speech forms.

South Africa appears, at this time, to be the most increasingly sensitive country to the linguistic problems inherited from the colonial period. In an article which appeared in the *Cape Argus* on 17 May 2005, it was reported that:

> The time has come to make the learning of an African indigenous language compulsory in all our schools, Education Minister Naledi Pandor declared today.
>
> The statement during her budget speech drew applause from visitors in the National Assembly gallery. […] Referring to news reports that English might become optional in schools, Pandor said requirements of the Further Education and Training (FET) Curriculum stated that at least two languages, one of which had to be the language of learning and teaching, had to be taken by pupils in their last three years of school. She said the new FET policy opened up the possibility of developing other official languages into languages of learning. The minister said that this was in no way an anti-Afrikaans campaign. 'All languages must be promoted and allowed to thrive.' Pandor did not indicate a time frame in which an African language would become compulsory. Although the language issue was one of the most contentious, Pandor spoke about other challenges facing the education system.

> She said it was clear that despite plans, an act, several initiatives and a quality assurance system, adult-based education and training targets for improving adult literacy were not working. She would therefore establish a ministerial committee to investigate other countries' models of mass literacy. 'I have signed a letter of intent with my Cuban counterpart, Dr Luis Gómez, which included an intention to investigate South Africa's adoption and adaptation of a Cuban-inspired mass literacy model currently in use in Venezuela and New Zealand.' Funding of adult learning centres was being finalized.
>
> Pandor said she was awaiting feedback from the SA Union of Vice-Chancellors about the department's proposals on limiting student enrolments to institutions of higher education.
>
> (Smith 2005)

A great number of concerned scholars have berated Africa's postcolonial leadership for its inertia towards the adoption and implementation of policies which will start the transformation of African societies for the better. For decades now, a host of voices and arguments have been made in favour of more Afrocentric language policies in Africa, but ostensibly all this has been to no or little avail.[3] Probably best known of these voices has been Ngugi Wa Thiongo who made the additional point that the decolonization of the African mind needs to involve prominently movement away from the usage of the colonial languages. It is an argument which has also been well articulated by Brock-Utne (Brock-Utne 2000).

Continuity and change in African-language policies

The history of this record starts from the earliest years of colonialism. In the pre-colonial era Africans used their languages for all socialization purposes. Without exception, this was the case. Where this was not the case, there was a situation one could describe as conquest or imposition by one group on the other. This is what Phillipson and Skuttnab-Kangas call *Linguicism* (Linguistic imperialism). Probably the most extensive and intensive process of linguistic acculturation and dominance before the colonial encounter was the impact of the Arab conquest of the northern part of the continent, starting from Egypt, into the Maghreb and into Spain. This is how the process of supplanting Amazigh with Arabic among the Berber started.[4]

The classic British colonial position on language policy was formulated in India, not Africa. But the outlines of the policy were relevant to the British colonial experience in Africa. As far back as 1835, in his famous '*Minute on Indian Education*' much of what comes through today as arguments for the displacement of the mother tongue for African education was offered by Macaulay. He argued that; 'We have to educate a people who cannot at present be educated by means of their mother-tongue.' What he meant by implication is that until such time that the mother tongue is equipped to do the job, the solution he is offering is second best. In this respect his position was more 'progressive' than many today. He was saying that in the absence of a mother tongue variously resourced and equipped to do the job, one had no alternative but to use a foreign language. He was not saying that the 'native' language was inherently ill-equipped. He went on to say:

> We must teach them some foreign language. The claims of our own language it is hardly necessary to recapitulate. It stands pre-eminent even among the languages of the west. It abounds with works of imagination not inferior to the noblest which Greece has bequeathed to us; with models of every species of eloquence; with historical compositions, which, considered merely as narratives, have seldom been surpassed, and which, considered as vehicles of ethical and political instruction, have never been equalled [,,,] In India, English is the language spoken by the ruling class. It is spoken by the higher class of natives at the seats of government. It is likely to become the language of commerce throughout the seas of the East. It is the language of two great European communities which are rising, the one in the south of Africa, the other in Australasia; communities which are every year becoming more important, and more closely connected with our Indian empire. Whether we look at the intrinsic value of our literature, or at the particular situation of this country, we shall see the strongest reason to think that, of all foreign tongues, the English tongue is that which would be the most useful to our native subjects.

This was long before Kipling wrote his panegyric extolling 'The White Man's Burden', or Elgar his Pomp and Circumstance marches. Macaulay's certitude and his ostensible feelings of the almost effortless superiority of his language and culture makes interesting reading.

> I certainly never met with any Orientalist who ventured to maintain that the Arabic and Sanskrit poetry could be compared to that of the great European nations. But when we pass from works of imagination to works in which facts are recorded, and general principles investigated, the superiority of the Europeans becomes absolutely immeasurable. It is, I believe, no exaggeration to say, that all the historical information which has been collected from all the books written in the Sanskrit language is less valuable than what may be found in the most paltry abridgments used at preparatory schools in England. In every branch of physical or moral philosophy, the relative position of the two nations is nearly the same.

Summing up Macaulay wrote that:

> [W]e are free to employ our finds as we choose; that we ought to employ them in teaching what is best worth knowing; that English is better worth knowing than Sanskrit or Arabic; that the natives are desirous to be taught English, and are not desirous to be taught Sanskrit or Arabic; that neither as the languages of law, nor as the languages of religion, have the Sanskrit and Arabic any peculiar claim to our engagement; that it is possible to make natives of this country thoroughly good English scholars, and that to this end our efforts

> ought to be directed. In one point I fully agree with the gentlemen to whose general views I am opposed. I feel with them, that it is impossible for us, with our limited means, to attempt to educate the body of the people. We must at present do our best to form a class who may be interpreters between us and the millions whom we govern; a class of persons, Indian in blood and colour, but English in taste, in opinions, in morals, and in intellect. To that class we may leave it to refine the vernacular dialects of the country, to enrich those dialects with terms of science borrowed from the Western nomenclature, and to render them by degrees fit vehicles for conveying knowledge to the great mass of the population.

There we have it. This was the classic formulation of the intentions and rationale behind British colonial educational policy and the pre-eminence of the English language in the education system they created. Throughout the colonial empire variations on this theme were implanted.

It is possible to dismiss all this as the suppositions of an imperialist of the pith helmet and jodhpurs kind, but, difficult to excuse Naomi Mitchison, more than a century after Macaulay, making more Eurocentric observations on the matter. Mitchison who is well-known in Botswana, writing her book *The Africans* which in my estimation was a rather ambitious undertaking because of the claim that it was written 'with a view to reinterpreting the history of Africa not only to outsiders but above all to the Africans themselves' (Mitchison 1970: 52). She unfortunately slipped up in her contention that African languages are not suitable as languages of science. She wrote that:

> Some languages develop in the direction of accuracy, and most European languages are of this kind. They break up words and ideas and partly analyse them … Words in ordinary use get shorter and simpler instead of longer. In English for instance we talk of an old red cow with straight horns or a young black cow which has been badly fed. But in some African languages there may be a single word for each kind of cow in which it can be quite hard to find the separate stems.
>
> (Prah 2000: 30).

In response to Mitchison, I have argued that this is a misreading of the character of language in general and African languages in particular.

> The German compound word 'Weltanschauung' is composed of two words, 'welt' for the world and 'anschauung' for view. The Dutch word 'binnehuis' is made up of two words, 'binnen' which is inside or interior and 'huis' which is house. In Afrikaans, a language with essentially Germanic roots, the term 'kragdadigheid' (tough, high-handed or mail-fisted approach) which in the heydays of the apartheid regime became a cherished notion of how to deal with resistance can be deconstructed as being composed of 'krag' for power or vigour, 'dadig' for deed or action, and 'heid' is a suffix for an abstract noun.

As examples of African words which represent single words for each kind of cow, Mitchison wrote that:

> [T]here are Setswana descriptive words: separate stems, prefixed by *kgomo,* the word for any kind of cattle beast: *kgomo e makoro* (with horns pointing inwards), *kgomo e kwebana* (plain read head, body red spotted on white but with streaks of plain red on back and belly), *kgomo e tshumuphefaadu* (ox with white fore-head and black and white body), or *kgomo e kgwanaphefaadu* (background red with white starry or triangular spots, but with a white wavy line of the side).[5]

This is supposed to be argument pointing out why Setswana is unsuitable for science. Mitchison goes on to suggest that Setswana for example is 'essentially good for poetry, singing and some kinds of conversation', but unanalytical. For her, Chinese ideographics where whole concepts are gathered up into a single written character 'is also bad for science'. She omits in this argumentation the fact that for centuries Chinese science led Western science at a distance. China today, in the scientific, technological and economic fields is outclassing the West. She added that:

> So nowadays Chinese is being altered accordingly. Perhaps African languages will be modified in the same way or perhaps they will be kept for speech, poetry, fiction and drama, while English or French is used as a useful written language for non-poetic communication.
>
> (Prah 2000: 31)

But if these are the absurdities of Mitchison's understanding, the father of Negritude in West Africa, former President Leopold Sedar Senghor of Senegal, the supreme Francophile, had this to say,

> [T]he syntax structure dominated by co-ordination and juxtaposition … make African languages particularly suitable for poetry, we would oppose the subordination feature specific to Indo-European language, which amounts to saying that those languages are basically scientific languages since they are suitable for reasoning,
>
> (Silue 2000: 113)

This viewpoint is both silently and volubly shared by some African elite and many Westerners. It is not a recipe or formula for progress in African education or African development. No language from Adam is made for science and technology. Languages of science and technology become so because they are consciously developed to become languages of science and technology. We would argue that education in Africa has to be built on African languages; that it is necessary for the whole of the educational system to be built in this Afrocentric manner. Mother-tongue education in Africa should be normal for Africans and it should stretch for the whole length and breadth of the educational system. That does not mean that Africans should not learn other languages. Other languages including other African and the colonial languages can easily be built into the educational system to permit this. Professor Masaoki Miyamoto of the University of Chubu some years ago at a CASAS conference he attended in Cape Town made the following observation, with humour that,

> I have to apologize for my bad English. I hope all of my friends here are tolerant enough to understand our almost mono-lingual situation in Japan where we can survive without any foreign language from kindergarten to university, from the cradle to the grave. In short, fortunately or unfortunately, we have never been colonized by the British, like most of you.
>
> (Prah 1997)

Need we remind ourselves that Japan is possibly scientifically and technologically one of the most equipped and accomplished societies on earth which studies, creates knowledge and produces technology solely in Japanese.

African elites and undemocratic language policies

A significant effect of colonialism on the cultural life of Africans was that it set into motion a process which led directly to a definite cultural division in the society between elites and the masses divided along language lines. The colonial process in all instances imposed languages of dominance on the colonized societies. The extent to which one acculturated was also a measure of the degree to which one acquired language skills in the colonial language. These languages became languages of administration, education, governance and the social life of the elites, and with them went a certain valorization of the colonial language above native tongues. The cultural bifurcation of colonial society laid the foundation for the socio-cultural division between mass society and the African elite in contemporary Africa. The constraints on social integration produced by this socio-structural contradiction are remarkable.

This process of producing natives who operated culturally and linguistically as their masters was consistently cultivated through educational systems, which rewarded adeptness in the use of the colonial language. With time and to great effect, the colonial languages became entrenched in the world-view of both the elites and the masses as languages of power. But these languages of power, per definition, excluded the culture and languages of the masses. In effect, under colonialism and neo-colonialism, the masses have been and are structurally excluded from active policy-making inclusion processes. So that, whereas in theory acknowledgement of mass participation in democratic institutions and policy-making may be acknowledged, in practice, the structure of post-olonial or neo-colonial society in Africa fundamentally excludes effective mass participation. This is in a world where, today, new concepts of 'interactive policy-making' are being bandied around.

The African media has a crucial role to play in African attempts to spread the use of indigenous languages and enable the African masses to participate more meaningfully in public discourse for democracy and development. Currently more than 95 per cent of African newspapers publish in the colonial languages. That means that the overwhelming majority of Africans are excluded from the constituency and market of these newspapers. It is impossible to develop a vibrant culture of democracy, public participation and sensitivity to issues affecting the lives of mass society, if such constituencies are fundamentally excluded from the readership of newsprint on the continent.

The European Commission on 3 April 2001 adopted a policy on 'interactive policy-making'. Its espoused aim has been to improve governance through the use of the internet for collecting and analysing reactions in the wide market place for use in the European Union's policy-making process. It is interesting to note that, the European Union's interactive policy-making initiative is geared towards assisting the European Commission in European Union policy-making through two principle approaches. First, a feedback system helps and facilitates the collection of spontaneous reactions in the market place. It operates through existing networks, contacts and linkage points as intermediaries in order to establish continuous access to the opinions and experiences of economic operators and European Union citizens. Second, it is fundamentally a consultation system designed to receive and store stakeholders' reactions to new initiatives. This modern approach to tapping into the opinions and views of relevant constituencies is grounded in the perception that policy-making should satisfy constituency needs and the informed constantly by constituency opinions. The underlining assumption in this is that the two-way traffic of views and ideas between the constituency and policy-makers is operated in language forms, including computer facilities, which are practically accessible to the two interacting parties. The whole process is premised on language accessibility and intelligibility. In Africa, with the cleavage existing between elites and mass society in language-use such modern approaches as have been adopted by the European Commission are currently well-nigh impossible. If the ethos of democracy is to imbue all governmental institutions and administrative practice, we need to start from the basic principle, which would allow mass society and the policy-making elites to communicate rationally and effectively. This requires the use of the languages of mass society.

In most instances in contemporary Africa, policy-makers are, not infrequently, people who cannot handle adeptly the languages of the constituencies for which they are supposed to devise policies. Culturally they are 'new near-Westerners', who are in charge of structures, which are supposed to cater for masses who are more thoroughly rooted in African culture and languages. Where the literature of administration and the instruments of administrative formations and practice are fashioned in colonially bequeathed languages, implicitly and structurally a neo-colonial condition is in place, and literacy is treated as a function of knowledge of the colonial language. Africans who can read and write their own languages remain, in effect, under such neo-colonial conditions 'illiterate'.

In Africa, the effects of linguistic neo-colonialism have been more profound and culturally debilitating than has been the case in much of formerly colonial Asia. In as much the same way that where hunter-gatherers have come into contact with agriculturalists they have tended to be culturally assimilated to the culture of the agriculturalists, and peasant societies become adjuncts to urban, industrial or industrializing societies, the oral cultures of Africa have easily succumbed to literate colonial cultures with revealed religions. In this respect, Asian cultures with their histories of literacy tell a different story. Gerald Moore has observed that;

> [I]n Asia [...] The withdrawal of imperial control revealed how precarious the situation of the (English) language really was. The volume of literary activity in languages such as Bengali, Tamil, Gujarati, Malay and Urdu, together with the gradual decline of English usage in public life, suggests that ultimately the imperial language may prove as marginal as the English presence itself; while in tropical Africa only the recent spread of mass education has offered the possibility of escape from an equally marginal role. For historical experience confirms that a language, which remains the property of a small elite cannot provide the basis of a national culture. A recent parallel would be the use of French by polite society in 19th century Russia.
>
> (Moore 1969: xi)

Perhaps, even more developmentally constraining in the African case is the fact that, the elites which are in charge of African countries are either oblivious of the strategic pitfalls of linguistic neo-colonialism or are for various reasons (mainly, power, privilege and interest) unwilling to adopt policies which will correct these strategic anomalies and culturally and linguistically empower the masses. The question is whether this situation can continue indefinitely.

If African languages in Africa are the languages of the masses, colonial languages are the languages of the elites. The use of Western languages in Africa serves as the cultural basis for dominance of the elites. Those who rule and control Africa today are those who speak the Western languages inherited from the colonial experience. In other words, today (as was the case under colonialism) the language of power is the colonial language. It is even possible to argue that generally those who speak these languages best are those closest to the heights of power. The premium put on the usage of colonial languages is not with respect only to its effective reading and writing, but also speaking like the westerner; speaking in 'his master's voice'. The acquisition of accents and expressions which are as close as possible to the Queen's diction or French *á la Académie Française* are not only profoundly valued, but also enormously admired. In the *heteroglossia* of the colonial language in Africa, yesterday and today, the diction of the metropolitan upper and middle classes have become the equivalents of Bakhtinian 'posited unitary language' or Gramsci's 'normative grammar', in short, the voice of superiority, power and hegemony.

In the colonial and neo-colonial situations of Africa, a further complicating dimension is the fact that the ultimate physical association to the diction of power is white skin. A small minority of the elite are able to partake of and appropriate part of this culture. Because the elites serve as a reference group for the teeming masses, indirectly and almost inadvertently, they ensure in one blow the dalliance of both his 'master's voice' and skin colour in 'Darkest Africa'.

Judicious language policies, which are Afrocentric, apart from the great service they would provide for cultural empowerment of mass society and the strengthening of the cultural basis of democratic culture have also importantly an integrative function. Most of Africa is divided up into a mosaic of states which chop up ethno-cultural entities into little bits and pieces. This fractionalization of African cultures makes it easy for them to be used for political ends by rival elites. Furthermore, they prevent the economic use of resources for language and cultural activities. On the basis of harmonized spelling systems for African languages it will be possible on the economies of scale to produce literatures for large constituencies. Instead of producing books for 2 million Ashantis in Ghana it would be possible to produce books for 15 million Akans in Ghana, Togo and the Ivory Coast. Instead of producing less than a quarter of a million Tswana books for Tswanas in Namibia, one could produce 10 million books which will serve Sotho-Tswanas in the whole sub-region including speakers in Zambia, Botswana, Namibia, Lesotho and South Africa. Recently, (June 2005) as part of the cooperative work between, *Laboratoire de recherche sur les langues Gbe*; LABO-Gbe (Benin) and CASAS, Professor Capo the Director of LABO-Gbe submitted for publication three manuscripts written in the harmonized Gbe orthography (1. AgbetƆ Bé Kúreká Yinyin, 2. Gbefán tsƆ Kuré KasimekplƆtƆwó Mé AkƆ 2002tƆ Wúnti: Mimé AfƆróphéwó 3. Dó Ló aló Acyangbe). These texts have potential reading audiences in four countries in West Africa: Nigeria, Benin, Togo and Ghana.

In a recommendation made by Eric Sibanda and Nomsa Zindela, the authors suggested that:

> There is need to promote collaboration between siSwati Language Boards in Swaziland and the Mpumalanga Province in South Africa. Thus we believe that any standardization of the Nguni languages should take into account that siSwati is actually spoken in two different countries and language practitioners of both countries should be involved in the harmonization process.
>
> (Chebanne, Jokweni, Mokotimi, and Ngubane 2003: 190)

For similar reasons, Ngunga and Sitoe have argued that

> [W]e want to propose the harmonization of the orthographic systems of cross-border languages on the light of principles established by UNESCO (1987) for the African Reference Alphabet (ARA). The cross-border harmonization comes about because Tsonga, although spoken mainly in Mozambique, is also spoken by over three million people in the neighbouring regions of South Africa, Swaziland and Zimbabwe. Mozambique alone has 1,638,479 native speakers of the Tsonga languages.
>
> (Chebanne, Jokweni, Mokitimi, and Ngubane 2003: 41, Sitoe and Ngunga 2000)

Almost all the principal linguists in the Southern African region today who have pronounced on the issue have pointed to the same direction. Miti 'strongly recommended' that,

> Local organizational structures for the siSwati, isiNdebele, isiXhosa and isiZulu varieties be involved in the harmonization of Nguni speech forms and/or orthography; for isiNdebele, which is a cross-border variety, a workshop/conference involving South African and Zimbabwean linguists and other language practitioners be organized to discuss harmonization of speech forms and / or orthography; investigation into and description of the spontaneous Nguni variety believed to be developing in Gauteng should be funded and undertaken in the very near future.
>
> (Chebanne, Jokweni, Mokitimi, and Ngubane 2003: 71)

Clearly the way forward lies in first the use of African languages and then second the use of African languages which have been orthographically harmonized. The sharing of cultural affinities and cultural attributes across borders will, additionally, serve to bring Africans closer and minimize ethnic conflicts through the celebration of cultural and linguistic diversity on regionalized bases.

Banda has observed that although the task of harmonizing and standardizing orthographic conventions is a daunting one:

> [I]t was also clear that in spite of the more than ninety dialects spoken in the two countries, it was possible to come up with a single orthography and spelling system for the two countries. Also apparent was the fact that for efficient and economic use of African languages, there was need for collaboration that went beyond colonial borders. The significance of cross-border research and collaboration was also underscored as it became evident that harmonization of languages and orthographic conventions requires cross-border solutions rather than those from country to country.
>
> (Banda 2002: 4)

I have had occasion to observe that, as of necessity, the solution to the challenges of African education and development cannot be resolved on a country-to-country basis. African languages in all countries straddle and cross borders. Indeed, the notion of cross-border languages in Africa is in a sense tautological since almost all African languages transcend the colonially bequeathed borders. Therefore cooperative and Pan-African solutions are called for. It is our view that the search for solutions across borders will help reduce the ethnic tensions which historically arbitrary borders foster, and which plague contemporary Africa in the societally crippling ways we are witnessing in our time (Prah 1998a: 9, 1998b: 68–99). As Ron Simango has rightly pointed out,

> [W]e bemoan the fact that our former colonial masters used a system of divide and rule to weaken us as a people. Yet in our discussion of language and

> identity we tend to forget that the different orthographies have remained potent instruments for perpetuating those divisions. In my view, resisting orthographic reforms on the grounds that one might lose his or her linguistic identity is a glaring contradiction: we cannot claim to hate a system (that divided us) yet at the same time adore the very instruments which perpetuate it.
>
> (Chebanne, Jokweni, Mokitimi, and Ngubane 2003: 38)

In times when the call for an African renaissance has been made in many circles including the call by ex-President Thabo Mbeki of South Africa, we need to remember that a renaissance is not possible without a renaissance of the African languages. An African regeneration is only possible on the basis of African languages (Kurimoto 2001). The logic of this is clear. It is the logic of democracy and self-assurance for the masses that make up the overwhelming majority in Africa. Attention has also to be drawn to the succinct point made by Miyamoto that; 'the most important factor which guarantees success of any language plan is that it should create larger and better job-markets for the common masses who will speak and write it'.[6]

Notes

1 Gregory Kamwendo, 'The slow march towards mother tongue instruction in Malawi: another case of "declaration without implementation"?' Paper presented to the Regional Mother Tongue Education Conference. 1–2 June 2005, Gaborone, Botswana (unpublished).

2 African Academy of Languages (ACALAN) Meeting. 'Linguistic diversity and literacy in a global perspective a comparative look at practice in Europe and Africa'. Project for the Study of Alternative Education in South Africa (PRAESA). University of Cape Town. 8 December 2004.

3 Regarding the inertia and diffidence shown by African leadership in this respect, see for example (Bamgbose 1982: 6–14; Ansre 1976; Apronti 1978; Adeyanju 1986).

4 Amazigh is a language of the Berber of North Africa. It is the main indigenous language in the area which predates Arabic. Largely suppressed over the centuries from the time of the Arab conquerors it is in recent years in experiencing a renaissance and is part of the cultural movement of the Berber people of North Africa for recognition. For a good introduction to the grammar of this language see (Sadiqi 1997; Abdelmassih 1971; Sadiqi and Ennaji 2004).

5 (Prah 2000: 30–31). In Tswana society, cattle are a central feature of social and economic life. Status and wealth are measured on the basis of cattle of cattle-holding. My contention is that, in old-fashioned Herskovitsian language, pre-capitalist Tswana society was a 'cattle complex'. Cattle colouring serves as a classifactory index, and apart from being descriptions, they also have symbolic value. Cattle colouring has bearing on ritual practice. For example a gift to a visiting monarch must in most instances be a black bull. This is also true for some other southern Bantu.

6 This very important remark appears in Masaoki Miyamoto's contribution, 'The modernization of the Japanese language in comparison to KiSwahili', in Prah (1998a: 274).

References

Abdelmassih, E. (1971). *A Reference Grammar of Tamazight: A Comparative Study of Berber Dialects of Ayt Ayadre and Ayt Seghrouchen – Middle Atlas Berber*. Ann Arbor, MI: University of Michigan.

Adeyanju, T. K. (1986). Language policy in Nigeria. (Public Lecture – Ahmadu Bello University). Mimeo.

Ansre, G. L. (1976). National development and language: prologue to language policy formulation and implementation (12th West African Languages Congress; University of Ife).

Apronti, E. O. (1978). The linguist as a democrat. (Unpublished Paper – 13th West African Languages Congress, Fourah Bay University, Sierra Leone)/

Bamgbose, A. (1982). When is language planning not planning? *Journal of West African Languages*, XVII(1): 6–14.

Banda, F. (2002). *Language Across Borders*, CASAS Book Series No.12. Cape Town: CASAS.

Brock-Utne, B. (2000). *Whose Education for All? The Recolonization of the African Mind.* New York: Falmer Press.

Brock-Utne, B. and Koloti, M. S. (eds) (2000). *Education for All – In Whose Language?* Report No. 6, Education in Africa, Vol. 8. Oslo: Institute for Educational Research, University of Oslo.

Brock-Utne, B., Desai, Z. and Qorro, M. (eds). (2003). *Language of Instruction in Tanzania and South Africa (LOITASA).* Dar es Salaam: E & D. Limited.

Chebanne, A., Jokweni, M., Mokitimi, M. I. and Ngubane, S. (eds) (2003). *Unifying Southern African Languages: Harmonization and Standardization*, CASAS Book Series No. 32. Cape Town: CASAS.

Kurimoto, E. (ed.) (2001). *Rewriting Africa: Toward Renaissance or Collapse?* JCAS Symposium Series 14. Osaka: The Japan Centre for Area Studies, Osaka, Japan.

Granqvist, R. (ed.) (1993). *Culture in Africa: An Appeal for Pluralism.* (Seminar Proceedings No. 29. Uppsala: The Scandinavian Institute of African Studies, Nordiska Afrikainstitutet, Uppsala.

Limage, L. (ed.) (1998). *Comparative Perspectives on Language and Literacy*. (Selected Papers – Language and Literacy Commission of the 10th World Congress of Comparative Education Societies). Cape Town: UNESCO.

Mitchison, N. (1970). *The Africans: A History*. London. Anthony Blond.

Moore, G. (1969). *The Chosen Tongue*. Harlow: Longman.

Ntahombaye, P. (1999). La langue au service de la paix au Burundi. (Communication presentée lors de l'atelier LINGUAPAX sur les languages nationals et la consolidation la paix en Afrique. Ouagadougou, Burkina.14–17 June 1999).

Prah, K. K. (1995). *Mother Tongue for Scientific and Technological Development in Africa*. Bonn: DSE.

Prah, K. K. (1996). *African Languages for the Mass Education of Africans*. Bonn: DSE.

Prah, K. K. (ed.) (1997). *Between Distinction and Extinction*. CASAS Book Series No.1. Cape Town: CASAS.

Prah, K. K. (ed.) (1998a). *Between Distinction and Extinction: Harmonization and Standardization of African Languages*. Johannesburg: Witwatersrand University Press.

Prah, K. K. (1998b). *Beyond the Colour Line: Pan-Africanist Disputations. Selected Sketches, Letters, Papers and Reviews*. Trenton: Africa World Press, Inc.

Prah, K. K. and King, Y. (eds) (1998). *In Tongues: African Languages and the Challenges of Development*, CASAS Monograph Series No.1. Cape Town: CASAS.

Prah, K. K. (2000). *African Languages for the Mass Education of Africans*, : CASAS Book Series No.7. Cape Town: CASAS.

Sadiqi, F. (1997). *Grammaire de berbère*. Paris: L'Harmattan.

Sadiqi, F. and Ennaji, M. (2005). *A Grammar of Amazigh* (Pars Lettres 25: Publications de la Faculté de Lettres et des Sciences Humaines. Shar El Mehraz. Fez).

Silue, S. J. (2000). *Education, Literacy and Development in Africa*, CASAS Book Series No.10. Cape Town: CASAS.

Sitoe, B. and Ngunga, A. (eds) (2000). *II Seminario sobre a Padronização da Ortografia de Línguas Moçambicanas*. Maputo: NELIMO/Universidade Eduardo Mondlane.

Smith, T. (2005). African language for all kids, *Cape Argus*, Cape Town: 17 May, 2005.

Whiteley, W. H. (ed.) (1974). *Language in Kenya*. London: Oxford University Press.

Part III
Latin American discourse studies

7 Latin American cultural-critical studies

In Latin America, modern and postmodern cultures have not been alien to our path and have both left their mark (Borón 2003). Their passing falsely inscribes us in glocalizations that, supposedly, make us better adapted to the already known globalization by means of the apparent particular features of our countries' cultures (Cvetkovich and Kellner 1997). These undertakings, of course, collapse: for example, when the time comes to use a language, and everything is given to us in a 'neutral Spanish' that none of us speaks. Or in the settling of coffee shops, fast food franchises, department stores, home-items megastores and so many others that from their façades and advertisements, regardless of their tiny variations, scream at us that we should not be confused: for it is not diversity knocking at our door but globalization and the culture that goes with it, postmodernity. The differences that enrich us and give us an identity beyond our continent remain invisible and hard to grasp for the ones who wish to conquer us.

At this particular moment, where everything seems to be in the custody of postmodernity or nihilism, modernity is still present and battling on in many spaces and sites.

The following two chapters in this book – the one on homeless people's concept of 'work' (see Pardo 2001) and the one on the Malvinas/Falklands narratives – point out in an evident way the cultural changes that have put modernity and postmodernity face to face. Occidental culture (but also, I believe, Oriental culture) cannot be conceived today without regarding these changes.

Although both modernity and postmodernity respond to the logic of capitalism, their differences are also important, not only as regards economy and politics but also, and more specially, culture. The whole process of occidentalization and hegemonization, metaphorically termed 'globalization' (actually, colonial neo-liberalism), is necessarily accompanied by a cultural transformation.

Modernity comprehends two homogenization periods. The first one begins in 1870 and ends around 1914 (though in Argentina it begins in 1880). The second period or postmodernity goes from 1945 to the present (Mignolo 1998: 32). The first modern globalization ends with the beginning of World War I, has French as its cultural language and English as its lingua franca, is Prussian regarding the military, liberal as far as economics are concerned, and initiates the creation of the nation state. The second globalization, the postmodern one, has English as both its cultural language and lingua franca, is neo-liberal regarding economics, seeks to minimize the state, is inclined toward the state of 'happiness' (individual satisfaction) instead of collective security (or welfare state) that is typical of liberalism, and is characterized by the nihilist philosophy (postmodernity) which accompanies this late capitalism. Also typical of this period are the so-called ethnic wars, framed by 'cold war' (cf. Pardo and Lorenzo-Dus 2010).

Globalization entails, for the subjects, an awareness or perception of the world being unique (Robertson 1992) and of each and every one of us being part of it, where everything affects everything. But it would be naïve to think that this perception is easily accepted by everyone. For this reason, in the face of globalizing or hegemonizing processes we also see the rise of exacerbated nationalisms and of developments that entail regionalizations (see Schaeffer 1997; Ortiz and Pardo 2006).

Latin America is currently at a time when, even though it cannot remain indifferent to these changes, it is for its most part an axis of opposition to globalization, an example of regionalization and, as much as possible and can be attained, of anti-neoliberal ideologies (Minsburg and Walle 1994; Legé Harris and Seid 2000). This is mainly the case of countries like Argentina, Bolivia, Peru, Ecuador, Venezuela and Cuba. As regards economics, we could say that Mercosur (Mercado Común del Sur [Southern Common Market]) unites these member states as taking part in common conceptualizations; other countries like Colombia and Chile, though associated with this organization, are in no real opposition to the hegemonic movements. Mexico presents this non-oppositional trait, too, and s not part of Mercosur.

As was already mentioned, this regionalization process, like many others, does not assume the same form in every country and even cultural forms of modernity and postmodernity coexist throughout every imaginable place in the globe. Nothing can be thought of as being either modern or postmodern, for many things are changing or reacting in opposition to postmodernity even when experiencing it, a fact that produces really interesting combinations.

As Fairclough (2000) claims, language materializes the new capitalism. The new neo-liberal order seeks to impose new representations of the world (Kiely and Marfleet 1998) through new discourses. It is obvious that, for this purpose, it must rely on old discourses and use them as pivots to generate new texts that make this change possible. This is why, without performing a deep linguistic discourse analysis in the chapters that comprise this section, I deem it important to give an account of what the people who are protagonists of our theories express, as it is in this discursive practice, together with the social practice, where we can find the representations that the actors in question have about themselves and their world. These representations form belief systems which are hard to catalogue, but there lies their richness, for they show us the coexistence of cultural differences in the frame of modernity and postmodernity.

One of postmodernity's characteristics is the end of a history that is unique, supposedly true and objective, and official with regard to the states, a history which has been in the hands of a learned, rich and powerful elite. As opposed to this, something emerges that has been called 'giving voice to the voiceless', where those who, up to now, had been excluded from the media and the public circulation of their sayings, start having vast audiences and become the protagonists of this new discursive order. The supposed 'minorities' are usually real majorities, as is the case with people living in extreme poverty or indigence, who represent more than 50 per cent of the world's population. These voices rise as a trait of postmodernity, where their sayings will actually be used to stigmatize these groups but also to oppose globalization as the creators of regional identities, triggering the various studies typical of these times. It can be said, then, that my present chapter on the concept of work is in some way rooted in postmodernity, even though I think of it as a text that criticizes it. However, it is important to point out that one of the topics I intend to analyse in that text is how modernity and postmodernity coexist in a cultural opposition within Argentina, one that stresses the way the so-called 'marginalized' are excluded not only on the economical but also on the cultural plane.

Now, what makes the encounter of these two cultures possible? It is probably different historical conditions, doubtlessly framed by the same capitalist logics, but with the peculiarities of what took place in Argentina, inherent to its own development.

It was Sarmiento, writer and former president of the republic, who, in his book, *Facundo o civilización y barbarie en las pampas argentinas (1845),* created a dichotomy which would haunt Argentina up to today. As Mignolo (1998: 33–34) points out, this was a canonical image of Latin American culture and, at the same time, a justification of internal colonialism. The colonized world intellectuals maintained that civilization was the process and that culture was its product. This allowed them to confront the supposed barbarism with the quest for European 'civilization' as the starting point for understating their own culture. We could say that this is the birth of an initial discourse which emphasizes difference, always so useful to homogenization and marginalization processes, as both sides of the same coin (Pardo and Lorenzo-Dus 2010).

However, postmodernity brings 'barbarism' and conflates it with 'civilization', taking it into the cultural axis. It entices 'barbarism' to become a spectacle (Debord 1994). Poverty, illness and death can then become a part of a spectacle that feigns popular culture. From there comes the endless succession of reality shows, the success, in Latin American countries, of 'cumbia villera'[1] and of police officers and thieves who display their behaviours in different shows, the exposition of private life and the sexual objectification of women. Though in a different tone, something similar happens with memory, conceived as a means of homage and of not forgetting, and with museums and monuments created on these premises, a memory which also aims at remembering wars, natural disasters, crimes and important catastrophes that tormented society. However, defying all predictions, the pain caused by the military dictatorships and the desaparecidos, the vindication of human rights, the trial and punishment of those found guilty of committing tortures, abuses and crimes against humanity, all of these did open a unique space for memory and gave it a reason to exist: that all that happened shall never happen again ('nunca más'). Thus, the negative quality of postmodernity is reversed so as to retrieve the positive and, in this way, generates a reform which helps not to repeat the same mistakes.

In the case of marginality there could also be something positive, the emergence of a different voice amidst a society of consumerism, a voice that could bring some contrast to the frivolity of prejudice, an attempt to change that logic of the capital. Nevertheless, more often than not these goals succumb to a postmodernity that trivializes and silences everything.

As pointed out earlier, there might be a better perspective as regards memory, because in many cases, like my present work on the Malvinas War, there is a certain amount of historical revision of the facts and alternative positions on the war. But even a contrary position to postmodern philosophy cannot help being attached to it.

On the other hand it must be noted that, at least in many Latin American countries, the situation of gazing at Europe or the United States as models has greatly changed, insofar as, in more cases than before, the aim is no longer to replicate their models but rather to turn away from them; even if we always remain more or less subject to capitalism, new trade alternatives in Latin America itself, China, the Arab Emirates and others begin to be sought (Sohn 2012).

Consequently, the two chapters that follow are linked with the phenomenon of the opposition between modernity and postmodernity (Pardo 2008), but what we are interested in showing is that such a dichotomy does not exist; instead, there are degrees of a continuum. We are also interested in showing that, in its glocalizations, globalization often fails its purpose, as is the case with private or public projects for assisting the homeless. The realization of these glocalizations begins with a priori, deductive theories, without ever going out into the field to find out what the needs of people living in marginality and poverty are and thus without obtaining any results. These people unconsciously resist, on the periphery, the neo-liberal logic their lives are immersed in. Robertson (1992) would not consider these people to be globalized precisely because of their non-awareness of globalization. However, this claim is highly questionable, as the very fact of being on the periphery is a direct consequence of neo-liberalism.

For the subsequent chapter on people experiencing homelessness, we use life stories. In postmodernity, these narratives acquire a new significance. On the one hand, this corresponds with the fact of giving voice to the voiceless, on the other, it highlights the idea of the postmodern hero (Forster 2002), insofar as the protagonists are ordinary men and women whose heroism lies in surviving the daily life and hopelessness of this world. Also (though not shown here), it is common in postmodernity to present the poor as those who narrate their 'minimal stories' revealing the lack of a collective project (Pardo and Massone 2008). In the leading roles of their postmodern progression, they lose strength as the resistance to the capitalist system. The intention of the chapter is to give evidence of the spatial and cultural eviction of the social actors who succumb to the neo-liberal system, but, at the same time, it aims to alert the authorities, when it comes to create public policies in correspondence with those who are subject to them, in such a way that these policies may become effective through field research and discourse studies. Though not presented here in their entirety, these studies reveal the linguistic forms whereby late capitalism is embodied and, at the same time, those which are resisted even in situations of such defenselessness.

The next chapter on the Malvinas War is situated in the space of war spectacularization and commemoration. Different narratives intertwine, becoming a true sample of the struggles between modernity and postmodernity. The relevance of the details and facts of each battle constitute yet another way of consecrating a new postmodern hero: the soldier in his fight to survive, amidst the worst conditions, a war born out of a dictator's madness.

The awareness of writing on these topics while at the same time being immersed, as a scholar, in the very facts under discussion and the knowledge of cultural occidentalization and of the logics of capitalism are exercises the researcher must do every time he/she develops or begins a research project. This consciousness allows one to settle in a space of criticism of one's own work and of the academic world in general. Although it appears to be impossible to escape the philosophy and practices inherent to this culturally globalizing system, the knowledge thereof will allow us to try ways and strategies which may at least enable us to stay alert and attempt cultural movements that are capable of alternative scholar reflections and practices.

Cultural studies need this continuous revision of the place they occupy in the neo-liberal cultural model, as well as of the form and ways of their resistance (a consequence of any homogenizing process). Cultural resistance cannot be reduced to a series of practices which are functional to globalization: it must search for an alternative sphere enabling it to perform actions which, even from inside the cultural system of late capitalism, could be defined as options that discuss the processes of colonialist occidentalization and seek new horizons for their practices (Escobar 2004).

The creation of the Red Latinoamericana de Análisis Crítico del Discurso de la Pobreza Extrema (Latin American Network of Critical Discourse Analysis of extreme poverty, REDLAD) is one of these new practices. This network is nine years old and consists of Latin American researchers from Argentina, Brazil, Chile, Colombia and Mexico, who devote their studies to the discourses that people undergoing situations of marginality produce about themselves and their surroundings (Coraccini 2011; Marchese 2011; Pardo Abril 2008, 2010; Garcia da Silva and Pardo Abril 2010; Quiróz and Samaniego 2010). The way the mass media refer to these actors is also analysed (Pardo and Buscaglia 2011; D'Angelo 2012). This network, unique in the sphere of critical studies and of cultural studies connected with the study of discourse, demonstrates how some scholars from the so-called 'First World' lack any interest in the consequences that the policies developed there and in the United States have brought, not only on the so-called 'Third World' but on the whole world as regards poverty.

Step by step, in the annual meetings that take place in the form of congresses and colloquiums, and in the visits of members of the network to its member countries, a historical, political, social, economical and, above all, cultural knowledge is being attained, revealing the convergences and divergences between each member country. Though we all suffer the consequences of globalization (Stiglitz 2003), our specific histories and cultures leave us in different places when it comes to giving an account of our cultural ways of confronting globalization.

However, this network is not only about achieving awareness or studying these cultural problems; it also acts politically in different organizations, government agencies, field work (from high school teaching in shanty towns, workshops, private lessons, purchasing products generated in shanty towns for academic events, to assessing governmental laws dealing with homeless and extremely poor people).

The experience of many REDLAD researchers on the theoretical and methodological planes has also been rich and valuable, for it has enabled them to create theories, methods and analysis techniques (cf. Barros 2010; D´Angelo 2012; de Melo Resende 2009; Molina 2012; Pardo 2012; de la Vega 2011) out of their own research in their countries and field work. As an example, linguistic analysis carried out in Chapters 8 and 9 is based on Information Hierarchy Theory and, specifically within it, upon what it focuses on (Pardo 2011) (see Chapters 8 and 9).

As regards cultural studies in each of the member countries, it has been one of our decisions to undertake comparative studies between them, so as to respect the diversity we find in our group. The so-called 'informants' are also a fundamental part of this process, as they participate in round tables at some of our congresses; they are a theoretical source for our works and some of them have produced papers with us as co-authors (cf. Ortiz *et al.* 2012). This, which should not draw much attention, is nevertheless one of the most difficult tasks to realize, not just through our fault of seeing them only as the narrators of experiences which 'we' later analyse, but also with the distance that is put in check by economical and cultural issues every time different social classes cooperate.

Just like Bauman (2003) who says that a 'society that is insecure about its survival develops the mentality of a besieged fortress', we could say that a large part of the academy, specially the one not located in the so-called 'First World', does the same. Being the only difference that, instead of fighting its demons outside (as is the case with society), these ghosts, which are in fact the Latin American academic community's own fears, and threaten its survival, have been living inside this community for years. That explains its admiration and enduring attentive gaze at Europe and the United States. That is why collaborations such as the ones put forward in this book, which open up new opportunities for academic and cultural exchange between Asia, Africa and Latin America, are challenges that enrich us by showing other ways of knowing the world, apart from occidentalism.

There are countless projects in Latin America that, just like REDLAD, without fearing their space of identity, and though the recognition of Latin America's own topics instead of the ones born of the 'civilization that opposes barbarism' is still hard to obtain, begin to tread the road of their roots, of their identity, of their pagan gods who dwell in their pyramids and their lands. This itinerary, not alien to postmodernity, mocks it by transforming it, by using it for its own benefit, by rewriting it, thus giving birth once again to that culture that was concealed by colonization through invasion and death.

Notes

1 Cumbia villera is a kind of music and dance that reflects certain aspects of the lives of people living in slums.

2 This chapter was produced conjointly with one of the leaders of the Mapuche community. These indigenous people, who live in the south of Argentina and Chile, have been persecuted for years and still are fighting for their lands and rights.

References

Barros, S. (2010). Realismo Crítico (RC), Análise de Discurso Crítica (ADC) e Gramática Sistêmico-Funcional (GFS): reflexões para a formação do educador de línguas em processo de emancipação e transformação social. In L. Montecino (ed.), *Discurso, pobreza y exclusión en América Latina*. Santiago de Chile: Cuarto propio, pp. 293–309.

Bauman, Z. (2003). *Trabajo, consumismo y nuevos pobres*. Barcelona: Gedisa.

Borón, A. (2003). *Estado, capitalismo y democracia en América Latina*. Buenos Aires: CLACSO

Coraccini, M. J. (2011). Historias de vida e pobreza: por una (intro)dução. In M. J. Coraccini, *Identidades silenciadas e (in)visíveis: entre a inclusão e a exclusão (identidade, mídia, pobreza, situação de rua, Mudança social, formação de professores)*. Campinas, SP: Pontes, pp. 17–28.

Cvetkovich, A. and Kellner, D. (eds). (1999). *Articulating the Global and tLocal. Globalization and Cultural Studies* Political and Culture No. 5. Boulder, CO: Westview Press..

D'Angelo, G. (2012). Procedimiento alternativo: método de análisis de discurso Audiovisual. In Abril N. Pardo, *Discurso en la web: pobreza en YouTube*. Bogotá: Universidad Nacional de Colombia (sede Bogotá), pp. 97–124.

Debord, G. (1994). *The Society of Spectacle*, New York: Zone Books.

de la Vega, L. (2011). *Embarazo, adolescencia y violencia intrafamiliar en* contextos *de pobreza: ACD en Historias de vida*. Buenos Aires: Tersites.

de Melo Resende, V. (2009). *Análise de discurso crítica e realismo crítico. Implicações Interdisciplinares*. Campinas, SP: Pontes Editores. .

de Melo Resende. V. 2010. A crise do Movimento Nacional de Meninos e Meninas de Rua no Brasil e o protagonismo juvenil: uma crítica explanatória con base em análise discursive. In L. Montecino (ed.), *Discurso, pobreza y exclusión en América Latina*. Santiago de Chile: Cuarto propio, pp. 349–364.

Escobar, A. (2004). Beyond the third world: imperial globality, global coloniality and anti-globalisation social movements. *Third World Quarterly*, 25(1): 207–230.

Fairclough, N. (2000). El lenguaje en el nuevo capitalism. In M. L. Pardo and V. Noblia, (eds), *Globalización y nuevas tecnologías*. Buenos Aires: Biblos.

Forster, R. (2002). La muerte del héroe. *Crítica y sospecha*. Buenos Aires: Paidós.

Garcia da Silva, D. and Pardo Abril, N. G. (2010). Miradas cruzadas hacia la pobreza desde una perspectiva crítica transdisciplinaria. *Cadernos de Linguagem e Sociedade*, 11(1): 66–90.

Kiely, R. and Marfleet, P. (eds) (1998). *Globalisation and the Third World*. Abingdon: Taylor and Francis Group.

Legé Harris, R. and Seid, M. J. (eds) (2000). Critical perspectives on globalization and neoliberalism in the developing countries. *International Studies in Sociology and Social Anthropology*, 16(1): 1–180.

Marchese, M. C. (2011). *El texto como unidad de análisis socio-discursiva. Una propuesta a partir del método sincrónico-diacrónico de análisis lingüístico de textos*. Buenos Aires: Tersites.

Mignolo, W. (1998). Posoccidentalismo: el argumento desde América Latina. In S. Castro-Gómez and E. Mendieta, *Teorías sin disciplina. Latinoamericanismo, poscolonialidad y globalización en debate*, México: Miguel Ángel Porrúa-University of San Francisco.

Minsburg, N. and Walle, H. W. (eds) (1994). *El impacto de la globalización. La encrucijada económica del siglo XXI.* Buenos Aires: Ediciones Letra Buena.

Molina, L. (2012). *La argumentación en las noticias. Una aproximación al análisis* de *la estructura argumentativa a partir del modelo de Toulmin*. Buenos Aires: Tersites.

Montecino, L. (ed.) (2010). *Discurso, pobreza y exclusión en América Latina*. Santiago de Chile: Cuarto propio.

Ortiz, T., Pardo, M. L., Fink, A., Noblia, V. Landau, M., Perotti, R., Carrizo, A. and Antinao, N. (2001). Globalización, modernidad y derechos humanos.*Versión*, 11, 335–351.

Ortiz, T. E. and Pardo, M. L. (eds). (2006). *Estado posmoderno y globalización. Transformación del estado-nación argentino*, Buenos Aires, Departamento de Publicaciones Facultad de Derecho de la Universidad de Buenos Aires.

Pardo Abril, N. (2008). *¿Qué nos dicen? ¿Qué vemos? ¿Qué es pobreza? Análisis crítico de los medios*. Bogotá: Antiquus Editores.

Pardo Abril, N. (2010). Filogénesis y transformaciones del concepto de pobreza. In L. Montecino (ed.), *Discurso, pobreza y exclusión en América Latina*. Santiago de Chile: Cuarto propio.

Pardo, M. L. (2001). La expresión discursiva del mandato. Análisis lingüístico del texto de la ley de reforma laboral argentina. In M. L. Pardo (ed.), Special Issue. *Derecho y Lenguaje. Revista Iberoamericana de Discurso y Sociedad. Lenguaje en Contexto desde Una Perspectiva Crítica y Multidisciplinaria*, 3(2): 2001, 117–137.

Pardo, M. L. (2008). La estetización y espectacularización de la pobreza: análisis crítico del discurso postmoderno televisivo en la Argentina. In T. Ortiz and M. L. Pardo (eds), *Desigualdades sociales y estado. Un estudio multidisciplinario desde la posmodernidad.* Buenos Aires: Facultad de Derecho de la Universidad de Buenos Aires, Departamento de Publicaciones.

Pardo, M. L. (2011). *Teoría y metodología de la investigación lingüística. Método sincrónico-diacrónico de análisis lingüístico de textos*. Buenos Aires: Tersites.

Pardo, M. L. 2012. Innovación teórica y metodológica en los estudios críticos del discurso de la pobreza extrema: contribuciones de la REDLAD. In V. de Melo Resende (ed.) Special issue: Análise de discurso crítica e extrema pobreza. VII Colóquio da REDLAD. *Cadernos de Linguagem e Sociedade*, 15–37.

Pardo, M. L. and Massone, M. I. (eds) (2008). Special Issue: Análisis crítico de la cumbia villera en la Argentina. In *Revista de la Asociación Latinoamericana de Estudios del Discurso (ALED).* Caracas: Venezuela.

Pardo, M. L. and Lorenzo-Dus, N. (2010). The Falklands/Malvinas heroes 25 years on: a comparative analysis of commemorative TV documentaries. In M. L. Pardo, Guest Editor. Special Issue: *Critical and Cultural Discourse Analysis from a Latin American Perspective. Journal of Multicultural Discourses*, 5(3): 253–270

Pardo, M. L. and Buscaglia, V. (2011). Delirio, pobreza y televisión: análisis del discurso y psicoanálisis. In M. J. Coraccini, *Identidades silenciadas e (in)visíveis: entre a inclusão e a exclusão (identidade, mídia, pobreza, situação de rua, Mudança social, formação de professores)*. Campinas, SP: Pontes, pp. 113–126.

Quiróz, B. and Samaniego, J. L. (2010). Sobre la teoría lingüística y el estudio del discurso de personas en situación de calle: algunos apuntes. In L. Montecino *Discurso, pobreza y exclusión en América Latina*. Santiago de Chile: Cuarto propio, pp. 331–349.

Robertson, R. 1992. *Globalization, Social Theory and Global Culture*. London: Sage.

Sarmiento, D. F. (1845). *Facundo o civilización y barbarie en las pampas argentinas*. http://bibliotecadigital.educ.ar/uploads/contents/DomingoF.Sarmiento-Facundo0.pdf (last accessed 11/12/2014).

Schaeffer, R. K. (1997). *Understanding Globalization. The Social Consequences of Political, Economic, and Environmental Change*. Lanham: Rowman and Litttlefield.

Sohn, I. (2012). After renaissance: China's multilateral offensive in the developing world. *European Journal of International Relations*,18(1): 77–101.

Stiglitz, J. E. (2003). *Globalization and Its Discontents*. New York: W. W. Norton.

8 Culture and political challenges

Television narratives about the thirtieth anniversary of the Malvinas/Falklands War

Introduction

A war can change a country's history and culture and this depends to a large extent on whether that war has resulted in a victory or a defeat. The Malvinas/Falklands conflict is an ideal case study, by means of which we can ask ourselves how the discursive representations of this war have been constructed in Argentina on this new anniversary (Pardo and Lorenzo-Dus, 2010a) and how this event is commemorated. These representations have been constructed throughout Argentine history and give shape to different cultural currents in Argentina.

The aim of this chapter is to examine the ways in which television commemorated the thirtieth anniversary of the Malvinas War at the discursive level, how, in so doing, it contributed to generating new narratives based on Argentine culture and its links with the Malvinas Islands, and how, 'new memory' (or memories) have been attempted (Hoskins, 2001), both discursive and social. Rather than stressing the media issue, this chapter aims to delve into the various narratives that expose the cultural changes which succeed one another in the social and the political planes.

The theoretical and methodological frameworks of this research are taken from Cultural Discourse Studies (Shi-xu 2015). From such a discourse perspective, further, we emphasize the Information Hierarchy Theory (especially as regards focal zones) in order to analyse the discourses upon which our current views on war and heroism in Argentina are based.

What we talk about when we talk about the Malvinas Islands

Before going any further, it may be necessary to specify some historical facts about the islands that even many Argentines tend to ignore. These facts will allow us to understand why these islands are part of a controversial situation. Some of them were taken from the excellent book on the islands by R. Terragno (2002: 29–33).

The Malvinas are located in the South Atlantic, 500 km away from Argentine territory and 350 km away from Isla de los Estados (Argentina). They are located 13,000 km away from the United Kingdom. They consist of 20 islands, including those over 20 km^2. The archipelago has a total area of 15,800 km^2. The largest islands are East Falkland or Soledad, measuring 6,350 km^2, and the West Falkland or Gran Malvina, measuring 4,500 km^2. The capital, Stanley, is on Soledad Island. However, since 1966 some Argentine media have called it Puerto Rivero. It was in that year that an armed group diverted a plane and forced it to land on the Malvinas. There they raised an Argentine flag that flew for 36 hours in the capital, renamed 'Rivero' in memory of a gaucho who was arrested by the British and taken to London in 1833. Rivero was a labourer for the Vernet Company. Along with other gauchos and Argentine creoles, in response to the fact that they were not being paid and were only allowed to eat the wild animals they could hunt for themselves, they killed the islands' administrators, despite having very few weapons, and raised the Argentine flag. This narrative would be retaken into consideration in postmodern times, making Rivero a hero to remember. The islands were French for three years (1764–1767). Only in 1765 did John Byron arrive at the islands, not knowing that there were Frenchmen there. But Spain claimed the islands as it considered them a part of its colonies. Since 1776, when the Viceroyalty of the Río de la Plata was created, they depended on the viceroy, whose seat was at Buenos Aires. Finally, the French left the islands because the Spanish paid them to do so. The cession took place on 1 April 1767. Argentina became independent from Spain in 1810 and formally declared its independence in 1816. Britain did not recognize Argentine independence until 1825. The United Kingdom did not assert any claim over the islands, neither at that time nor when the Treaty of Amity, Commerce and Navigation was signed, later that same year. The first British claim dates from 1829. It was in 1833 that the British troops led by John James Onslow overthrew Governor Pinedo and took possession of the islands. Before that date there had been six Argentine governors. Those born on the islands did not have British citizenship and Argentina never ceased to assert its demands.

The islands, commemoration and memory

Memory is an important topic in this work, as the corpus consists of texts that were published to commemorate the place the thirtieth anniversary of the Malvinas War.

Two periods can be identified in the Western world as memory resurgences: the first from 1890 to 1920 and the second from 1960/70 to the present (Winter 2006). The first began with World War I and is crucial for the construction of national identities. The second commenced with the memories of World War II and the Holocaust and continued with Eastern Europe revolutions (1989). The second phase is characterized by a constant revision of the twentieth century's wars and catastrophes. This period also includes televising of wars and is therefore visualized by all countries involved in them and also by those that were not involved but nevertheless participate in the commemoration.

During this second memory resurgence, oral testimonies, as well as testimonial films, become a typical feature of this phase. In the case of wars, testimonies come not only from war veterans, the military and their relatives, but also from war correspondents, something that creates a new way of giving testimony to modern (Hoskins and O' Loughlin, 2010) and postmodern conflicts. The Malvinas War commemorations were held in the same way, though in Argentina television commemoration was always the predominant form, as can be seen in this chapter and in Pardo and Lorenzo-Dus (2011).

Hoskins and O' Loughlin (2010) state that there was also a third memory resurgence that posed a challenge to the current, second resurgence. Unlike the second, the third resurgence does not seek to forget the past. On the contrary, it rushes to establish a commemoration as part of the twenty-first-century policies of memory, especially those connected with the legitimation and de-legitimation of long sustained wars (like Iraq), in the case of Europe. The third memory resurgence is widely spread thanks to the connectivity provided by digital media, which led to an increase in commemorative practices.

Due to Argentina's territorial location and history, some European commemorations are observed here, though they do not merit any television or local commemorating. Argentina has not participated in many commemorations (the World War II, the Holocaust, VE Day, the Hiroshima bombings) held in Europe, Asia or the United States. In recent years, though, Argentina began to participate in this type of collective memory, albeit with other references such as Cromañón (where 194 people died during a rock concert caused by a fire in the premises, on 30 December 2004), the AMIA attack, la noche de los lápices [the night of the pencils], of the beginning and the end of the military dictatorship, some national holidays, scandalous crimes committed by police officers or citizens, plane crashes. All these, and many others, are remembered. The Malvinas War has its own peculiarities, one of which is being the country's only modern war. Memory and commemoration are very local. Even though research into this war has increased during recent years, it has not produced anything significant (Bietti 2009: Vitale 1999; Sábato 1995; Varela 2000; Guelerman 2001; Vezzetti 1998, 2002; Martins 2003; Sarlo 2005; Guber 2001; Vitullo 2012).

Simultaneously with the memory phenomenon there have been changes in the concepts of 'hero' and 'heroism' in Argentina. Forster (2002) goes through the transformations that this concept has undergone in literature, from the Greeks up to the present. This is very useful for our analysis since a correlation between fiction and reality can be observed and it is also very clear when it comes to comparing what could be called 'a modern hero' versus 'a postmodern hero'. For Forster, the modern hero represents the birth of the autonomous individual, one that becomes the maker of his/her own destiny by defeating the conjoint forces of gods and nature (Forster, 2002: 76–77). On the contrary, the postmodern hero represents the triumph of nihilism: he/she becomes what he/she is by simply surviving his/her daily routine. According to Forster, the emergence of this hero is another transmutation that characterizes postmodernity, specifically, the substitution of the extenuating enumeration of life's trifles for the tragedy of history. Forster points out that:

> the everyday scenes, the countless accounts of family life, of love, of the details of trivial, ordinary, common existences, human lives (have replaced) those stories (of tragic-modern heroes) which have become inexplicable and unintelligible for men and women today.[1]
>
> (Forster 2002: 184)

Culture and memory: historical, political and social phenomena

Since we were children, it has been repeated 1,000 times that the Malvinas are Argentine. Schools had a more or less explicative narration as to why it was so. It appealed to the nationalistic sentiment of students and parents and exhibited strong nationalistic features. There were many maps. special attention was paid to geography and to the events that took place in 1833,[2] and the fact that the nation state had been asserting its sovereignty claim over the islands to different organizations was insisted upon. Many schoolbooks, especially those from the 1950–1960s,[3] centre on the territorial and the military-political narrations of the time. Thus, a cultural trait was born that persists to the present, a trait that conflates homeland with territory as a synonym of the national (a typical feature of modernity). This discourse remained the same throughout the dictatorship (1974–1984).

Contrary to this type of education, there is a discourse that emphasizes war in the islands (warfare) and the military junta's interference in it. This junta declared the war in 1982. The school discourse from that time indicated that there were at least two opposite cultural positions in Argentine society. That change began with the emergence of democracy (1984). It could be said that this new way of teaching and this partial cultural restructuring constitute a de-malvinization movement opposed to the pre-democratic primary and secondary. This movement would later bring relevant social and political consequences to Argentina.

Leaving the schools aside, the advent of the Malvinas War became the first completely mediatized major event (Sarlo, 1997: 2). Like the British, the Argentines saw for the first time images of the South Atlantic, of the ships, planes and soldiers that took part in the war. While television, which answered to the de facto government, hid information from the citizens, making them believe that battles were successful, the British were already preparing the attack that would lead the war to its end. Abruptly and to their surprise, television had to show the Argentine surrender, for many had believed in the triumph spread by the media.[4]

In contrast to this, schoolbooks from these last 30 years that narrate the Malvinas history show very few images of the war and the islands (only maps showing the combat zones). Curiously, most importance is now given to the narrative aspects of the war, rather than the geographical, historical or chronological ones.

The reaction of children and young people today is similar to that of some schoolbooks, as they seem to attach little importance to the islands and to Argentina's claims, asking why so small a territory should be annexed and why the islands are Argentine. But this is not just a budget-motivated change in the schoolbooks (fewer illustrations and commentaries); rather, it would appear that there has been a change in the state's policy regarding this Argentine cultural feature.

To comprehend these facts, it should be noticed that in Argentina the majority of those involved in the Malvinas War were conscripts who were still undergoing military training and who, therefore, were not proper soldiers. These 18-year-olds were sent with very few months of training, without the necessary economic and military resources[5] to fight a war that was born of the need to sustain the dictatorship through a nationalistic discourse (learnt in schools before the war) which was the media's job to spread. This explosive combination of media and dictatorship deprived Argentina of another young generation, again.[6]. Most of their contemporaries hold a nationalistic view about the Malvinas cause.

Having lost the war, these young men were hidden by the same people that had sent them to fight. They literally came back through the back door, with no recognition and no acceptance from society. It took many years until this was reversed and they were considered heroes. It was a long wait for vindication because, among other things, private soldiers and the military were conflated in the social imaginary and many of them supported extreme nationalistic discourses.

It was a strong, progressive cultural effort, especially promoted by the state during the last ten years, that created the possibility of somehow separating one group from the other, acknowledging good actions from both sides as well as condemning their bad actions. There were also several economic recognitions given to the families and the war veterans. Therefore, there are at least two coexisting cultural positions on the Malvinas, which move gradually between two extremes, extreme nationalism and complete demalvinization. In what follows, I shall try to expose some of the narratives that configure these cultural positions, explaining their characteristics and the facts that trigger each of them.

The narratives about the Malvinas War on Argentine television

Much has been written about the Malvinas War, from many different perspectives and standpoints, but very little about the commemoration of this event, specifically by on television. Although the media in general played a preponderant role during the Malvinas War (Sarlo 1997), the same cannot be said of commemorations.

Five years ago, television barely dared to reflect upon the Malvinas. While there were documentaries, novels and films on the subject, the war was not discussed publicly or at a massive scale. Too much pain and shame and too many unresolved core problems made it impossible to even think about the Malvinas.

As has already been mentioned, our aim in this work is to present, after the analysis of the discourses produced by each of the television shows and some exploratory research, the narratives that, expressing different cultural positions, were constructed around the Malvinas War on Argentine television during its thirtieth anniversary commemoration, for these narratives show a gradualness that goes from the triumphalist, nationalistic discourse to the discourse of a new vision, the diplomatic way, where the war is not against the British or the islands' inhabitants, but against the British colonial policy (even though this is not explicitly mentioned).

This gradualness provides evidence for the coexistence (within Argentina) of narratives and cultures that still promote 'modern' values, that step by step attempt a postmodern view of the war and start building a different representation of the hero. Though it could be said that, one way or another, all of them are directly or indirectly inscribed in the big narrative of history, some changes do not entirely leave this axis (it could hardly be otherwise, for the historical, cultural and social characteristics of Argentina do not seem propitious for breaking this axis), not only as a way of revalorization of a nationalist narrative, but also because this responds to Argentina conforming to a group of resistance to 'globalization' or neo-liberalism by means of the UNASUR[7] and MERCOSUR[8], namely the regionalization that is also a result and/or a consequence in the face of hegemonic movements.

Methodology and corpus

Within the broad cultural discourse studies framework (Shi-xu 2015), the methodology being used here is eminently qualitative and constitutes a case study, while the theoretical perspective largely a Latin American one (Pardo Abril 2007; Garcia da Silva 2009; Resende and Ramalho 2006; Pardo 2011).

The corpus consists of four television programmes, each of them corresponding to one of the terrestrial Argentine channels, broadcast in commemoration of the Malvinas War during 2012 ana programme broadcasted by a cable channel for the same reason and on the same date as the others.

The linguistic analysis conducted here is based upon the Information Hierarchy Theory[9] and, specifically within it, upon its focuses.[10] We know that all languages create hierarchies, that is they mitigate or reinforce information. Speakers, then, decide consciously or unconsciously how they order the hierarchy of everything they say (orally or textually).[11] In addition, mitigations and reinforcements can be recognized at a micro level that corresponds to the utterance.

Terrestrial programmes

The analysed programmes, all of them broadcast during 2012, are as follows:

- 'Malvinas a 30 años, los debates necesarios' [Malvinas, 30 years on, the necessary debates), Channel 7, broadcast on the channel's central news programme, 'Visión siete'.
- 'Malvinas, herida abierta' [Malvinas, an open wound], Telefé, broadcast on the channel's central news programme.
- 'Televisión registrada' (TVR) [Registered television], without a name as it was a part of the programme TVR.
- 'Malvinas, 30 años' [Malvinas, 30 years], Canal América, broadcast on the programme 'Animales sueltos' [Loose animals].

Cable programme

- 'Los siete días que cambiaron la historia' [The seven days that changed history], TN (Todo Noticias) (repeated with minimum variations on the programme 'A dos voces' on the same channel).

The narratives

The narratives that emerge from the first analysis of the programmes here proposed for study are at least five, which in a very general way can be termed as follows:

1. The nationalist and triumphalist narrative.
2. The pity or lack narrative.
3. The narrative of the correlation between dictatorship – crimes against humanity – the Malvinas War.
4. The narrative of a new vision – diplomatic way – (war is neither against the British nor the islanders).
5. The narrative of the false way.

We will try to show briefly some of these characteristics, so as to observe their fundamental traits and how they construct a hero that accompanies each narrative according to its properties. It is important to clarify that, though we have looked for the most representative examples of each characterization, many of these narratives intertwine and coexist within the same text.

Culture and its expression in different narratives

N1. The triumphalist narrative and the modern hero

'30 años', 'Animales sueltos', Canal América. An example of the triumphalist culture and discourse is the one conveyed by the América channel during its commemorative show, broadcast on the programme 'Animales sueltos'. This discourse is defined by its pronounced nationalism, its search for reparation of the image of those who participated in the Malvinas War and the discursive construction of a hero typical of epic poetry.

Let us briefly examine the general context of this show and some fragments of this narrative (N) that exemplify the afore-mentioned discourse. Each narrative has been assigned a number to obtain greater explicative clarity (N1, N2. etc.). Letters 'U' preceded by a number indicate utterances and their corresponding number. The sign '–' indicates each speaker. The corresponding speaker's name and his/her text in the dialogue appear after this '–'.

Communicative situation

Alejandro Fantino, the show's presenter, introduces this thirtieth anniversary of the Malvinas War anticipating that the people who will shortly be surrounding him are 'heroes'. As he himself explains, it is his desire that this show will be useful to 'the schools', and he refers to the Malvinas War using the following words: 'struggle', 'feat', 'absolutely heroic deed', 'war heroes', 'to make history with this show'. It is easily seen that this is an epic narrative that seeks the construction of a modern hero (in opposition to a postmodern one), Ooe that is capable of great deeds in order to fulfill a collective wish. Though this is no longer a geographic narrative as it was in the modern school, it is indeed a discourse that vindicates Argentine sovereignty over the islands, added to the fact that the previous heroes were distant in time[12] and did not have real epic resources. However, given the existence of the war (where, besides, so many young soldiers perished), it functions as a reinforcement of Argentine sovereignty; for, even though the war was lost, 'one cannot lose what one doesn't have', and the only thing that justifies that war is the conviction that the islands belong to Argentina.

Going back to the narrative, some of the guests have participated in other commemorative shows, in the present as well as the twenty-fifth anniversary of this war such as Esteban Triex (who was a private during the war) and Sergeant Villegas (cf. the linguistic analysis of his narratives in Pardo and Lorenzo-Dus, 2010b). The narrative that unites both of them is the one that shows the solidarity (he is a 'brother that life gave to me'[13]) between privates and their superiors, as Triex saved Villega's life. This narration is fundamental since one of the objections to the so-called triumphalist narrative is the fact that the relation between the privates and their superiors was something more than bad. Villegas says: 'Hoy la bastardean (a dicha relación) y la llenan de basura' ('Today they bastardize (that relation) and fill it with filth'). This is a statement that separates the triumphalist account from the 'narrative of lamentation' (which we will examine later).

The other guests invited to the show are Private Di Sciullo (a soldier who stayed on the islands for 74 days), Jorge Ledesma (who killed a British man in the islands, now a poet); Víctor Villagra (a former combatant who fought the British hand-to-hand) and Nicolás Kasanzew[14] (a journalist who covered the war from the islands).

Sitting in a semi-circle, each of the participants tells an anecdote that shows their 'courage' during the war. The most remarkable testimony is that of Ledesma, who tells how he killed Colonel Jones, Chief of the Parachute Infantry of the British forces.

We shall now examine some fragments that exemplify the discourse described above (the underlinings show each utterance's focus):

E1: Fantino: ¿A quién abatió Ledesma?

E2: Kasanzew: Herbert Jones, un tipo mítico por su valor, amado por sus soldados, un legendario tipo que los ingleses lloraron mares de lágrimas cuando Ledesma lo abatió (mientras Ledesma sonríe).

E3: Ledesma: Eran dos soldados del regimiento 12 que ya se habían agotado sus municiones, habían agotado todo y miraban al inglés con una cara de terror impresionante. E4: Yo cuando lo tengo, cuando veo eso le disparo (F: ¿con tu ametralladora?). E5: Sí, con mi ametralladora. El inglés cae con sus pies mirándome, y yo escucho que grita y se manotea el cinturón. E6: Lo único que pienso es que está buscando una granada para tirársela a ellos, entonces, sí, levanto la MAG, apunto y cuando le hago la segunda descarga, veo que se queda quieto (F: Ja).

U1: Fantino: Who did Ledesma gun down?

U2: Kasanzew: Herbert Jones, a fellow who was famed for his courage, loved by his soldiers, a legendary[15] fellow the British cried their eyes out when he was gunned down by Ledesma (Ledesma smiles).

U3: Ledesma: There were two soldiers from the 12th regiment, they had already run out of ammunition; they had run out of everything and were looking at the Englishman with shockingly terrified expressions. U4: When I got him, when I saw that I shot him. (F: With your machine gun?) U5: Yes, with my machine gun. The Englishman falls, his feet facing me, and I hear him scream and he grabs at his belt. U6: The only thing I could think of is that he was looking for a grenade to throw at them, so then, yes, I raise my MAG, aim, and when I shoot at him for the second time, I see that he lies still. (F: Ha).

Suddenly, Kasanzew applauds and cries 'Bravo!' Not all the participants applaud. An awkward moment is created, but the applause is already happening. This reveals a feeling of discomfort, as there is some awareness among the participants that this applause goes beyond what can be accepted in Argentina today as a socially tolerable discourse about the Falklands/Malvinas War.

In U1 as well as in U2, the focus corresponds to the one who 'guns down', Ledesma, instead of the one that is gunned down. What the viewer receives as the most prominent (in terms of Information Hierarchy) information is the 'hero's' surname. This 'heroic' action present in the narrative (gunning down the enemy) is emphasized with reinforcements like 'mythical fellow', 'courage', 'loved by his soldiers', 'cried their eyes out'. In a war context, these virtues exalt Jones's figure, but above all they exalt the hero's: he who did not kill any man, but someone who was important to the enemy. This argument, that glorifies the enemy to reinforce the modern hero's virtue, is typical of the triumphalist and nationalist narrative. This narrative intertwines with the one taught at school, now exacerbated by war. It is a part of Argentine cultural, social and political identity.

Another programme that resumes the triumphalist narrative, at least to a great degree, is:

C5N: Malvinas a 30 años: historias de héroes (Malvinas 30 years on: Stories of heroes). The triumphalist affiliation of the programme can already be observed in the title. At the beginning, in dialogue with Colonel Ballesteros, Eduardo Feinman[16] says (notice how the focus corresponds to the defence of Argentine sovereignty over the islands):

E1: Feinman: Nosotros aquí vamos a homenajear a los héroes, a nuestros héroes, que pusieron lo que había que poner en ese momento para defender a nuestra tierra, a las Islas Malvinas'.

E2: Coronel Ballesteros: Con sorpresa, por supuesto, porque no lo esperaba y alegría porque, por fin, veía que se recuperaban las Malvinas. E3: Uno pensaba que un gobierno nacional y más, estando a cargo de militares, que conocen los problemas de la guerra, no se iban a largar a la locura, a la aventura.

U1: Feinman: Here we are going to pay homage to the heroes, to our heroes, who at that time had what it took to defend our land, the Malvinas Islands.

U2: Coronel Ballesteros: Surprised, of course, because I wasn't expecting it, and with joy because, at last, I saw the Malvinas being regained. E3: One thought that a national government, more so being led by the military, who know war's troubles, wouldn't go wild, into adventure.

Despite Ballesteros' awareness that going into war was something crazy to do (focus in U3), both of them feel joy over the recovery of the islands (focus in U1). Appealing to that culture learnt during modernity, both the first narrative and this one occupy one extreme of a continuum.

N2: the lamentation narrative

'Malvinas a 30 años. Los debates necesarios', Canal 7, broadcast on the channel's central news programme, Visión siete, on 2 April from 19.00 to 21.00.

This narrative is defined by its emphasis on the violent and low-income situation that young soldiers had to face during the Malvinas War. In this case, the special programme, not suitable for children and young people as indicated at its beginning, starts with a series of images of the islands and of soldiers, missiles, the wounded, trenches, dead soldiers' helmets that signal poverty and the military's neglect of the young soldiers (note that this discourse is at odds with the lack of images in 1960s schools). It is also important to point out that this lengthy programme includes a very well documented historical first part, dealing with why the Malvinas are Argentine. Even though Argentine schooling did not have historical narratives about the islands, it did have narratives about the reason for sovereignty. Thus Argentine modern culture appears in a text whose beginning is opposed to it, since the lamentation narrative, which focuses on the details of the soldiers' everyday lives and their survival instead of their heroic deeds, is typical of postmodernity. As a consequence, the linking of several narratives can be observed throughout the show. The rest of the narratives emerges from the reproduction of a speech given by the nation's president (a direct speech that functions as a reinforcement of the intended message). Her speech is framed by the now known 'lamentation narrative'. The next narrative links the Malvinas War with the theme of the return of democracy to Argentina. Lastly, another type of narrative is established from the claim that the diplomatic way appears as the only just way of claiming the Malvinas. It is stressed that in the present, just as it was before the war, but especially today, claims are made by means of diplomacy.

Fragment of the speech by the Argentine President, Cristina Fernández de Kirchner (CFK):

> E1: ¿Por qué será que la historia se lleva siempre a los más jóvenes en los momentos difíciles? E2: Por eso mi reconocimiento a esa juventud que marchó a las islas sin preparación, sin los pertrechos suficientes, sin la formación, yo diría también muchos con miedo, quién no tiene miedo de ir a la guerra. E3: Los que no sienten miedo no son los valientes, valientes son los que avanzan aún con miedo. E4: Esos miles de jóvenes, esos miles de jóvenes, esos cientos de jóvenes que estuvieron en las islas y dejaron su vida allí, hoy tienen para siempre no solo el reconocimiento sino la memoria eterna del pueblo argentino. E5: He dirigido una carta al titular de la Cruz Roja Internacional para que tome las medidas pertinentes e interceda ante el Reino Unido para poder identificar a los hombres argentinos y aún ingleses que aún no fueron identificados. E6: Cada madre tiene el derecho inalienable como Antígona de Sófocles de enterrar a sus muertos y llorar a sus muertos.

> U1: Why is it that history always takes away the youngest in difficult times?[17] U2: Because of that, my recognition goes to the youth that marched to the islands with no preparation, with not enough equipment or supplies, with no training, many of them, I would also say, with fear, who is not afraid of going into war? U3: The brave ones are not those who feel no fear, the brave ones are those who go on even in fear. U4: Those thousands of young men, those thousands of young men, hundreds of young men who were in the islands and left their lives there, today and forever they have not only the acknowledgement, but the eternal memory of the Argentine people. U5: I have addressed a letter to the principal of the International Red Cross so as to identify the Argentine men and even the British who have not yet been identified. U6: Like Sophocles' Antigone, each mother has the inalienable right to bury their dead and cry for their dead.

While this corresponds to the 'lamentation' or 'lack' narrative, as we already pointed out, it also shows important divergences. The focuses themselves indicate this. The fact that the young men have no equipment, no supplies and no training does appear, but they are also recognized in that they went without fear. This fear, though, is not experienced as a lack, but as a token of heroism and bravery (U3: 'the brave ones are those who go on even in fear'). Here it could be said that she joins the triumphalist discourse. It can also be observed that memory has great importance, for it is established as a way of acknowledging the young soldiers in the face of the indifference and even the rejection that characterized the war's first years (U4: 'but the eternal memory of the Argentine people'). What is here attempted is a reinterpretation of the facts and a discourse that appeals to cultural change. She then combines the lamentation narrative with the theme of dictatorship and crimes against humanity through an indirect reference to the disappearance of people during dictatorship times (U6: 'each mother… to bury their dead and cry for their dead'), even if, in so doing, she must ask for the search and recognition of the 'British who have not yet been identified' (U5). This international and humanitarian right puts the Argentines and the British on the same plane, in a view that is less nationalistic and more connected with human rights.

N3: The narrative of the correlation between dictatorship – crimes against humanity – democracy

In Channel 7, in another segment of the same recently analysed programme, we found a narrative that deepens the opposition between crimes against humanity (as the afore-mentioned disappearance of people perpetrated during the dictatorship) and democracy, placing the latter next to the 'fair cause' of the islands and its misuse by the dictators who led Argentina into a war: '¿Cómo fue posible que una dictadura usara una legítima causa?' ('How was it possible for a dictatorship to use a legitimate cause?') (said by one of the journalists in the channel's studio). At the same time, this phrase is reinforced by the testimony of Eduardo Ortuondo, who was tied to stakes and tortured by his superiors on the battlefield. He mentions the *desaparecidos* and compares the torture inflicted by the Argentine military chiefs to their soldiers, with the crimes against humanity they perpetrated through state terrorism.

> Luego del Acto del 25 de mayo […] y automáticamente cuando se rompió la formación fuimos a nuestras posiciones en donde me metieron en un pozo de agua helada hasta el cuello. Cuando llegó el telegrama de mi casa, aquel 9 de abril […] no quería volver al regimiento […] porque todo lo que ustedes saben de los desaparecidos, lo veíamos y veíamos el maltrato que tenían los testigos de Jehová, los cuales todos los días eran torturados a golpes.
>
> After the Ceremony for the 25th of May […] and automatically when the formation was broken we resumed our positions where they submerged me to the neck in a well full of frozen water. That 9th of April, when the telegram arrived from my home […] I didn't want to go back to the regiment […] because everything you know about the desaparecidos, we saw that and saw the mistreatment of the Jehovah's Witnesses, who were beaten and tortured on a daily basis.

Notice that what the focuses highlight is, precisely, the ways of torturing. In the commemorative show in TVR on Channel 9, the link between the Malvinas and crimes against humanity is manifested in the interview that the journalist Daniel Tognetti conducted with Benjamín Menéndez[18], where the latter is asked:

P (Periodista): ¿<u>Estaquearon</u>?, ¿los estaqueaban <u>a los soldados</u>?
BM (Benjamín Menéndez): Puede ser que alguien haya <u>estaqueado</u>. Es un castigo que figuraba <u>en el reglamento</u>.
P: Es un castigo, pregunto yo: <u>¿aberrante?</u>
BM: Si figura en el reglamento, <u>alguien lo puede hacer</u>.
J (Journalist): <u>Did you use stakes</u>? Did you tie the <u>soldiers to stakes</u>?

BM: It may have happened that someone used stakes. It's a punishment that was in the regulations.
J: It's a punishment, I ask you: is it aberrant?
BM: If it's in the regulations, anyone can do it.

The lack of precision in BM's answer (similar to Jorge Rafael Videla,[19] who referred to those murdered during the dictatorship with a metaphor, 'desaparecidos') admits to the use of stakes for torture during the war. This further connects the Malvinas War with the crimes against humanity perpetrated by the dictators.

Telefé, another private television channel, also presents, in different sections, a narrative that connects the themes of dictatorship and war:

> Si la dictadura tenía una forma de perpetuarse esa era la guerra de Malvinas (If there was a way for the dictatorship to perpetuate itself, it was the Malvinas War).

We can see, then, an oscillation: on the one hand, the war is associated with dictatorship, as the military's meddling is considered the only reason why there was a war; on the other hand, there is an effort to separate that deed from the dictatorship as regards the young and their heroism as soldiers (not as military), since their images could only be vindicated if that dissociation is achieved.

It is a cultural process that goes from attachment to the national, from the triumphalist and pro-war narrative, to achieving a culture that separates the war from the dictatorship, allowing the emergence of a postmodern, lacking hero who reaches his/her epopee in misery and through the worst combat conditions, returning, precisely, neither victorious nor triumphant, but a hero nonetheless. Step by step, these different cultural visions of the same phenomenon make their way. We shall examine two more of them.

N4: The narrative of a new vision – diplomatic way

Another recurring narrative maintains that the claim of sovereignty over the islands must be made through by diplomacy. This discourse has its roots in the education Argentines have always received. It cannot be said that this is a new narrative, only that it was revived, of course with greater strength, since the war began.

Brunstein, in Channel 7's commemoration, says:

> Reclamo diplomático continuó hasta ahora. Los que viven ahí saben que vivían en territorio en litigio (A continuous diplomatic claim up to the present. The ones living there know they are living in a disputed territory).

This can be also observed in TVR when part of a CFK's speech is reproduced:

> Sentarse a dialogar y negociar acerca de la cuestión de la soberanía de las Islas Malvinas (To sit down to discuss and negotiate the issue of the sovereignty over the Malvinas Islands).

N5: The narrative of the false way

What is next reproduced is not a television programme, but a document signed by different people who proposed an 'alternative vision' of the war. They are journalists, presenters, politicians and writers, many of whom are members of *Clarín* and *La Nación*, two right-wing newspapers suspected of complicity with the military dictatorship.

The following is a paragraph from this supposed option:

> A tres décadas de la trágica aventura militar de 1982 carecemos aún de una crítica pública del apoyo social que acompañó a la guerra de Malvinas y movilizó a casi todos los sectores de la sociedad argentina. Entre los motivos de aquel respaldo no fue menor la adhesión a la causa-Malvinas, que proclama que las islas son un 'territorio irredento', hace de su 'recuperación' una cuestión de identidad y la coloca al tope de nuestras prioridades nacionales y de la agenda internacional del país. (Three decades after the tragic military adventure of 1982 we still lack public criticism of the social endorsement that accompanied the Malvinas war and mobilized almost every group of the Argentine society. Not minor among the reasons of that endorsement was the adherence to the Malvinas cause, which claims that the islands are an 'irredenta', turns their 'retrieval' into an identity issue and puts it on the top of our national concerns and of the country's international agenda.')
>
> Going beyond what this text states, one of its promoters, the ex-congressman Fernando Iglesias, declared to Radio Continental that 'el hecho de que las Islas formen parte de Gran Bretaña y la existencia de una base militar ahí es injustificable y <u>forma parte de los reclamos absolutamente legítimos que hace la Argentina</u>' ('the fact that the Islands are a part of Great Britain and the existence of a military base there are unjustifiable, this <u>constitutes a part of the absolutely legitimate claims asserted by Argentina</u>').

With this, not only does he take back the main reasoning of the former statement; at the same time, he does not question the Argentine sovereignty over the Malvinas Islands (notice the focus and the reinforcement: 'absolutely'). In terms of Kohan, Blanco and Imperatore (1993), this narrative is still 'subject to the idea of a just cause' and is not an alternative narrative. I propose to call this 'the narrative of the false way'. It is a discourse that postulates an inexistent 'happy medium' that, from a postmodern and pro-hegemonic perspective, could get rid of national issues and of the idea of a just cause. Because of this, it does not relate to the Latin American anti-colonialist and resistance movements, of which Argentina is a part, that emerge precisely as counter to globalization. At the same time, though it seems to question that idea, this pretension remains nevertheless attached to it, as any argument in favour or against it is based on the belief that it is necessary to discuss the notions of identity and national sovereignty, which in turn support the assumption of a just cause.

Conclusions

It is important to notice that all narratives in the examined programmes respond to the idea of a just cause (the culture learnt in schools during modernity). A narrative that did not take this warrant (in argumentative terms) into account would not be possible, as in Argentina the ideas of national sovereignty, territorial outlines or frontiers have not yet been modified by postmodernity. On the contrary, present-day Latin America is experiencing one of the most important regionalization and anti-colonialism processes of its entire history, in counterbalance to European or American postmodernity. This war, the last of the wars that make up modernity, adheres to the idea of a sovereign nation state and also to a modern conception of the hero. It is the hero of the great deed that appears as 'postmodernized' in the lamentation or lack narrative. The non-triumphalist narratives can be considered as having some postmodern aspects, since they question the military's heroism, fully support the claim over the islands through diplomacy and require a new rights-based vision on war crimes as crimes against humanity. The narrative of the false way pretends to be set in a more postmodern perspective but fails before the idea of a just cause and the (untidy) arguments of the peoples' supposed right to self-determination. This narrative would be the counterpart of the triumph, for behind its arguments is a pro-colonialist posture typical of the pan-American modernity. In the modern-postmodern counterpoint, this somewhat leaves it tied to the old ideas.

In addition to this it is worth mentioning that, with the exception of the triumphalist and the false way, these narratives do not appear as 'pure' forms; rather they form a continuum which goes from triumphalism through the narrative of pity, lamentation or lack, the connection dictatorship–crimes against humanity–the Malvinas War, a new vision through diplomacy and, finally, in counterpoint but also closing a circle, to the narrative of the false way. There is still a long way to go between modernity and post modernity in Argentina on this and many other topics.

Notes

1 To observe the differences between the ways of representing heroes in Great Britain and Argentina, see Pardo and Lorenzo-Dus (2010a).
2 See section 'What we talk about when we talk about the Malvinas Islands' in this chapter.
3 It should be noted that, in those years also, there were de facto military governments.
4 To read about the military's anecdotes and life experiences of the Malvinas war, cf. Corbalán (2011). For the view of the Argentine military commandos, cf. Ruiz Moreno (1986).
5 All these circumstances that soldiers had to undergo would bring as a result the emergence of the 'lamentation narrative', which will be discussed later in this chapter.
6 I say 'again' because Argentina had already lost the young generation that the Dictatorship 'disappeared' (that is, murdered).
7 The Union of South American Nations (UNASUR) is an international organization whose objectives are building a South American identity and citizenship, as well as developing an integrated regional space. It is formed by the 12 countries of South

America. These population of these countries amounts to 400 million inhabitants, that is, 68 per cent of the total population of Latin America.

8 The Southern Common Market (MERCOSUR) is a sub-regional block formed by Argentina, Brazil, Paraguay (now in process of reincorporation), Uruguay and Venezuela. Bolivia, Chile, Colombia, Ecuador and Peru are its associate members And New Zealand and Mexico are its observers. Its official languages are Spanish and Portuguese.

9 The Information Hierarchy Theory, called Functional Sentence Perspective, was developed by the Prague School. It posits a hierarchical division of sentences in theme and rheme (or topic and comment). The former has lesser informative strength than the rheme. Its application to the utterance (sentences put to use) and to the text has been developed by Pardo (1986, 1996, 2011).

10 Focuses are located in the rhemes and respond to Spanish word order, in which the information with the greatest degree of communicative dynamism (what makes the utterance go on until it is completed) goes at the end and closure of each utterance.

11 Given the Spanish word order, VsO (verb, subject in the desinence, object), the most focal zone is the one realized at the end of each utterance. It is generally preceded by a comma or by a relativizer plus complement construction with an adverbial function.

12 See the Rivero gaucho's case in 'What we talk about when we talk about the Malvinas Islands'.

13 All quotations in this paragraph are attributed to Sergeant Villegas.

14 Nicolás Kasanzew is a journalist who covered the Malvinas war from the islands on television (for the official channel at the time, ATC) and who was accused of giving a triumphalist version of the war when the country was in fact facing defeat.

15 It is important to remember that at the time of his death Colonel Jones was 30 years old.

16 A journalist known for his controversial statements on different subjects. Regarding the Malvinas, he adheres to the triumphalist narrative.

17 Here, the president refers to the *desaparecidos* ('missing people', most of whom were young) during the military dictatorship (1974–1984).

18 Brigadier General and military governor of the islands during the war. He was the one who surrendered the Islands to the British.

19 President of the military junta during the dictatorship, found guilty of crimes against humanity and died in prison.

References

Bietti, L. (2009). Entre la cognición política y la cognición social: el discurso de la memoria colectiva en la Argentina. *Discurso & Sociedad*, 3(1): 44–89.

Corbalán, L. (2011). Malvinas en primera línea. *Vivencias y anécdotas de integrantes del Regimiento de Infantería 4.* Buenos Aires: Edivérn.

Forster, R. (2002). *Crítica y sospecha.* Buenos Aires: Paidós.

Garcia da Silva, D. E. (2009). Representações discursivas da pobreza e discriminação na mídia. In *Discurso em questão: representação, gênero, identidade e discriminação.* Goiânia, GO, Brasil: Cãnone Editorial, pp. 63–74.

Guelermanm, S. J. (ed.) (2001). *Memorias en presente: identidad y transmisión en la Argentina posgenocidio.* Buenos Aires: Grupo Editorial Norma.

Guber, R. (2001). *¿Por qué Malvinas? De la causa nacional a la guerra absurda.* México: FCE.

Hoskins, A. (2001). New memory: mediating history. *Historical Journal of Film, Radio and Television*, 21(4): 333–346.

Hoskins, A. and O'Loughlin, B. (2010). *War and Media*. Cambridge: Polity Press

Kohan, M., Blanco, O. and Imperatore, A. (1993). Trashumantes de neblina, nos las hemos de encontrar. De cómo la literatura cuenta la guerra de Malvinas. *Revista Espacios*, 13 (dic. 1993–marzo 1994), Buenos Aires, Facultad de Filosofía y Letras, Universidad de Buenos Aires, pp. 82–86. Available online at: http://golosinacanibal.blogspot.com.ar/2008/12/trashumantes-de-neblina-no-las-hemos-de.html (last accessed 2 August 2012).

Martins, L. (2003). Estragos de la experiencia y cuerpos re(in)sistentes (notas sobre narrativa argentina). *Espéculo: Revista de Estudios Literarios*. Madrid: Universidad Complutense de Madrid. http://www.ucm.es/info/especulo/numero25/lmartins.html (last accessed 25 August 2012).

Pardo, M. L. (1986). Hacia una redefinición de las nociones de tema y rema. De la oración al discurso, *Filología*, 21(1): 25-55

Pardo, M.L. 1996. *Derecho y lingüística: Cómo se juzga con palabras*. Buenos Aires: Nueva Visión.

Pardo, M. L. (2011). *Teoría y metodología de la investigación lingüística. Método sincrónico-diacrónico de análisis lingüístico de textos*. Buenos Aires: Tersites.

Pardo, M. L. and Lorenzo-Dus, N. (2010a). The Falklands/Malvinas 25 years on: a comparative analysis of constructions of heroism on Argentinean and British television. *Journal of Multicultural Discourses*, 5(3): 253–270.

Pardo, M. L. and Lorenzo-Dus, N. (2010b). El ACD y el discurso televisivo sobre la guerra de Malvinas. Un análisis comparativo argentino-británico de cómo se construye nuestra memoria social. *Texturas. Estudios interdisciplinarios sobre el discurso*, 9(9/10): 223–252.

Pardo Abril, N. (2007). *Cómo hacer análisis crítico del discurso. Una perspectiva latinoamericana*. Santiago de Chile: Frasis.

Pérez, M. V. *et al.* (2012). Memoria y pedagogía: el abordaje de Malvinas en las escuelas balcarceñas antes y después de la guerra. ISFD Sede: Instituto Superior de Formación Docente y Técnica No. 32. Región 20. Balcarce. Provincia de Buenos Aires. Available at: www/TRABAJOS%202014/INFD_investigacion_v2012b3.pdf.

Ruiz Moreno, I. (1986). *Comandos en acción*. Buenos Aires: Editorial Heliasta.

Resende, V. de M. and Ramalho, V. (2006). Análise de discurso crítica. São Paolo. Editorial Contexto.

Sábato, H. (1995). Las vueltas de la memoria. *Ciencias Sociales*, 22. Buenos Aires: Facultad de Ciencias Sociales. Universidad de Buenos Aires.

Sarlo, B. (1997). *¿La voz universal que toma partido? Crítica y autonomía*. Nueva sociedad, 150, julio–agosto.

Sarlo, B. (2005). *Tiempo pasado. Cultura de la memoria y giro subjetivo. Una discusión*. Buenos Aires: Siglo XXI.

Shi-xu (2015). Cultural discourse studies, in K. Tracy, C. Ilie and T. Sandel (eds), *International Encyclopedia of Language and Social Interaction*. Oxford: Wiley-Blackwell.

Terragno, R. (2002). *Falklands*. Buenos Aires: Ediciones de LaFlor.

Varela, M. (2000). Memoria y medios de comunicación, o la coartada de las identidades. V Congreso Latinoamericano de Ciencias de la Comunicación, organized by ALAIC (Asociación Latinoamericana de los Investigadores de la Comunicación), Chile: Santiago de Chile.

Vezzetti, H. (1998). Activismos de la memoria: El 'escrache', *Punto de Vista* 62: 1–7.

Vezzetti, H. (2002). *Pasado y presente. Guerra, dictadura y sociedad en la Argentina*. Buenos Aires: Siglo XXI.

Vitale, M. A. (1999). Los discursos golpistas en la prensa gráfica argentina. Las memorias discursivas del golpe militar de 1930. In G. Soto (ed.), Discursos para el cambio. Selection of the articles presented during the III Coloquio Latinoamericano de Estudios del Discurso. Santiago de Chile. Universidad de Chile y Pontificia Universidad Católica de Chile. CD-ROM.

Vitullo, J. (2012). *Islas imaginadas. La guerra de Malvinas en la literatura y el Cine Argentinos.* Buenos Aires: Corregidor.

Winter, J. (2006). *Remembering War: The Great War between Memory and History in the Twentieth Century.* New Haven, CT: Yale University Press.

9 Modernity, postmodernity, culture and representations of work in the discourse of the Argentine extreme poor[1]

Introduction

This chapter intends to analyse the cultural differences between modern and postmodern capitalist logic (Ángulo Aguilazocho y Lozanía Casares 2005) in relation to the way in which work is represented in the discourse of the homeless inhabitants of Buenos Aires. Modern society is slowly but surely turning postmodern, thereby changing 'from a producers' into a consumers' society, from a work ethic-orientated society into one ruled by consumer aesthetics' (Bauman [1998], 2003: 12).

Homelessness is essentially linked with extreme poverty. In Argentina, an adult who cannot afford a basket of basic goods and services (food, clothing and public utilities) with an estimated cost of 566.43 pesos is considered extremely poor. Most of these adults live on the streets, are out of work and have no roof over their heads – even if they do own a dwelling, it is currently inhabited by others, be they family members or not related.

We aim to show that their life stories reflect the cultural differences between the modern and postmodern view of work, with various consequences. They contain two main discursive representations:

1 Work as seen from the 'modern' perspective, i.e. as entailing both physical effort and personal involvement in the creation of a product, as well as enabling individuals to plan for a stable future and helping construct their identity;
2 Work as considered from the 'postmodern' standpoint, i.e. as immaterial and approached without personal commitment, unstable, precarious, associated with welfare benefits or charity aid and providing no basis for future planning.

Since 2003 our team have been conducting life-story interviews with over 60 homeless people over 17 living in Buenos Aires. The examples with which this chapter is concerned are drawn from this corpus.

Our theoretical framework has been provided by cultural discourse studies and we have used qualitative methods to examine the data. The linguistic analysis I conduct is based upon the Information Hierarchy Theory and, specifically within it, upon the focuses (Pardo 2011). In this respect we have taken up and reformulated (Pardo 2011) the notion of information hierarchy as conceived by the Prague School (Mathesius 1939; Firbas 1992). We have drawn on Shi-xu's (2013) concept of culture

To start with, culture, and for that matter, East, West, Chinese, Asian, the global South, and the like, should not be seen essentialistically as a reified, monolithic or homogeneous entity. Moreover, it should not be conceived of metaphorically along national, gender, generational, professional or organizational lines, such as 'national culture', 'gender culture', 'corporate culture' (Gunnarsson 2000). Rather, culture is to be understood holistically, and so, historically, socially, economically, politically, ethnically, locally and globally (Robertson 1992; Tomlinson 1997). Thus, 'culture' is a set of concepts, representations, attitudes, values, symbols, styles, rules, patterns, (power) relations, and so on, of particular social communities, which evolve through human civilizations and the world's local and global histories on the one hand, and are created, maintained, contested and transformed in and through both human (inter)actions and artefacts on the other (Pang 1993; Shi-xu 2005). In this light, the contemporary world may be seen as one in which the American-Western cultures dominate, repress, and prejudice against the rest of human cultures and the latter realign themselves and resist against that unequal order.

Information Hierarchy Theory and focus

Information Hierarchy Theory is a linguistic approach (Pardo 1992, 1996, 2011) inspired by Functional Sentence Perspective (Firbas 1992; Mathesius 1939; Pardo 1996, 2011; Weil 1844). Information hierarchy is a language principle according to which the information that language users provide is presented in a certain sequence that depends both on the word order of the language spoken and on the speaker's intention to highlight certain features. It is also linked to cognitive processes in which old information is replaced by new information through the repetition of forms and meanings. In Romance languages like Spanish, as Functional Sentence Perspective scholars (Weil 1844; Mathesius 1939; Firbas 1964) have shown, the most significant information is placed at the end of the utterance, called rheme. Within it a focus can be identified, usually preceded by some supra-segmental element, such as a pause. The focus constitutes the point of orientation of the utterance – its most dynamic, communicative part (Firbas 1964, 1992). In Romance languages, speakers use mandatory pauses to mark these focal points, which, needless to say, speech transcriptions should reflect in order to preserve the meaning of the utterance. In the following sentence, for instance, the theme is 'Those who live in this shanty town', and the rheme (i.e., the remaining part of the utterance), contains the focus: 'the government to help them':

Example

Rheme in bold, Focus in bold italics

> The poor of the [Argentine] capital **feel excluded from the system because the City Government *has forsaken us***
>
> *Poverty, extreme poverty and culture in Argentina*

To discuss extreme poverty in Argentina, Latin America or even the world at large in terms of cultural studies is not easy. The survival strategies deployed by those who suffer from it do not, in our view, constitute a culture but alternative ways to deal with a situation in which their human rights are violated.

There can be no culture of hunger, life on the streets, or extreme poverty, just as there can be no culture of forced disappearance, torture or child theft. These are crimes, plain and simple, even if those who perpetrate them may share certain features. In the present case they are an outcome of the capitalist system, which pays lip service to the human rights to work, housing and health, but fails to enforce them, because, within its logic, inequity and exclusion are foreseeable consequences (cf. Goldin and Reinert 2012). Capitalism, whether modern or postmodern, sees no crime in poverty; in this respect, it may be considered as a 'culture', namely a way of looking at life or the world. The poor, on the other hand, merely endure the situation in which they have been placed, creating values that express ways of surviving an unwanted state of affairs rather than a culture of their free choice.

Among the writers who do speak of a culture of poverty is Oscar Lewis (1959), who draws a distinction between poverty and poverty culture (cf. Mohan 2011), an idea that has been received with as much praise as criticism. Such culture has been handed down throughout the generations through enculturation,[2] a process that resembles a vicious circle. This would explain why the economic conditions for its eradication have never been created.

To Lewis poverty culture is most likely to be developed by the lower strata of fast changing societies. It cannot take place in primitive or caste societies, whereas in fascist and socialist countries, as well as in advanced and prosperous capitalist ones, this life style tends to disappear. Only 20 per cent of the urban poor are true poverty culture bearers, while infrastructural and structural conditions would account for the other 80 per cent, whose customs and behaviour would not be deeply rooted or inherited.

Lewis's interpretative model is made up of some 70 long-lasting inter-related psychological, social and economic features, which are particularly related to the worldviews, aspirations and character of the people living in such 'culture'. Grigulevich and Veselkin (unpublished manuscript) compared Lewis's abject poverty culture to a 'hereditary disease', believing that his theory served to reinforce the status quo and mollify the class struggle. In the United States, Lewis's views were adopted in racist and reactionary circles.

Gunnar Myrdal (1962) introduces the notion of underclass.[3] This does not apply to the materially poor, but to groups of young people and ethnic minorities characterized by habitual drug abuse, criminal activities, high unemployment and broken homes. Wilson (1987) sees it as a new form of poverty brought about by deindustrialization. Auletta's typology (1992) distinguishes between (1) the passive poor (long-time welfare beneficiaries); (2) street criminals, school drop-outs, and drug addicts; (3) those who live by stealing or work in the black economy; (4) the 'traumatized', namely the homeless, the mentally ill, the elderly and the helpless. These groups would possess the abnormal/antisocial behavioural traits that define 'abject poverty' (Monreal 1996). We wonder whether we might talk of an abject culture. Might we even conceive an antisocial culture whose members would range from criminals to those suffering from psychiatric disorders? Might people with a certain mental condition share a culture of their disease?

The poor have often been socially excluded from an increasingly unfair and polarized Argentine society. The term 'exclusion' refers to the conditions that encourage or make possible the rejection or separation of certain members, who are stigmatized and denied access to institutional or other benefits.

Poverty is nowadays an unusually complex phenomenon (Rudra 2005), difficult to approach from a single, all-encompassing perspective. Quantitative estimates based on socio-economic variables afford only a prima facie view of the structural conditions that determine its nature and extent. They provide, at most, an outline of the situation and trends, being more than inadequate to account for poverty dynamics or its consequences for the lives of those who suffer from it. The traditional and most widespread ways to define poverty are the Unsatisfied Basic Needs (UBN) and the Poverty Line (PL) methods. Both have been questioned, however, and consensus has been reached on the need for an all-embracing methodology that might enable us to assess 'social exclusion'. This would point to the suitability of micro-level case studies of the people living in poverty, with discourse analysis as a useful tool, since macroeconomic indicators have proved insufficient.

The term 'poverty' must therefore be re-conceptualized: to ascertain its real dimensions we must enquiry into needs that cannot be translated into figures, as well as into the relations between the poor and the non-poor (Pardo 2013). A new, more heterogeneous profile of poverty would entail a re-examination of social policy, which may tackle either its causes or its effects by focusing on the traits of those who live in it or on the structural conditions that have placed them in such situation (Valentine 1992).

Work vis-à-vis modern and postmodern culture: the Argentine case

From a modern perspective, the importance of work lies in its transformational capacity. This affects not only the material objects to which it applies, work in the classical sense, but also individuals and their social relations, generating a structuring structure (Giddens 1995) relation that is reshaped through a feedback process.

Hardt and Negri (2002) and Virno (2003) suggest that the classical notion of work has been increasingly replaced by a more disembodied view that matches a new reality: work is being considered more and more as an 'intellectual, immaterial, and communicative' force (Hardt and Negri 2002).

This immaterial view of work tends to subsume all previous kinds of work, and is linked to the postmodernization process driven by information technology.

Just as modern production tended to become industrial, postmodern production is service-orientated and IT-dependent (Virno 2003). This transformation has been taking place globally, with major social consequences. The growth of the service sector, both in absolute and relative terms, has led to a redefinition of the classical manufacturing process (Hermo and Wydler 2006; Irogbe, 2005).

These changes have not happened overnight: the two models coexist in various ways in different countries, according to the socioe-conomic and educational make-up and needs of the social groups that inhabit them. Thus, they operate at the same time and within the overarching capitalist system, albeit with marked differences. On the other hand, since any change, particularly in the technological and economic fields, 'affects ethics, values, and religion' (Lerner and Schramm 1967), this process has sparked huge cultural transformations.

In Argentina, perceptions of work started to change significantly in 1991 with the so-called Employment Act, which introduced flexibility[4] in employment contracts, stating that fixed-term employees would have no right to redundancy pay when the agreed end date was reached[5]. A deregulation process was thus ushered in that involved a severe reduction in the protection afforded to workers under Argentine law. Limits were set on redundancy pay for permanent employees and the president was allowed to curb the right to strike by decree.

Argentine workers had to adapt to the growing precariousness of labour brought about by the new legislation. The 1990s were characterized by high unemployment (18 per cent) as well as by the meeting of the modern and postmodern work cultures. Updating became essential: the workings of technology and financial systems had to be mastered. Manufacturing was neglected and the service sector focused on. As ways of living, working and schooling changed, many were unable to rise to the challenge. The devastating economic crisis of 2001 brought about street protests followed by a deadly crackdown and the resignation of a president who fled the scene by helicopter. Many Argentines were thrown out of the system and urban poverty[6] reared its ugly head.

The newly impoverished middle class encompassed bricklayers, butchers, factory workers, horse trainers, pizza cooks, barbecuers, architects and other professionals, art students, taxi-drivers and artists. Extreme poverty forced many of them to live on the streets. A clear distinction appears in the discourse of those who took part in my research project between work as a manual activity that creates a product (work in the classical/modern sense) and immaterial work, such as selling a magazine when they have not been involved in editing and production.

The magazine *Hecho en Buenos Aires*[7] is not, as we might think, a home-grown phenomenon but was rather inspired by *The Big Issue*. Towards the end of the 1980s, the homeless of New York started selling the *Street News*, a newspaper set up to provide them with employment. The initiative was met with mixed reactions, rejected by the police and feared by certain members of the public concerned about harassment. Though eventually publication ceased, the idea was taken up in Europe. In 1991 Gordon Roddick, owner of The Body Shop, and John Bird launched *The Big Issue* magazine in London, establishing the International Network of Street Papers three years later (Noblía 2003).

Hecho en Buenos Aires was brought out for the first time in 2000, funded by the British Council, the World Bank and the Lévi-Strauss Foundation. Originally conceived as a way of helping the homeless into a job and out of the streets, its sale has come to be seen as immaterial work, since they do not contribute to its contents or to the editing process. They tend to view it as charity rather than as proper work.

The relations between the homeless, NGOs, and public policy are thus fragile and unstable, since what is offered as a job is not considered as such. A culture clash takes place between those who embrace the dual (material/immaterial) understanding of work and those who stick to the classical view, since they are currently unemployed and the tasks they used to perform answered that description. They take pride in their handmade products, value a regular income that might enable them to plan for the future, and see their trade as something that is learnt through training or long practice. Street selling, on the other hand, is work in the postmodern or immaterial sense. It does not produce any goods; nor can it be learnt by study or experience. It cannot guarantee a regular income, as its success depends on the goodwill of passers-by and cannot therefore secure a future for those who rely on it. Beyond the immediate consequences for job adjustment, these contrasting approaches reveal a difference in social values.

Participants' positive attitudes towards the *Hecho en Buenos Aires* project translate into expressions of gratitude to the state and sponsoring NGOs for the opportunity to earn their daily bread.

The following examples have been drawn from the life-story interviews (LSI) we carried out and analysed by applying Information Hierarchy Theory.

Initials have been substituted for names to protect interviewee identity. A 'u' followed by a numeral indicates utterance number within a particular LSI. Rhemes are underscored and foci are marked with underlined italics. M stands for male and F for female subject and the numbers next to them indicate age.

CR (M, 34)

CR (u60) Most new vendors, who come from the street, from the place from which we came too, *think that selling the magazine is like begging, get it?*

Interviewer (e61) Of course selling is ... it's a job. Things are sold everywhere: here they sell coffee; over there they sell honey ... that is...

CR (u62) It is a job ... Of course, but it's a psychological issue, because you feel ... I'm telling you because *the same's happened to me, like you're asking the community to help you.*

Our analysis of these utterances yielded four topics: *magazine, charity, work,* and *community*. Rather than losing face in front of the interviewer, CR admits to having a psychological issue that prevents him from considering street selling as a proper job, since he cannot account for it in any other way. This would point to the two cultural views of work discussed above: the postmodern and modern perspective. In refusing to regard his current occupation as work, he is inwardly and dialogically comparing it with an alternative notion that he fails to spell out. The interviewee focuses on the idea of street selling as begging (*charity*): you're asking the community to help you, which introduces the *community* as a topic. He then agrees with the interviewer (*It is a job ... Of course),* which could be construed as a compliance strategy, also aimed at keeping his good image (Brown and Levinson 1987) Finally, he insists on the idea of selling as asking for help (something he has already experienced in the form of begging and receiving charity aid), and is therefore placed once more in a defensive position concerning his image. Again the reference to charity constitutes the focus of the utterance.

M (F, 50)

M (u44) I'm grateful to everybody [at the magazine] because they're helping me, *they're giving me a hand.* But what I need above all is to have a job, regular wages for me to be able to count on, *and to get out of this.* Because I think nobody likes this life, *even though they give you* [money]. Precisely because you have to go around asking [people to buy the magazine]... it's ... *it's not very pleasant.* [To] those of us who are used to always working, this is, like, depressing. Things pile up *and the pain, the annoyance, is heightened.*

Utterance foci show M shares CR's opinion on the street selling of *Hecho en Buenos Aires*. The adversative 'but' highlights the cultural opposition between street selling (work in the postmodern sense) and a regular, stable job (work in the modern or classical sense) that would enable its holder to plan for the future. M sees the latter as a way out of extreme poverty, her wishes in this respect being further stressed by the postpositive use of the first-person singular subjective pronoun.[8] Being helped and given money causes dejection and increases both physical and psychological suffering because the speaker considers herself as someone who has always worked, regardless of the time she has been living on the streets. Though the job she longs for is in the past, it still gives her an identity, as well as the hope that keeps her going.

OC (M, 46)

OC (u55) I... when ... I don't know... when I was ... I went from home to the stud farm by private hire car: I had my own money and I knew that I ... went and *bought my own clothes*. It was then that I started to value things, *as I must*. But because I was... *I worked by the sweat of my brow* [sic]. But that ... when that ... happened, I said: 'well, *I've got ill again.*'

Interviewer: You can sell the magazine.

OC Yes, walk, all those things, *sell a little ... light* [work]. I'd *very much like to train horses*. I know that *as a horse-trainer I* [can] *earn money*.

OC employs the first-person singular pronoun[9] to state that he used to follow a daily routine (i.e. going from his house to the stud farm). He would have been relatively well-off, as he was able to travel by private hire car. The same pronoun is used to talk about having owned money, bought clothes and worked. He adds that he learnt to appreciate things as he ought to. The expression 'to earn one's bread by the sweat of one's brow' points to a cultural value typically associated with the modern notion of work and deeply rooted in Argentine social imagery. Linked to other values such as family and education, its significance can be traced back to immigration times. This reference is in focal position, as are his idea of the duty to become aware of the vaue of things and the mention of his ability to purchase clothes.

When the issue of street selling is raised again, he contrasts it with his previous occupation, though acknowledging that now, as a result of his illness, he can only perform light tasks. The references to horse-training and to the money he used to earn constitute the foci of the respective utterances, which stresses the modern perspective.

A (M, 38)

A (u33) Wishes? Yes, *to be* well-off, *without this magazine*. I want a job, to study ... I, who *studied up to the age of 20 ... doing ... to create something new, something productive*.

Interviewer (u57) What is a job to you?

A (u58) *What is* a job? Work *dignifies the person*. You work and you have what you want; *it's going to be hard, but all of a sudden, see? It gives you ... this...* You plan your future, *that of your family* ... It dignifies ... gives dignity.

A's speech is quite impressive. Not only does he not want to sell the magazine, but he also stresses his aspiration to create something new and 'productive', as the first two foci indicate. This train of thought leads to the well-known idea that work confers dignity on human beings, which is tantamount to saying that it gives them an identity, another cultural value linked to the modern notion.

AC (F, 53)

AC: What was I going to say? It's a job too ... h'm ... *but it's a job, see? that ... that...*

Interviewer More of a free-lance nature ...

AC: Of course it's up to you, see? If you sell you earn money, if you don't sell you don't earn. It's a job, *but no one pays you to sell*.

Like CR, AC uses the adversative 'but' after admitting that street selling is a job, thus denying what she has just acknowledged. What she actually desires is to work in an employed capacity, earning regular wages that might enable her to plan for the future.

Conclusions

In the modern or industrial age, the cultural notion of work was crucial to the way in which individuals gave meaning to their own lives and constructed their identities. Apart from the fact that it provided them with a living, work had ethical value as a source of personal dignity and social worth. It was stable, as people remained with the same employer for most of their working lives, enabling employees to plan for the long term and laying the foundation for other virtues, such as sacrifice, effort and saving. Postmodernity, by contrast, has been characterized by rapid technological, political and cultural change. Loss of job stability has led to a feeling of uncertainty about the future. Work and professional career are no longer appreciated and identity is rooted in consumption.

The extreme poor of Buenos Aires take the modern view of work, and their goals and actions are inspired by modern values. They want to produce, follow a daily routine, and plan for the future – a recurring idea across the interviews. They see themselves as living on charity, selling something in whose creation they have not taken part, under 'flexible' conditions, without a proper workplace, bonuses, health insurance, or pension contributions, and therefore unable to plan even for the short term.

Although *Hecho en Buenos Aires* has been devised as a means of improving this precarious state of affairs, their belief systems have not been taken into account. Both public policy and private schemes are grounded in preconceived notions about what the poor need, which are often at odds with what the recipients of their aid think and wish. In order to bring views closer together we would suggest active involvement in publication content; as featured in similar cooperative projects, as well as encouraging vocational education and the creation of small businesses. There is no reason why the two cultures cannot live side by side and poverty would be best approached by listening to those who suffer its consequences.

Notes

1 The present chapter is the result of the author's work with the Centre for Research on Philosophical and Cultural Anthropology and the National Council for Scientific and Technological Research of Argentina, as well as with the Latin American Network for the Critical Analysis of Poverty Discourse, of which she is a founding member. It is also part of the project Discourse and Social Change: Three Basic Problems of the Latin American Urban Poor, funded by the University of Buenos Aires, Arts School.

2 We define it as the educational process by means which a culture is instilled since childhood.

3 The term refers to poor and marginalized social groups. The concept had been used in the 1960s poverty debates, but Gunnar Myrdal was the first to define it clearly and apply it meaningfully to a new social group situated on the fringes of the labour market. Among its main features were the inadequate cultural and vocational training of its members, as well as their overlap with the homeless, lack of political organization and little social participation. The underclass tended to inhabit the city areas worst affected by economic crises and by the overcrowding resulting from urban renewal projects. Myrdal particularly mentioned the African-American and Hispanic minorities as the worst hit by unemployment and underemployment, and female household heads, who

had been further marginalized from the labour market and constituted an at-risk group. Most of these characteristics have been discussed in poverty debates since the 1980s, although their structural connection with the economy and the labour market has been largely ignored of late.

4 The process had actually begun during the 1976–1983 military dictatorship, when 25 articles of the Employment Contract Act were amended and 97 repealed in order to curtail workers' rights, a reform that affected over 40 per cent of the legal text.

5 This legal provision enabled what became known as 'junk contracts'.

6 This new poverty was the outcome of middle=class impoverishment, a process that had begun by the mid-1970s. Kessler and Di Virgilio (2008) show the strategies deployed by the new poor to adjust to their situation, stressing the erosion of their social identity.

7 Made in Buenos Aires (translator's note).

8 In the Spanish text the first-person singular subjective pronoun yo is used after the verb poder in 'para poder yo contar,' which has been rendered as 'for me to be able to count on' (translator's note).

9 The speaker uses the personal pronoun yo ('I'), which might have been omitted in Spanish (translator's note).

References

Ángulo Aguilazocho, M. S. and Lozanía Cazares, M. A. (2005). The human integral development: a challenge for the communitarian development in the globalization processes. *Ra Ximhai*, 1(3): 509.

Auletta, K. (1992). *The Underclass*. New York: Random House.

Barbieri, E. and de Castro, R. (2001). Algunas posturas y polémicas alrededor de los conceptos de pobreza y cultura de la pobreza. *Sobre excesos y exabruptos*, 2:1. Available online at: http://www.vivilibros.com/excesos/02-a-06.htm (last accessed 4 August 2013).

Bietti, L. (2005). El trabajo como categoría en conflicto y transformación: análisis lingüístico de su representación discursiva. Actas del III Coloquio Nacional de la Asociación Latinoamericana de Estudios del Discurso, ALED. Buenos Aires: Argentina.

Brown, P. and Levinson, S. (1987). *Politeness: Some Universals in Language*. Cambridge: Cambridge University Press.

Firbas, J. (1964).On defining the theme in functional sentence analysis, *Travaux Linguistiques de Prague* 1: 267–280.

Firbas, J. (1992). *Functional Sentence Perspective in Written and Spoken Communication.* Cambridge: Cambridge University Press.

Frescura Tolosa, C. D. (2005). La representación discursiva del trabajo en las historias de vida de los indigentes. Actas del III Coloquio Nacional de la Asociación Latinoamericana de Estudios del Discurso, ALED. Buenos Aires: Argentina. Available online at: http://www.academia.edu/572267/La_representacion_discursiva_del_trabajo_en_las_historias_de_vida_de_los_indigentes

Gunnarsson, B-L. (2000). Discourse, organizations and national cultures, *Discourse Studies,* 2(1): 5–33.

Giddens, A. (1995). *La constitución de la sociedad.* Buenos Aires: Amorrortu editores.

Goldin, I. and Reinert, K. (2012). *Globalization for Development: Meeting New Challenges.* Oxford: Oxford University Press.

Grigulevich, J. and Vesilkin, E. ¿La antropología social de Oscar Lewis y el colonialismo? Unpublished manuscript.

Hardt, M. and Negri, T. (2002). *Imperio*. Buenos Aires: Paidós.

Hermo, J. P. and Wydler, A. (2006). Transformaciones del trabajo en la era de la 'modernidad líquida' y el trabajo 'inmaterial'. *Herramienta,* 32. Available online at http://www.

herramienta.com.ar/revista-herramienta-n-32/transformaciones-del-trabajo-en-la-era-de-la-modernidad-liquida-y-el-trabajo

Irogbe, K. (2005). Globalization and the development of underdevelopment of the Third World. *Journal of Third World Studies*, XXII(1) 41–68.

Kessler, G. and Di Virgilio, M. (2008). La nueva pobreza urbana: dinámica global, regional y argentina en las últimas dos décadas. *Revista CEPAL*, 95: 31–50. Available online at http://www.eclac.cl/publicaciones/xml/9/33749/RVE95KesslerDiVirgilio.pdf

Lerner, D. and Schramm, W. (eds) (1967). *Communication and Change in the Developing Countries*. Honolulu, HI: University Press of Hawaii.

Lewis, O. (1959). *Five Families: Mexican Case Studies in the Culture of Poverty*. New York: Basic Books.

Mathesius, V. 1939. On the so-called Functional Sentence Perspective. *SAS*, 5: 171–174.

Mohan, B. (2011). *Development, Poverty of Culture and Social Policy*. New York: Palgrave Macmillan.

Monreal, P. (1996). *Antropología y pobreza urbana*. Madrid: Los libros de la Catarata.

Myrdal, G. (1962). *Challenge to Affluence*. New York: Pantheon.

Noblía, M. V. (2003). La privatización de la desocupación y la pobreza: el rol del estado y de la empresa social en las representaciones sociales de la indigencia. In T. Ortiz and M. L. Pardo (eds), *Origen y transformación del estado argentino en períodos de globalización.* Buenos Aires: Biblos.

Pardo, M.L. (1992). *Derecho y Lingüística. Cómo se juzga con palabras*. Buenos Aires: Centro Editor de América Latina.

Pardo, M.L. (1996). *Derecho y Lingüística. Cómo se juzga con palabra*s. 2nd edition. Buenos Aires: Nueva Visión.

Pardo, M. L. (2011). *Teoría y metodología de la investigación lingüística. Método sincrónico-diacrónico de análisis lingüístico de textos*. Buenos Aires: Tersites.

Pardo, M. L. (2013). Innovación teórica y metodológica en los estudios críticos del discurso de la pobreza extrema. *Cadernos de Linguagem e Sociedade*,14 (Special Issue) pp. 15–37.

Robertson, R. (1992).*Globalization: Social Theory and Global Culture*. London. Sage.

Rudra, N. (2005). Are workers in the developing world winners or losers in the current era of globalization? *Studies in Comparative International Development*, 40(3): 29–64.

Shi-xu. (in press). Cultural discourse atudies. In K. Tracy, C. Ilie and T. Sandel (eds), *International Encyclopedia of Language and Social Interaction*. Oxford: Wiley-Blackwell.

Tomlinson, J. (1997). Cultural globalization and cultural imperialism. In A. Mohammadi (ed.). *International Communication and Globalization: A Critical Introduction*, (pp. 170–190). Thousand Oaks, CA: Sage.

Valentine, C. (1969) [1992]. *La cultura de la pobreza, crítica y contrapropuesta*. Buenos Aires: Amorrortu.

Virno, P. (2003). *Gramática de la multitud. Para un análisis de las formas de vida contemporáneas*. Buenos Aires: Colihue.

Vilagrasa Ibarz, J. (2000). *Los debates sobre pobreza urbana y segregación social en Estado Unidos.* Scripta Nova, IV, 76. Available online at: http://www.ub.edu/geocrit/sn-76.htm

Weil, H. (1844.) *De l'ordre des mots dans les langues anciennes comparées aux langues modernes. Questions de grammaire générale.* Paris: Joubert.

Wilson, W. (1987). *The Truly Disadvantaged: The Inner City, The Underclass and Public Policy*. Chicago: University of Chicago Press.

Epilogue

The three of us communication scholars from the continents of Asia, Africa and Latin America, respectively, decided to join hands in an attempt to create a concerted and integrated programme of studying the new and emerging developing world, not just because we are interested in the discourses of our cultural communities per se, but more because we share a deep conviction that our non-Western, developing, Third World, despite its current difficulties and crises of various kinds, represents an immense hope of forming a human-cultural Great Wall that may prevent our planet from going down a spiral of neo-colonialist and neo-imperialist globalization and recreate a more balanced world order that can sustain the growth and prosperity of our common humanity (see also Injoo 2012; Van der Putten 2013).

But, for the time being and most urgently, what are the socioeconomic conditions of the developing world like? What are their major concerns, views and aspirations? What are the general strategies and norms underlying their actions and activities and what are the barriers to them? What are the commonalities as well as differences between the Asian, African and Latin American communities in those aspects? How can we developing world researchers go beyond academic Westcentrism and listen to and tell their stories, so to speak, in their own terms and from their own perspectives? It is theoretical, empirical and methodological questions such these that concerned us and prompted us to search for answers.

Consequently, it became obvious to us that, in order to help edify a post-Cold-War, post-globalization, and new developing world as envisaged above, the first and foremost step for us developing world researchers of discourse and communication to take is to drawn attention to the actual socio-cultural practices of the non-Western, developing, Third World and, in conjunction with that, to create a new research paradigm that is capable of culturally consciously and critically examining and evaluating those practices and so a mode of research that will ultimately help the developing world to better understand itself and the wider international community to better understand the emerging world.

On the 'non-Western', 'developing', 'Third World', including its 'discourses', there have of course been prior studies (e.g. Lent 1978; Melkote 1991; Reeves 1993; Rudra 2005). Many are even optimistic, compassionate or constructive (e.g. Cho 2005; Harris 2005). And yet the acute problem still is that the extant international mainstream scholarship on globalization, development and communication has more often than not been parochial, Western or essentially Westcentric (Taylor 2005). It is imperative, both methodologically and cultural-politically, that researchers based in the developing world must become the primary agents to identify the topics of concern and construct culturally appropriate and effective systems of research, after having deconstructed the globalized Westcentric scholarship.

There is yet another, no less complicated and challenging, problem for the present endeavour: The cultural and scholarly legacies of the developing world are rich and varied to the extreme on the one hand and on the other the phenomena and problems of developing societies are as complex as they are diverse. How can we adequately and justifiably accomplish the envisaged task?

Against the backdrop of the current state of art, it seemed to us that native researchers, case studies, socially broad issues, major countries from the Asian, African and Latin American communities concerned, and of course historically and culturally appropriate perspectives and tools, would be essential and fundamental constitutes and tools of such an ambitious enterprise, though still many others should be included.

Thus, the trio of us from China, South Africa and Argentina, respectively, formed a collective authorship and agreed on the common principles of research as follows: (1) to place the peoples and cultures of the developing world at the centre of research and so to make sense of and account for their lives and practices in their own terms and from their own perspectives; (2) to draw upon culturally pluralist, creative and critical tools wrought with local wisdoms, norms and objectives; and (3) to cooperate in building a common programme of development discourse studies that serves to consolidate and empower the developing world on the one hand and to transform the viral imperialist world order on the other.

From the studies presented in this volume, a number of observations and conclusions may be made. First, this is a first attempt of collaboration between scholars from the developing world in charting a new course of development discourse studies. Here not only are common themes of development research explored, but also building a development-oriented paradigm attempted at. Hopefully, such Third World academic cooperation will gather momentum to transform the asymmetrical order of international scholarship on development (and) communication.

Second, the developing world, both ordinary and scholarly, has ample reasons to be discontented with the Western cultural impositions – neo-colonialist and neo-imperialist. We argued that the dominant Western scholarships are insufficient or inappropriate for understanding our realities. Similarly, European languages can be an impediment to local African education, science and development more generally. Consequently, the non-Western developing world must reinvent itself on its road of development.

Third, Asian, African and Latin American communities, their intra- and intercultural diversity and complexity notwithstanding, contain sufficient grounds for forging a collective discourse research paradigm that will not distinguish their common scholarly identity, but also tackle their societal and cultural concerns more productively. Our research has shown that there are shared, real and urgent needs to open up new theoretical spaces and create locally relevant tools for studying development. At the same time, we argued that the developing world also contains rich cultural and scholarly legacies and resources for constructing a culturally innovative and inclusive system of research.

Fourth, the present study has been able to broach a range of native developing world topics and issues that have hitherto been largely eclipsed or absent from international literature and, in particular, local and cultural-political voices and suggestions are brought forth. International branding of a Third World city, standardization of non-European, indigenous languages for science and technology, concepts of the work of homeless people, and so on, are cases in point. New questions call for attention, reconceptualization and methodological invention.

Fifth, various chapters have demonstrated that the developing world, like the rest of the world, is undergoing, and has undergone, vast, fast and profound changes, whether in economy, science and technology, and cultural ideologies. Development provokes rethinking of the question of language and educational policy in Africa; postmodernity transforms the cultural mentality of Latin America.

Sixth, our studies have also shown that the developing world has mutually instructive and beneficial experiences and lessons in development including development discourse research. The practices of international branding of the Chinese city can have valuable implications for other cities in the developing world. The question of indigenous languages for development in Africa can raise similar interrogation in Asia and Latin America. The cultural historical ways that an Asian paradigm of development discourse studies is constructed can inspire African and Latin American researchers of discourse and communication.

Seventh and evidently, the developing world faces common challenges and barriers in the way of Third World development: Western colonial, neo-colonial and imperialist impositions in society and scholarship, lack of cultural investment, internal ideological contradictions, poverty, and many others that are not dealt with here. Problems such these require urgent attention and search for solutions.

Last but by no means least, the discourses of the developing world exhibit cultural strengths and potentials that can constitute one important bulwark against America-dominated globalization. Our studies have demonstrated that non-Western cultures of the developing world contain spiritual resources, communicative tools, business means, and so on, to compete with the workings of globalization.

Future agenda

It will have been realized that the present volume is but a brief, tentative and in many respects imprecise and incomplete attempt at forging a new approach to human (development) discourse and communication studies. Partly owing to our limited knowledge and experience and partly because development discourse studies is a completely new field, many cultural and scholarly legacies may have been neglected, multifarious and complex issues and phenomena excluded, differences and commonalities ignored. Indeed, for the historic task of searching for a development discourse studies programme in support of a new and emerging developing world against an American- superpower-dominated order, there are many urgent actions still to be taken and we suggest a few in closing.

The first and foremost move to make is to un-learn, de-construct and de-colonize the Westcentric universalizing ways of studying the non-Western, developing Third World. Second, culturally conscious and critical scholars and students the world over should strive to rejuvenate the forgotten, marginalized, disappearing heritages of native, non-Western, Third World scholarship. Third, they should start in earnest investigation into unfamiliar, indigenous, especially non-Western discourses with a view to finding locally practical, acceptable and constructive solutions. Fourth, scholars and students everywhere, but most relevantly now, from the developing world should learn from and collaborate with one another, in order to create a common research paradigm that effectively addresses their societal and cultural concerns. Finally, they should try persistently to disseminate their culturally innovative work on the international stage in order to move forward inter-cultural dialogue in development (and) discourse research.

References

Cho, H.Y. (2005). 'Second death', or revival of the 'third world' in the context of neo-liberal globalization. *Inter-Asia Cultural Studies*, 6(4): 497–509.

Harris, J. (2005). Emerging third world powers: China, India and Brazil. *Race and Class*, 46(3): 7–27.

Injoo, S. (2012). After renaissance: China's multilateral offensive in the developing world. *European journal of international relations*, 18(1): 77–101.

Lent, J. A. (1979). Mass communication in the Third World: some ethical considerations. In J. A. Lent, (ed), *Third World Mass Media: Issues, Theory and Research*. Studies in Third World Societies No. 9 (pp. 1–16).Willamsburg, VA: College of William and Mary.

Melkote, S. R. and Steeves, H. L. (2001). *Communication for Development in the Third World: Theory and Practice for Empowerment*. New Delhi: Sage.

Reeves, G. (1993). *Communications and the 'Third World'*. London: Routledge.

Rudra, N. (2005). Are workers in the developing world winners or losers in the current ear of globalization? *Studies in comparative international development*, 40(3), 29–64.

Taylor, I. (2005). Globalisation studies ad the developing world: Making international political economy truly global. *Third World Quarterly*, 26(7): 1025–1042.

Van der Putten, F. P. (2013). Harmony with diversity: China's preferred world order and weakening western influence in the developing world. *Global Policy*, 4(1): 53–62.

Index